P9-ASD-864

Celebrating
Diverse
Voices

THOUGHT AND PRACTICE
FIRST ANNUAL YEARBOOK
OF THE BANK STREET COLLEGE OF EDUCATION
1992

Editors:
Frank Pignatelli, Susanna W. Pflaum
Board of Advisers:
Nancy Balaban, Harriet Cuffaro, Barbara Dubitsky,
Linda Levine, Maritza McDonald, Susanna W. Pflaum,
Sylvia Ross, Steven Schultz, Edna Shapiro, Bernice Wilson
Readers:
Nancy Balaban, Marvin Cohen, Barbara Dubitsky, Helen Freidus,
Lonnetta Gaines, Lisa Garrison, Lia Gelb, Claudia Grose,
Mary Hilles, Marian Howard, Nina Jaffe, Nina Jensen,
Kenneth Jewell, Fern Khan, Joseph Kleinman, Linda Levine,
Leah Levinger, Claudia Lewis, Nancy Nager, Katherine O'Donnell,
Madeleine Ray, Esther Rosenfeld, Sylvia Ross, Gil Schmerler,
Steven Schultz, Edna Shapiro, Jo Straceski, Susan Sullivan,
Nola Whiteman, Bernice Wilson, Claire Wurtzel

Celebrating Diverse Voices

Progressive Education and Equity

Editors:
Frank Pignatelli
Susanna W. Pflaum

SCCCC - LIBRARY
4601 Mid Rivers Mall Drive
St. Peters, MO 63376

WITHDRAWN

CORWIN PRESS, INC.
A Sage Publications Company
Newbury Park, California 91320

Copyright © 1993 by Corwin Press, Inc.

All rights reserved. No part of this book may be reproduced or utilized in any form or by any means, electronic or mechanical, including photocopying, recording, or by any information storage and retrieval system, without permission in writing from the publisher.

For information address:

 Corwin Press
A Sage Publications Company
2455 Teller Road
Newbury Park, California 91320

SAGE Publications Ltd.
6 Bonhill Street
London EC2A 4PU
United Kingdom

SAGE Publications India Pvt. Ltd.
M-32 Market
Greater Kailash I
New Delhi 110 048 India

Printed in the United States of America

Library of Congress Cataloging-in-Publication Data

Celebrating diverse voices: progressive education and equity / edited by Frank Pignatelli, Susanna W. Pflaum.
    p. cm. —(Thought and practice)
Includes bibliographical references and index.
ISBN 0-8039-6038-7. —ISBN 0-8039-6039-5 (pbk.)
    1. Educational equalization—United States. 2. Progressive education—United States. 3. Educational change—United States. I. Pignatelli, Frank. II. Pflaum, Susanna W. III. Series: Thought and practice (Newbury Park, Calif.)
LC213.2.C45 1993
370.19'342—dc20   92-30439
                                                               CIP

94 95 96 97 10 9 8 7 6 5 4 3 2

Corwin Press Production Editor: Tara S. Mead

Contents

Preface

Celebrating Diverse Voices: Progressive Education and Equity moves away from one vantage point and instead argues from, and for, a multiplicity of perspectives. Hence this volume includes scholarly chapters as well as policy and advocacy chapters. Authors address both practical and more theoretical concerns and, in totality, consider different levels of schooling as well as disciplines. They also analyze issues of school reform from points both internal and external to the school. The common thread throughout these chapters is an attentiveness to the *effects* of actions by educators and others in the light of concern for equity. Secada (1989) helps us understand what a concern for equity entails:

> The heart of equity lies in our ability to acknowledge that, even though our actions might be in accord with a set of rules, their *results* may be unjust. Equity goes beyond following the rules, even if we have agreed that they are intended to achieve justice. . . . Educational equity, therefore, should be construed as a check on the justice of specific actions that are carried out within the educational arena and the arrangements that result from those actions. (Secada, 1989, pp. 68-69, emphasis added)

AUTHOR'S NOTE: Headnotes for the chapters were written collaboratively by Susanna W. Pflaum and Frank Pignatelli.

ix

Equity, as I see it, is mobile, probing, an act of critical intervention in prevailing but unacceptable socially constructed arrangements. It involves, as Aristotle (1925/1963) put it, "sympathetic judgement" (p. 152). Within this context, the challenge for progressive educators emerges: How can progressive educational practice, policy, and theory be grounded, shaped, and driven by considerations of educational equity? How can complex and oftentimes volatile issues of diversity be negotiated so that those who are methodically silenced or marginalized are heard? Are traditionally disenfranchised members of the educational community—whether they are teachers, students, parents, or members of community groups concerned about education—being encouraged to participate in the educational process and particularly in matters of school governance?

The urban context—in particular, New York City—frames several of the discussions in this volume. If we have learned anything during this past year of turmoil, it is that the social fabric of our large urban centers is badly frayed and in desperate need of renewal. The schools are not immune. The "savage inequalities" so vividly and movingly reported by Kozol (1991) that are allowed to persist in public schools across the United States stand as proof positive. The disturbing, troubling consequences of not building strong, healthy communities across differences—or, at least, workable, effective alliances—beset our cities as well as our public schools. The rage, destruction, and violence that erupted in Los Angeles recently is not unrelated to the senseless shootings and stabbings by and against young people that have occurred in and around public schools in New York City.

Although it would be foolish and wrong to argue that schools alone bear the burden of responding to the erosion of a humane, democratic culture, educators do have a vital role to play. The progressive impulse in education is about remembering the salience of equity. Thus stories of professional responsibility sensitive to issues of equity need to be told. And concerns about the need for educational renewal must be voiced in a language that is richer, more encouraging, more inclusive than the monotonous tones of "more accountability," "more efficiency." Progressive educators, such as those represented here, therefore look to shape an educational discourse that prizes and notes acts of collective responsibility. For, more than merely tolerating differences, we need a discourse capable of sustaining an ongoing mutual regard for the other (especially when "the other" is regularly less heard and less visible).

Several chapters in this book are analyses of the past; they turn to periods and events when progressive educators furnished new images and new realities. From the beginning, one of the early progressives, Lucy Sprague Mitchell, founder of Bank Street College of Education and, before that, chairman of the Bureau of Educational Experiments, was looking outward, to what her work and that of her progressive colleagues could mean to a larger audience. Joyce Antler, historian and biographer of Mitchell, talks about the bureau, officially organized in 1916, being intended to serve "as a coordinating agency of educational renewal" (Antler, 1987, p. 224). And Mitchell, herself, was very clear about what she saw as the bureau's mission. Commenting about the bureau's laboratory school, for example, Mitchell's eyes were fixed upon the implications of the work for public education. She also recognized that the bureau needed to assume an activist position if it hoped to contribute effectively to school reform. She wrote:

> We think of all our work ultimately in relation to public education. We wish to keep constantly in mind and to be ready to attack whenever there seems to be a real opening those unsolved social and administrative problems of the public schools which will need attacking before anything we may work out in our laboratory school can be made effective. (Antler, 1987, p. 285)

Later, as founder of Bank Street College of Education, when she turned her energies toward the challenge of developing teachers capable of effecting deep change in the education of children, Mitchell framed her vision in a dynamic, engaging, open way. "We are not interested," she said, "in perpetuating any special 'school of thought.' Rather, we are interested in imbuing teachers with an experimental, critical and ardent approach to their work" (Antler, p. 309).

Not long ago, Perrone (1991) reminded progressive educators of their history. As Perrone notes, it is a history marked by deep commitments and the inevitability of struggle and conflict:

> Progressivism in education was guided historically by a belief that schools needed social power and at their best were rooted in cultural understandings, ethical commitments, and an ongoing struggle for democracy—in other words, large purposes that transcend mere materialism. (Perrone, 1991, p. 9)

In a real sense, Dewey, Counts, Mitchell, and other past progressive educators provide us with a needed history. Granted, theirs was not a unitary voice. Amidst accusations of advocating indoctrination in the schools at the expense of what others called democratic schooling, the well-known "dare" issued by Counts (1932) to "build a new social order," for example, met with stiff resistance from a group of his progressive colleagues (Tanner, 1991). Nevertheless, historically, progressive educators have posed important, necessary questions and challenged aspects of the U.S. experience that continue to gnaw away at some of our most cherished democratic principles. It is our hope that the chapters in this yearbook take a step in the right direction and contribute to the discourse that is needed if educational renewal is to be taken seriously.

FRANK PIGNATELLI

References

Antler, J. (1987). *Lucy Sprague Mitchell: The making of a modern woman.* New Haven, CT: Yale University Press.

Aristotle (1963). *The Nicomachean ethics of Aristotle* (Sir D. Ross, Trans.). London: Oxford University Press. (Original work published 1925)

Counts, G. (1932). *Dare the school build a new social order?* New York: John Day.

Kozol, J. (1991). *Savage inequalities: Children in America's schools.* New York: Crown.

Perrone, V. (1991). Large purposes. In K. Jervis & C. Montag (Eds.), *Progressive education for the 1990s: Transforming practice.* New York: Teachers College Press.

Secada, W. (1989). Educational equity versus equality of education: An alternative conception. In W. G. Secada (Ed.), *Equity in education.* New York: Falmer.

Tanner, D. (1991). *Crusade for democracy: Progressive education at the crossroads.* Albany: State University of New York Press.

About the Authors

Terry Born has an M.A. in English from New York University. Currently a student in the Principals Institute of Bank Street College, she was a teacher of English, theater, and photography at Middle College High School. She is a curriculum developer and consultant in interdisciplinary education, performance assessment, and school-based management and has discussed these at local and national meetings. Her most recent research appeared in "An Evaluation of CUNY/NYC Board of Education Collaborative Programs," published by the Graduate School of Education of the University of Pennsylvania.

Anne Francis-Okongwu is Assistant Professor of Education at Queens College, City University of New York, School of Education. She received her B.A. from Boston University, an M.S.W. from Fordham, and her Ph.D. from the Graduate Center at City University of New York in anthropology. Research interests include comparative studies of urban, female-headed, single-parent families and the impact of race, class, and gender on family life, education, and social reproduction.

Norman Fruchter is the Program Adviser for Education at the Aaron Diamond Foundation, a Senior Consultant at the Academy for Educational Development, and President of Community School Board 15 in Brooklyn, New York. Coauthor of both *New Directions in Parent Involvement: A Policy Analysis* and *Choosing Equality: The Case for Democratic Schooling*, he has worked as a parent organizer in New Jersey and New York City, and directed an alternative high school for dropouts in Newark and an experimental college program for public sector workers in Jersey City. He is also the author of two novels, *Coat Upon a Stick* and *Single File*.

Maxine Greene has been teaching educational philosophy, literature, social philosophy, and aesthetics at Teachers College, Columbia University, since 1966. Currently Professor of Philosophy and Education emerita, she still teaches part time in the Division of Philosophy and the Social Sciences. Past president of the American Educational Research Association, she works in the fields of social theory, aesthetics, criticism, and educational history. She has published approximately 100 articles, a number of chapters in edited collections, and five books, the most recent being *The Dialectic of Freedom*. Her Ph.D. and M.A. were earned at New York University and her B.A. from Barnard College. She has honorary degrees from Bank Street College, Hofstra University, Lehigh University, and the University of Colorado.

Joseph Kleinman is currently a member of the graduate faculty at Bank Street College of Education. Prior to this, he served as assistant director, dean, and teacher in the New York City alternative schools in District 4, Manhattan. He received his M.S.W. from the Hunter College School of Social Work and an M.S. in Educational Administration from Bank Street College of Education. He is currently enrolled in the History Ph.D. program at the Graduate Center of the City University of New York. His research and writing interests are in the areas of African American urban communities and nineteenth-century U.S. history.

Linda Levine is an anthropologist on the Graduate Faculty at Bank Street College. She conducted ethnographic research for her dissertation at an East Harlem elementary school in New York City, earning her Ph.D. in anthropology and education from the University of Pennsylvania in 1988. Her dissertation study, titled "'Everyone Else . . . Including Me:' Learning to Value Diversity in School," reflects three interrelated research interests: intercultural communication, the social construction of literacy, and urban education. She coauthored two recent papers on career change. During 1991-1992, she served on the advisory board for the "Bridges and Boundaries" exhibition at the Jewish Museum and traveled to Bogotá as consultant to faculty investigating classroom discourse at the Universidad Nacional. At Bank Street, she has been an adviser in special education and museum education programs, instructor, and codirector for programs designed to attract liberal arts undergraduates to careers in urban teaching.

Claudia Lewis is an anthropologist and Distinguished Scholar in Children's Literature emerita at Bank Street. She began her association with the college as a student in the School for Teachers in Bank Street's second year of training teachers, 1932-1933, under the direction of Lucy Sprague Mitchell. After several years of teaching children, she joined the Graduate Faculty in 1943. She has taught courses (including language and literature, formerly taught by Mrs. Mitchell), advised students, and worked in the Divisions of Research and Publications. Currently, as an adjunct faculty member, she teaches courses in children's creative writing and cross-cultural studies of children and works with the Publications Group. She is the author of several adult books on anthropology as well as numerous books of poetry and stories for children. She received her Ph.D. from Teachers College.

Leonard S. Marcus is a writer, editor, and teacher with a special interest in children's literature. An adjunct lecturer at the New School for Social Research and the School of Visual Arts, he is

Parenting magazine's children's book reviewer; for many years, he also served as *The Lion and the Unicorn's* book review editor. His essays and reviews have appeared in *The New York Times, The Washington Post, Smithsonian, Horn Book,* and other publications. His own children's books include *Petrouchka* and *Mother Goose's Little Misfortunes.* His biography *Margaret Wise Brown: Awakened by the Moon* was published earlier this year. He holds a B.A. in history from Yale and an M.F.A. in poetry from the University of Iowa Writers Workshop.

Jon Moscow is the Executive Director of the Parents Coalition for Education in New York City, Inc. He has worked as the Parent and Community Coordinator in Manhattan's Community School District 2 and as Computer Resources Coordinator at the Literacy Assistance Center. The parent of two children in the New York City Public Schools, he was a founding member of the Parents Coalition. He is a member of the boards of Advocates for Children of New York and the Parents Resource Center. He has a M.S. in Education from Bank Street College.

Susanna W. Pflaum is Dean of the Graduate School of Bank Street College of Education. She received her B.A. from Radcliffe College, her M.A. from Harvard Graduate School of Education, and a Ph.D. from Florida State University. Earlier, she was Dean of the School of Education at Queens College and, prior to that, professor and administrator at the University of Illinois at Chicago. She has published books and research articles in the areas of language development and the reading behaviors of learning disabled children. She is concerned with teacher education and the preparation of teachers for work with all children.

Frank Pignatelli is Instructor and Adviser on the faculty of Bank Street College Graduate School, Department of Educational Leadership. Prior to this, he was an Adjunct Professor at City College of the City University of New York, where he taught courses in the social foundations of education. He has worked also in a variety of roles in the New York City public school system, including time as a founding member of, and teacher in, an alternative junior high school and as an administrator on the school, district, and central board levels. He received his Ph.D. in philosophy and education from Teachers College, Columbia University. His scholarly interests include the application of postmodern and poststructural theory to problems of education.

Tom Roderick worked full time at the East Harlem Block Schools from 1968 to 1975 as Director of the East Harlem Block Elementary School and served from 1975 to 1980 as consultant to its board of directors. Since 1983, he has been Executive Director of Educators for Social Responsibility in New York City (ESR Metro). A membership organization of educators, ESR Metro works closely with the New York City Public Schools as cofounder and cosponsor of the Resolving Conflict Creatively Program, a national model for school-based efforts to teach young people better ways of dealing with conflict. He has a B.A. from Yale University and an M.A. in education from Bank Street College.

Patricia Rogan Sherman is an Instructor and Adviser at Bank Street College, where she teaches Child Development. She received her Ph.D. in Counseling Psychology from New York University in 1988. She is a licensed psychologist. She has published and presented papers on the counselor as change agent.

Jonathan G. Silin is a member of the Graduate Faculty, Bank Street College of Education. He holds an M.S. from Bank Street and an Ed.M. and Ed.D. from Teachers College, Columbia. The former Director of Public Information Services for the Long Island Association of AIDS Care, most recently he has been a consultant to the Harvard AIDS Institute, VIII International Conference on AIDS. His publications include articles on teaching, professionalism, and AIDS. He is working on a book about the changing nature of contemporary childhood.

With this richly textured account of the potential of progressive education, Greene asks us to envision and work toward building a progressive agenda grounded in our ability and need to care, to be responsive to "the other." As we cherish common ground, we must also value the situatedness of persons and their need to make sense of and participate in the remaking of their worlds. In contrast with the "pathology" evident in widespread social neglect and self-righteousness, Greene finds cause for optimism in the emergence of teacher networks, the influence of feminist criticism, whole language curricula, and successful alternative schools. Further, she urges educators to recognize the value of the arts and literature to free the imagination and break through the givenness of an unacceptable current time.

1. Perspective and Diversity: Toward a Common Ground

MAXINE GREENE

This is a time of newly acknowledged diversity in U.S. culture. Voices are becoming audible; faces are becoming visible; and we are realizing, some of us for the first time, how many silences there have been in the past, how many blank spaces in our history. We

AUTHOR'S NOTE: This chapter is based on an address given by Maxine Greene at a conference titled "Common Ground: A Conference on Progressive Education," at Swarthmore College, October 25, 1991. It was sponsored by The School in Rose Valley in Moylan, Pennsylvania. This chapter will be published as a talk in *Living Voices: Proceedings of Common Ground: A Conference on Progressive Education.* The proceedings will be published with funds from The Pew Charitable Trusts and will be available by writing to The School in Rose Valley.

may have looked too long from monological points of view; we may have assumed consensus where it did not exist. Today we are being made sharply aware of multiplicity. We are discovering the range of perspectives that must be taken into account as we work to remake community, as we strive to achieve a common ground. Not only are we asked today to look through the lenses of gender and class and ethnic difference; not only are we provoked to pose questions to the "canon," the so-called tradition. We are being asked to re-create our "habits of the heart," to redefine our "habits of mind" and what we can communicate in schools.

Fundamental to a conception of progressive education, most of us would agree, is a conception of pluralism linked to a notion of a "great community." Concerned as John Dewey was about the "steadying and integrating office" of the schools, he never thought in terms of homogeneities or the kind of sharing that overwhelmed diversity. One of the ends in view where connectedness and cooperation were concerned was the release of individuality. He understood that situations have to be deliberately created if there is to be a play of difference, an expression of personal energy. At once he recognized that people abandoned to privacy and total self-reliance are unlikely to develop, to "become different," or even to achieve their freedom. Fabrics of care, networks, support systems, communication: All are needed for the growth of persons, for the pursuit of possibilities. He wrote one time that "only the voluntary initiative and voluntary cooperation of individuals can produce social institutions that will protect the liberties necessary for achieving development of genuine individuality" (Dewey, 1916, p. 115). He had choosing in mind and new beginnings; and he knew very well the "social pathology" that stood in the way—the kind of pathology that stands in the way today.

Responding to Social Pathology

In his words, it manifested itself

in querulousness, in impotent drifting, in uneasy snatching at distractions, in idealization of the long established, in a facile optimism assumed as a cloak, in riotous glorification of things "as they are", in intimidation of all dissenters, ways which depress and dissipate thought all the more effectually because they operate with subtle and unconscious pervasiveness. (Dewey, 1954, p. 170)

This in many ways characterizes what we see around us today in this peculiar moment of self-righteousness and social neglect. As we speak about progressive education, we must not allow ourselves to put aside the dreary realities of contemporary life—the violation of children, the drug epidemic, the spread of AIDS, homelessness, the erosion of services, the racism, the homophobia, the privatism, the lack of care. Nor ought we ignore the perspectives, the vantage points of those suffering violation, exclusion, humiliation, and neglect. They are as important as the perspective so many of us unflinchingly oppose: the perspective of the positivist, the instrumental rationalist, the Pentagon spokesman who translates wounded civilians into diagrams on a chalkboard for all to see.

I need to turn to literature to highlight what I am saying before continuing. I think of Joseph Conrad's Marlow in *Heart of Darkness* talking to the Director of Companies, the Lawyer, and the Accountant about the Roman conquest of Britain and the Roman officials' confrontation with "the mysterious life of the wilderness." Sardonically conscious that he is speaking to latter-day exemplars of imperial greed, Marlow tells them: " 'Mind, none of us would feel exactly like this. What saves us is efficiency—the devotion to efficiency' " (Conrad, n.d., p. 221). How can we who are in education not be attuned to those who use efficiency as test and mystifier at once?

And then I think of the moment late in Fitzgerald's *The Great Gatsby* when Nick Carraway realizes that Tom Buchanan's sending George to kill Gatsby seems entirely justified to Tom. "It was all very careless and confused. They were careless people, Tom and Daisy—they smashed up things and creatures and then retreated back into their money or their vast carelessness, or whatever it was that kept them together, and let other people clean up the mess they had made" (Fitzgerald, 1953, pp.

180-181). There are few of us today who do not feel the cold blast of such carelessness in streets, schoolyards, emergency rooms, libraries; it too is part of the pathology. And then there is that remark in Albert Camus's novel, *The Plague*, one I cannot but hope we people who care about progressive education take seriously. It is spoken by Tarrou, who is telling his friend Dr. Rieux about the vocation of true healing, which seems to him to be very hard. " 'That's why I decided to take, in every predicament, the victims' side, so as to reduce the damage done.' " Later, Dr. Rieux acknowledges Tarrou when he speaks of how important it is to bear witness in favor of the plague-stricken people and to state "quite simply what we learn in a time of pestilence: that there are more things to admire" in human beings than to despise (Camus, 1948). And, finally, there is Christa Wolf, whose woman narrator ponders in *Accident*:

> I was once more forced to admire the way in which everything fits together with a sleepwalker's precision: the desire of most people for a comfortable life, their tendency to believe the speakers on raised platforms and the men in white coats; the addiction to harmony and the fear of contradiction of the many seem to correspond to the arrogance and hunger for power, the dedication to profit, unscrupulous inquisitiveness, and self-infatuation of the few. So what was it that didn't add up in this equation? (Wolf, 1989, p. 17)

It may be our pedagogical responsibility to respond.

Moving from that reflection (generated, it happens, by the Chernobyl disaster of a few years ago), we might well think of the kind of critical intelligence (and, I would hope, critical dialogue) presumably fostered in progressive classrooms. In this case, there are implications for what Dewey called "social inquiry," what some of us—drawing out some of its strands—might call a form of ideology critique. Surely, given the persisting mystifications surrounding official formulators, men on platforms, and the rest, and adding to those the obvious desire for harmony and easy answers, educators have much to do in enabling the young to pose worthwhile questions having to do with what William Blake called "mind-forged manacles." There is clearly a bland coercion of consciousness going on that moves even adults to take shortcuts, to avoid examination of their own assumptions, to blind themselves to the consequences of thoughtless (or careless or manipulative) acts. Then, in addition, there is the implication for an encouragement of scientific literacy, linked to concrete experiences in what is thought to be "real" life.

Thinking and Care

Surely, the centrality of care in Fitzgerald's sense (and, probably, in the sense of feminist ethics) is connected with this. I am reminded of Dewey's discussion of mind in *Art as Experience*, where he says that mind ought to be thought of as a verb and not a noun. "It denotes," he wrote, "all the ways in which we deal consciously and expressly with the situations in which we find ourselves." He said mind is "care in the sense of solicitude, anxiety, as well as of active looking after things that need to be tended" (Dewey, 1934, p. 263). It was, for Dewey, an activity that was intellectual, volitional, and (as he put it) affectional; to be mindful in the most significant sense was to be responsive to norms, to take careful heed, to use intelligence in the funding of meanings, personally to attend. To speak this way is to abandon the enclaves of academic specialism as it is such values as detachment and "objectivity." The mindful individual is engaged in participant thinking in the midst of life. She or he is at the furthest remove from the spectator or the abstract observer or experimenter. For Dewey, and for progressive educators generally, the thoughtful person is not only grounded, she or he is given to relational thinking, contextualized thinking. Unlike the Buchanans, she or he cannot retreat, no matter how great the confusion; she or he is required to "stop and think" (Arendt, 1978, p. 4) in part because she or he is in the world with others, connected with humankind.

That is why it is as natural as "2+2 is 4" for Dr. Rieux to fight the plague in Camus's novel, because it "is his job." There is no likelihood that the plague can be overcome by medical efforts; but it nonetheless remains necessary, if one is a physician, to struggle against the pestilence. Similarly, in that novel, sanitary squads were in time organized by the citizens to play their part in the fight. Most of the townsfolk ignored the plague when it first arrived; they were so devoted to "cultivating habits" that they could not arouse themselves at first from resignation or indifference. The squads did finally enable those people to come to grips with the disease and convinced them that, because plague was among them, "it was up to them to do whatever could be done to fight it." Because it became in that way some people's duty, "it revealed itself as what it really was; that is, the concern of all" (Camus, 1948, p. 121).

The Literacy of Technology

Now I realize it is extreme to assert that, in fighting for progressive education, we may well be fighting the pestilence. It is perfectly clear that the concerns I have been identifying are not part of the dominant discourse in education today. There is considerable pressure in many quarters (federal, corporate, even local) to orient education to the achievement of technical expertise. The end most often defined has to do with economic competitiveness or technological and military primacy in the world. Mathematical and scientific failures are lamented (as they probably should be) but not for reasons that have to do with young persons' understanding of their lived worlds. Rather, the reasons have again to do with extrinsic factors: the need for "world-class" achievement in the interests of the nation; the importance of U.S. leadership in an "undeveloped" world. The messages that come to young people have little to do with the values of extending their own repertoires or reducing their powerlessness. Almost nothing is said about the connections between mathematical and scientific literacy and ecological issues, health and nutritional problems, pregnancy, demographic matters, nuclear threats. Low test scores are made to appear a sign of disloyalty; the decline of functional literacy, evidence of impiety. There are suggestions, sometimes explicit, sometimes hinted at, that those who do not "pass," who do not "live up" or pull themselves up "by their bootstraps," will simply be left by the wayside. Several of the educational reports actually assert that society can no longer afford to support those who cannot cope with the new technologies.

Somewhat the same implications can be detected when people in official positions speak of "cultural literacy" and "what every American needs to know" (Hirsch, 1987). Overtly fearful of what is called "multiculturalism," there are many who try to legislate a predefined literacy, to encapsulate the "American heritage." They become protectionist, defending the canon or the tradition against the onslaughts of multiplicity and perspectivism. There are those, in fact, who have begun associating problem posing in the classroom or what is conceived of as critical inquiry with what is called "politically correct." We are seeing a reemergence of what used to be named essentialism in schools where the establishment of unified language communities is more important than young persons' thinking about their own thinking, reaching out from their own places to interpret and make sense of the world. Almost nothing is done to enable the young to deal thoughtfully and critically with the media. It follows that attitudes of passive receptivity are allowed, if not encouraged; consumerist and formulaic responses are taken to be the norms. Ironically, in the midst of all this, there are complaints that we are working to create communities of the competent rather than communities of citizens. In spite of this, few speak of educating what Dewey called an "articulate public." Few seem openly to want to break with what looks more and more like a monological mold.

There is certainly considerable agreement that progressive education does indeed break with that mold in its stress upon the dialogical, the experiential, the alternative possibility. If we do succeed in finding common ground, it will be one—it ought to be one—on which many voices can engage in dialogue, on which many perspectives are continually revealed. Questions about what constitutes the literacies required in the contemporary world ought to take us beyond considerations of purely functional literacy. We know something about the kind of learning that involves continuities and connections in lived experience. We know something about windows opening in consciousness, about what it means to look at things as if they could be otherwise. We learn more and more from Eleanor Duckworth, for example, about "wonderful ideas" and about questioning and about the uses of figuring things in complex ways, of "keeping it complex" (Duckworth, 1991, p. 24).

Toward the Common

We need to explore the ways in which the local and particular can feed into what we cherish as common, what we define and redefine as common ground. We need to discover how the particular can fertilize the common, how new perspectives and new visions can enrich the familiar landscapes, how the landscapes themselves can set off and highlight the new visions, enclose them in wider and wider frames. We may find that the crucial problems of cultural literacy can best be dealt with in such contexts, where diverse voices can be celebrated, where (as Marianne Moore once said) confusion itself can be celebrated. They may be dealt with in contexts where different voices join now and then in reciprocity, where they make contact in conversations stemming from dimensions of what they share. Confronting pluralism as seldom before, we have to ponder what it actually can mean for a common world to emerge from so many meaning systems, such a spectrum of "realities."

It is interesting to note the many voices, speaking in a range of idioms, concerned with overcoming fragmentation and incoherence in our nation today, and it is difficult not to hear them as voices of resistance to the plague. There are Robert Bellah and his colleagues calling for a transformation of the culture through a reconstitution of what they call the "social world." Like Dewey, they write of how individuals need the nurture of groups that carry a "moral tradition reinforcing their own aspirations" (Bellah, 1985, p. 141). The philosopher Richard Rorty, seeking a contemporary significance for pragmatism, writes both of contingency and of solidarity (Rorty, 1989). *Contingency* refers to the variability of languages and identities that becomes clear when we recognize the dependence of points of view on biography, on lived situation in the world. It connects with what I am attempting to say about perspectivism: the relation between vantage point and sense making; the role of standpoint when it comes to interpreting what comes into focus, what reveals itself before our eyes. Rorty speaks of *solidarity* as well as an alternative to objective certainties. For him, it implies a sharing of beliefs among those who share a community's story. Such sharing, such reciprocity, may be the only reasonable goal at a moment marked by so much multiplicity. Certainly this coheres with the thinking of the ethnographic thinker Clifford Geertz, who writes of translation and intersubjectivity and who raises what becomes for us a pedagogical question—"how separate individuals come to conceive, or do not, reasonably similar things" (Geertz, 1981, p. 156).

We find, wherever we look, an increasing interest in what is called "conversation." We find persons responding to the critic Mikhail Bakhtin and his explorations of the dialogical and the multiple voices engaged in sense making, within personal consciousness and without (Bakhtin, 1981). Even in art criticism, in a book like Lucy Lippard's *Mixed Blessings*, we find a call not merely for respect for differences but for an area between the familiar and the unfamiliar: a "fertile, liminal ground where new meanings germinate and where common experiences in different contexts can provoke new bonds" (Lippard, 1990, p. 9). All this connects for me with the notion of common ground, as it does with the nurture of learning communities, always in the making, always in process, like democracy itself.

Networks and Choices

There is a moral intention visible in the forming of such communities, and it has to do with solicitude and care, and with resistance to what is perceived as plague. Of course, the tension is great, the afflictions multiple. The scholarly interest in dialogue and connection has not yet undermined the corporate and technicist oratory or the management ethos that has so little use for active citizenship, or what Bellah and his colleagues call "communities of memory." Still, there are memories, and there are renewals. There are persons in education choosing themselves again, collaborating voluntarily in regard for the experiential, for the kinds of questioning that arise out of lived actualities in all their ambiguity and complexity.

As I ponder the new schools networking around the country, I am reminded of Dewey again, writing in *Democracy and Education* about the fact that the self is not ready made, "but something in continuous formation through choice of action." He associated the self with what he called interest and said that "the kind and amount of interest actively taken in a thing reveals and measures the quality of selfhood which exists" (Dewey, 1916, p. 408). There are numbers of teachers today forming their selves through an active interest in persons, in children, in consciousness, in experience, in dialogue, in community; and something remarkable may be happening (*America 2000* or no *America 2000*) in many parts of the country, in small spaces, numerous spaces, totally in contrast to the places where heartlessness and efficiency rule.

We might summon up the names, the faces of numerous teachers and principals resisting technical rationality as they refuse exclusion, breaking with the deadening consequences of traditional scheduling and specializing, trying for interdisciplinary vistas and forms. Many are deliberately creating small communities in their schools: "family groups," collaborative teams among teachers and parents (and sometimes with people from universities). Many are reaching beyond the walls of the schools, as young people move out into their own neighborhoods to work in child care or among the homeless or in tutoring centers or in places where they can do field research, do interviews, take down stories, plant seeds. There is Deborah Meier, who began her work at Central Park East in New York, surely a place where progressive education occurs. There are small groups meeting there, dialogue of many kinds. Students are offered a "promise" that they will be enabled to use their minds. It is necessary, realizing that, for us to picture the urban environment in which this takes place—not only the treeless streets, the litter, the traffic, but the worn-down housing projects, the drug salespeople, the crack houses. And, downtown, we must remember the constant beckoning of an unattainable consumerist paradise. Ann Cook in the Urban Academy urges her students on to many-faceted inquiries in the city, in museums, theaters, side streets, hospitals. In Bronx Regional High School, cement gray and graffiti scarred, young people came together to learn how to create a mural rendering Rosa Parks's refusal—with their own faces in the windows of the celebrated bus. In that school too, students took the initiative to learn how to construct a shelter for their homeless classmates. They worked with construction men to learn the crafts they required; their community was a working community as well as a moral one; and they involved, as collaborators, the homeless youngsters who were to be served—so, one of them said, "they won't be embarrassed." There is, of course, Eliot Wigginton's remarkable work in Georgia, known to the nation through the Foxfire books the students have written and prepared for publication themselves. Their particular field research, their studies of strip mining and health programs and union histories, have opened new dimensions of the common ground, especially as what is done in practice is made to radiate outward to the thinking of "complex things" Eleanor Duckworth describes and recommends.

There are more, many more, in a largely invisible network of individuals held together (I would guess) by a conception of some common ground. Strangely enough, what they are saying in their small communities, and on occasion simply to one another, is affecting the language of what is called "restructuring," the latest wave of school reform. The emphasis on collaborative learning, flexible scheduling, work experiences, community activity, field research, and—perhaps most centrally—what is called the "active learner"—all are consonant what has been said or is being said with respect to progressive education.

This may be the case as well with newer approaches to assessment and evaluation, as portfolios are used in the place of multiple choice tests, as qualitative or naturalistic inquiries are used. We hear increasingly of "learner-centered schools," alternative schools, magnet schools, "site-based management," teacher autonomy; and it may be that those involved have the values of democratic education in mind. There is no assurance, however, that this is the case. There are too many examples left of sexist and racist practices, class discrimination, tracking, and bureaucratic controls. The so-called free market society still exists with its condemnations, its exclusions, its use of young people as means rather than ends. We might hope, however, that some of the new language in use and some of the new research feeding at some levels into school practice might provoke greater resistance, even as it enables more educators to see.

Crossing Disciplines

Some of the inquiries in the fields of psychology, philosophy, and literature seem to have become peculiarly relevant even for what we would like to think of as a rebirth of progressive education. I have in mind the attention being paid to narrative and storytelling as ways of knowing, ways of learning and sense making. It connects at many junctures with the swelling interest in texts and textuality, as it does with the emphasis on dialogue. Jerome Bruner's interest in storytelling (Bruner, 1986, pp. 11-43) as a way of knowing has drawn many kinds of attention; so has Charles Taylor's treatment of narrative as a mode of imparting meaning to experience and working out the moral purposes of human lives (Taylor, 1989, pp. 51-52). Martha Nussbaum's turn toward imaginative literature for images of how we ought to live those lives adds another level to this movement (Nussbaum, 1990) as does Rorty's recent insistence on the importance of poets and novelists as guides to the doing of philosophy (Rorty, 1991). Whether influence can be identified or causes and effects defined, all this seems to connect in some dimension to the work of Donald Graves, Donald Murray, James Britton, Jane Hansen, Lucy Calkins, and the many young women instrumental in forming what is called the "whole language" movement in the teaching of writing. This, along with the new approaches to reading and to "language-based classrooms" that distinguish what has been called the "new literacy," overlaps at many points with some of the basic concerns of progressive education (Willinsky, 1990).

It is not accidental that one of the leaders in taking experiential approaches to reading and writing was Louise Rosenblatt, whose first book, *Literature as Exploration* (1938), appeared under the sponsorship of the Progressive Education Association. In recent years, her work has been widely recognized as instrumental in the development of what has been called "reader reception theory." This is an approach to literature very evocative of Dewey's *Art as Experience* (Rosenblatt, 1978) in part because of its stress on the importance of any work of art becoming an object of a reader's experience if it is to be realized and in part because of its acknowledgment of the importance of perspectives when it comes to the achievement of meaning. When we relate all this swelling reaffirmation of experience and point of view to the engagement with journal writing among children and adults, to the attentiveness to life stories and lived landscapes, we cannot but feel a gulf (perhaps a healthy gulf) between the preoccupation with behaviorisms and measurement and what might be called existential reality in all its variety. When we turn our attention at once to the life stories being disclosed in women's studies, to the probing of connectedness and relationality in feminist literature, we may experience a kind of meshwork among us, something that may bring the common ground into view.

If there are indeed distinguishable threads connecting those who share and are beginning to articulate progressive values and norms, they may resemble what Hannah Arendt had in mind when she spoke of the "web of relations" that forms when persons begin speaking to one another as "who, and not what they are" in their efforts to bring into being—among themselves—what Arendt called an "in-between," an "inter-est," perhaps a metaphor for what we are calling a common ground (Arendt, 1958, pp. 182-184). We may in fact try to render it continuous with some of the efforts being made, being chosen in democratic education. In any event, the themes of communication and articulateness appear and reappear; they are beginning to distinguish the most significant talk of our time. Suddenly, it seems that all sorts of persons are struggling to give shape to the flux of their lived experiences, reaching beyond where they are in response to their own puzzlements, their own shared questionings.

Art and Imagination

To wonder at all this makes some talk of the arts irresistible, especially as I try to think what is involved in achieving a common ground. Dewey certainly realized that inquiries can be freed and consciousness of judgment find deeper levels when persons involve themselves in some informed fashion with the several arts. He wrote, for example, that the function of literature, like the function of art in general, is "to break through the crust of conventionalized and routine consciousness" (Dewey, 1934, pp. 35-37). He knew the importance of imagination when it came to rendering art forms objects of experience, enabling persons to break through the "crust" when they did. He knew too that imagination, which is a cognitive capacity, is what frees persons to look at things as if they could be otherwise. If young persons are to be aroused to come together in learning communities and open spaces among themselves, if they are to be awake enough to take heed of the pestilences in the world, they have to be aroused to stop and think on occasion. They have to be enabled to look through the windows of the actual, to perceive what might be, perhaps what ought to be. Imagination is the capacity to reach beyond in that manner. It is imagination that permits us to break with what Virginia Woolf called "the cotton wool of daily life," the grip of the overly familiar—yes, and comfortable (Woolf, 1976, p. 72). Only when imagination is released are people likely to notice enough and risk enough to want to fight the plagues, to side with the victims of pestilences. But, in these days, what with the constant bombardment of conventional television images, we can no longer rely on children becoming authentically imaginative, shaping "as-if's" in their own particular ways. This is another argument for early and continual exposure to the arts, which cannot be realized without the ability to posit alternative realities. Even in elementary school, children are able—if introduced to paintings or melodies or stories or plays—to create their own visions of experiential possibility. Gradually, as they grow, they become conscious of looking through unaccustomed lenses; they begin to understand how and why encounters with art forms defamiliarize what lies around. Things obscured by routines and habits surge into presentness before them; and in some way they understand. Understanding, they are awakened to pay heed.

A scene from *Romeo and Juliet* or *The Glass Menagerie* or *Gawain and the Green Knight* may, if seriously attended to, reveal shapes and colors and nuances of relationships never noticed before. Edward Hopper's rendering of a city in *Sunday Morning*, or Cezanne's *Lac d'Annecy* or Martha Graham's *Appalachian Spring* will permit the appearing world to disclose more depths and shallows, shades of movement, glimpses of passion than might ever have been suspected by the one paying heed. Elizabeth Bishop's "At the Fishhouses," Toni Morrison's *Beloved*, Tillie Olsen's *Tell Me a Riddle*, Jamaica Kincaid's *Lucy*: Anyone can make a person "see" in her or his own memory, her or his own experience, passages, collisions, flashes, vacancies never noticed before; her or his life was loaned to the text. Perhaps, as Jean-Paul Sartre said with respect to literature, a work may appeal to a reader's or perceiver's freedom. It may move her or him to choose in some unpredicted fashion, to take action in a realm of possibilities, to try to repair. There may be an abrupt awareness of the abandoned droop of someone's hand, of an empty window like an eye socket in a burned-out building, the sadness of departing footsteps, the explosion of a child's red ribbon in the sun, the tremulous sculpture of linked arms. Some persons will want to create, to make, to bring something new into the world by shaping a medium: sound, perhaps, language, clay, their own bodies in movement. Others may find sufficient occasions for transformation in reading fictions or visits to museums and concert halls. What is important is their realization that it is up to them to achieve the works they encounter as meaningful, to transmute them into aesthetic objects for themselves.

These are, in many senses, private transactions, but they become increasingly meaningful if they are talked about later on, if they can be shared. The play, the novel, the painting, the sonata are, after all, emergent from human making in other social contexts; they belong to a community stretching back in time. Attending, taking note along with others, persons cannot but find more doorways opening. Personal encounters may be complicated and enriched the more they are opened to what others see and feel and know. "The Possible's slow fuse," wrote Emily Dickinson, "is lit/by the imagination." In classrooms thought to be progressive, thought to be educative, we need to open spaces of possibility. It is with the consciousness of possibility that persons experience their freedom. It is with such a consciousness that they are moved to engage in dialogue with others, to reach toward what is not, what might be—what seems decent, valuable, humane.

Public Spaces

These are the kinds of spaces that may become public spaces, where diverse beings come together to articulate their concerns and, perhaps, to take action to make change. For Dewey, democracy had much to do with the bringing into being of such spaces, even as it had to do with a community in the making. This may be where the richest vein of progressive thinking is to be found. Today, particularly, it seems so deeply important to break with the silences of apathy, the silences of indifference and of powerlessness. When Dewey wrote of an "articulate public," he had in the mind the necessity for communication, for the kind of communion that sustains a common ground. Dewey would have been as appalled as we are by what he would call an "eclipse of the public" (Dewey, 1954, p. 183) that always leads to feelings of pointlessness and inertia on the part of many young people. The "eclipse" today not only refers to the widespread speechlessness and, yes, the anesthesia with regard to wars and social ills and what some have called "the needs of strangers." It refers as well to a felt incapacity to exert power, to resist the diffusions of power, to make oneself felt by one's representatives, by anyone claiming authority.

For Dewey, publics are formed and public spaces opened when people associate with one another in response to perceived crises or deficiencies—homelessness, we might say, child abuse, street crime, AIDS—and find out how to speak up in such a fashion as to draw the attention of officials and representatives responsible for taking action to remedy such ills. To become a member of such a public, an individual has to be able to communicate as well as to reflect and to know and to imagine. Dewey wanted to see "the highest and most difficult kind of inquiry and a subtle, delicate, vivid, and responsive art of communication" (Dewey, 1954, pp. 110-112), something he knew depended upon atmospheres of cooperation, sympathy, and care. He surely would have understood and responded to the idea of the "sanitary squads" in Camus's *The Plague*. And I believe he would have seen the pedagogical implications of sanitary squads and opening public spaces, especially in times of public passivity, group antagonisms, consumerism, banality, and malaise. It seems to many that progressive education, with its conceptions of active learning, dialogue, and problem posing, may be literally understood to represent public education at its best—education for the nurturing of an articulate public reaching toward a common ground.

If more and more people can resist what Dewey called the "inertia of habit," if they can truly choose to take the side of the victims, if they can choose for vitality and action and critique, there may be a common ground emerging from a great diversity of vantage points. Persons have to be released to see and speak and imagine and think as situated beings; and situated beings look toward each other through their own distinctive perspectives, even as they look toward possibility. The themes may converge and part and converge again as time goes on and the world keeps changing. Progressive education is and will be education for reflective practice and for wide-awakeness and for social concern. It will be carving out wider and wider spaces for freedom and the bite of possibility. Its relevance, like the common ground, continues to lie ahead. It can be, though, education for the resurgence of a public that may take a new responsibility for the world. Perhaps Václav Havel said it best, imagined it most ardently, when he was in prison before the revolution in Czechoslovakia with no clear idea of what was coming and little expectation of his own release. Havel wrote often about the human journey from the injunction to pay attention to the voice that everywhere calls persons to take responsibility and what it means when such responsibility brings home the feeling of being alive. Wondering whether there were indeed any signs of an existential revolution (even as we wonder whether there are indeed signs of a firm progressive common ground), he wrote:

> I can't help feeling that if you are open to hope, you can find timid signals in many things: in movements of youth in revolt such as have broken out periodically since the 1950s, in genuine peace movements, in varied activities in defense of human rights, in liberation movements (as long as they don't degenerate into mere attempts to replace one kind of terror with another) . . . in ecological initiatives, in short, in all the constantly recurring attempts to create authentic and meaningful communities that rebel against a world in crisis, not merely to escape from it, but to devote their full efforts—with the clearsighted deliberation and humility that always go with genuine faith—to assume responsibility for the state of the world. (Havel, 1983, p. 372)

Now I know Havel was not and is not a progressive educator; but the ground he stands on and the hope he acts upon are what many of us would choose to share. What he wrote in his own dark time seems consonant to me with what we are doing here—trying to choose ourselves as responsible, determining to fight the plague. He was showing forth the juncture between personal possibility and the public space; doing so, he was offering hope to anyone willing to make a commitment in the midst of multiplicity—a commitment to remake and remake again a democratic community. This is how we in our own fashion can rebel against a world of carelessness, a nation in crisis, as we reach out together toward our common ground and toward what we hope might be.

References

Arendt, H. (1958). *The human condition.* Chicago: University of Chicago Press.

Arendt, H. (1978). Thinking. In *The life of the mind* (Vol. 1). New York: Harcourt Brace Jovanovich.

Bakhtin, M. (1981). *The dialogic imagination.* Austin: University of Texas Press.

Bellah, R. N., et al. (1985). *Habits of the heart.* Berkeley: University of California Press.

Bruner, J. (1986). *Actual minds, possible worlds.* New York: Cambridge University Press.

Camus, A. (1948). *The plague.* New York: Knopf.

Conrad, J. (n.d.). *Heart of darkness.* In *Three great tales.* New York: Modern Library.

Dewey, J. (1916). *Democracy and education.* New York: Macmillan.

Dewey, J. (1934). *Art as experience.* New York: Minton, Balch.

Dewey, J. (1954). *The public and its problems.* Athens, OH: Swallow.

Duckworth, E. (1991). Twenty-four, forty-two, and I love you: Keeping it complex. *Harvard Educational Review, 61*(1).

Fitzgerald, F. S. (1953). *The great Gatsby.* New York: Scribners.

Geertz, C. (1981). *Local knowledge.* New York: Basic Books.

Havel, V. (1983). *Letters to Olga.* New York: Holt.

Hirsch, E. D., Jr. (1987). *Cultural-literacy: What every American needs to know.* Boston: Houghton Mifflin.

Lippard, L. (1990). *Mixed blessings.* New York: Pantheon.

Nussbaum, M. (1990). *Love's knowledge: Essays on philosophy and literature.* New York: Oxford University Press.

Rorty, R. (1989). *Contingency, irony, and solidarity.* New York: Cambridge University Press.

Rorty, R. (1991). *Objectivity, relativism, and truth.* New York: Cambridge University Press.

Rosenblatt, L. (1938). *Literature as exploration.* New York: Appleton Century.

Rosenblatt, L. (1978). *The reader, the text, the poem.* Carbondale: Southern Illinois University Press.

Taylor, C. (1989). *Sources of the self.* Boston: Harvard University Press.

Willinsky, J. (1990). *The new literacy.* New York: Routledge.

Wolf, C. (1989). *Accident: A day's news.* New York: Farrar, Straus & Giroux.

Woolf, V. (1976). *Moments of being.* New York: Harcourt Brace Jovanovich.

Fruchter takes a policy perspective to examine how school restructuring efforts must be combined with the particular kinds of curricular change recommended by parents, advocacy groups, and reform-minded educators. Currently, school restructurers and curricula activists are not moving forward together but must, according to Fruchter, to achieve the kind of reform both groups want. Of particular concern is the need for restructurers to consider curricular revision in light of diversity. Fruchter calls for new school-based alliances among people with different roles but similar aspirations.

2. Restructuring and Multiculturalism: A New Alliance to Shift the Power Balance?

NORMAN FRUCHTER

The Bush administration's major policy initiative, *America 2000: An Education Strategy* proposes new accountability and improvement plans for current schools and the "invention" of "a new generation of American schools." Specifically, the Bush initiative proposes:

- new academic standards in English, math, science, history, and geography;

AUTHOR'S NOTE: Shorter versions of this chapter appeared in *Social Policy* (Winter 1992) and *School Voices* (Winter 1991); used by permission of the publisher.

- new American Achievement Tests based on those five subjects;
- new incentives for programs of school choice, including revision of Chapter I (federal remedial education aid) to allow funding of eligible children in private or parochial as well as public schools;
- a New American Schools Development Corporation, funded by business and industry, to support the 535 New American Schools to be created in each congressional district;
- congressional start-up grants of $1 million for each of those 535 schools.

Criticism of the Bush plan is growing within the nation's education community. Most of the educators in the Grant Foundation's *Voices From the Field: 30 Expert Opinions on America 2000* (1991) indict the plan's failure to recognize the role of poverty in educational underachievement, its avoidance of student diversity as a fundamental challenge to traditional curriculum and pedagogy, its inability to build on successful existing models of school restructuring, its single-minded (and probably unconstitutional) championing of choice, its regressive notions of raising achievement through national standards and a national testing program, its top-down implementation, and its failure to provide the scale of funding necessary to renew U.S. schooling.

Yet the poverty of Bush's program does not diminish his administration's power to impose its solutions on U.S. schooling. Though the choice components of the Bush program face the same congressional defeats such proposals have previously suffered, competition for the research and development centers and the 535 New American Schools may drain important reform energies. Moreover, the Bush proposals have generated powerful and well-funded efforts to set national standards and develop assessments to measure how well students, schools, school districts, and states meet those standards.

Chester Finn (1989) champions national standards and assessment in a symposium, National Standards for American Education. Finn argues that improvement in student academic performance depends on clearly articulated national standards "expressed in terms of outcomes, the actual skills and knowledge to be acquired, not just intentions, exposure, time spent studying, or courses taken" (Finn, 1989, p. 6). High expectations lead to high results, in this formulation, only if high standards are promulgated and then reinforced by assessment. Opposition to Finn's arguments in the symposium focused on three sets of problems:

- *The issue of authority:* Who decides the standards, structures the decision-making process, and determines the resulting breadth or narrowness of the definition of what counts as the knowledge and skills to be measured?

- *The issue of diversity and pluralism:* What happens to those students and families whose traditions, knowledge, capacities, and skills are at risk of being excluded from the national standards, and what happens to those schools whose distinctiveness and achievements are at risk of being homogenized by top-down mandates and bureaucratic standard-setting and assessment processes?

- *The issue of the relationships between new standards and assessment and the necessity to improve failing schools and dysfunctional school systems:* This includes the possibility that such standard-setting processes constrain rather than improve all schooling and particularly ineffective schooling.

Thus Maxine Greene argues that "the challenge, as I see it, is to devise the kinds of pedagogies that might provoke young people to develop a sense of oughtness, to think (if things were otherwise) about the kinds of human beings they would like to be" (Greene, 1989, p. 9). Greene urges the rooting of standards in communities of value and achievement that create "capacities like critical thought, autonomy of choice, creativity, integrity, persistence, strength of will" (Greene, 1989, p. 13).

Sara Lawrence Lightfoot argues:

As our country's schools incorporate increasingly diverse student populations, the old definitions of excellence are challenged by the competing values, styles and "frames of intelligence" (in Howard Gardner's terminology) of people from different origins ... [which necessitates] a discerning and critical reinterpretation of standards that incorporate a broader, more complicated view of intelligence and achievement. (Lightfoot, 1989, pp. 15-16)

And, finally, Deborah Meier of the Central Park East Secondary School and founder of the Center for Collaborative Education, a New York City-based network of innovative public schools, argues that "if the problem is trying to figure out the connection between teaching and learning, how schools can get young people to use their minds well, then working out ahead of time what everyone should know by twelfth grade is not a solution" (Meier, 1989, p. 26). Meier argues that schools must develop ways to challenge, question, prod, and engage students. "To do this right is going to be an enormously difficult task. If we are serious about this task, many revolutions must take place in our educational system; this is where we have to put our attention—not on the divisiveness of developing a national curriculum" (Meier, 1989, p. 27).

School Restructuring

Meier's "many revolutions" defines restructuring as the slow process of changing individual schools. This process seeks to transform instruction, curriculum, classroom, and school organization as well as teacher preparation and support so that students' capacities and needs, in all their diversity, become the compelling focus of schooling. Transforming the hierarchical and passive relations that characterize most U.S. schools requires the many revolutions Meier envisions as well as a steady commitment to individual school change.

Thus James Comer's School Development Program, Ted Sizer's Coalition of Essential Schools, Henry Levin's Accelerated Schools Program, and Don Davies's League of Schools Reaching Out all define and provide school-based training and support for comprehensive change *processes*. Restructuring in these programs is a school-by-school engagement in which the school's constituencies assess, analyze, and reshape the school's regularities to better meet their students' needs. For this school-by-school, long-term effort, the issue of national standards and accompanying assessment is at best an ancillary support, at worse a draining diversion.

Therefore we can expect a continuing conflict pitting progressive school reformers seeking the resources, legitimacy, and time to expand and consolidate their initiatives against proponents of national standards and assessments. This conflict may well prove unequal; the forces calling for national standards can draw on considerable political and economic power, as well as national media, to advance their position. Progressive reformers have achieved a remarkable degree of national visibility and legitimacy for school-based changes once dismissed as Deweyite utopianism, but their resources, political support, and constituencies are still limited.

Yet there is another important movement—the demand for curricula of diversity and inclusion—whose voice is often distorted at national levels but is increasingly vibrant and militant in local settings. *If the constituencies demanding school reform and revision of curricula can join together to fight for educational change, the power balance might shift decisively toward comprehensive restructuring.*

The demand for curricula of diversity and inclusion is a bottom-up mobilization of anger and frustration at systemic school failure. This push to reformulate curricula, primarily by people and organizations of color, is based on several compelling claims:

- Many academic disciplines, particularly English, history, and the social sciences, are structured by a pervasive Eurocentrism that diminishes or dismisses the experiences of other cultures, races, and ethnicities, thereby fundamentally *distorting* the past and current realities all Americans need to study and understand.
- Basing school and college curricula on such distortions marginalizes students of color, stunts the discovery and exploration of their identity in academic settings, and increases their alienation from both public education and other mainstream societal institutions.

- In an era of changing demographics in which children of color will constitute the majority of many city and state school systems, continuing the traditional Eurocentric canon denies all Americans the intellectual and scholarly resources necessary to develop more effective ways of learning, working, governing, and living together.

Thus the revision of curriculum at Stanford University and demands for a Ujamaa Institute in New York City or an all-male African American school in Detroit are the public tip of a far more extensive debate about the necessity to transform curricula to reflect the realities of our pluralist national experience.

These changes suggest a common issue, the underlying fear of all groups confronting a schooling system controlled by dominant others. The groups seeking change to reflect broader perspectives are raising challenging questions for school people:

- Are you prepared to understand and accept my child for who she is and where she comes from?
- Are you capable of perceiving her real strengths and weaknesses, valuing her as you correct her, helping her grow, and supporting that growth?
- Or will your social, cultural, and economic distance from my community, group, and family produce stereotyping, negative judgments, lowered expectations, and ritualized effort that will limit her development, stunt her capacities, and damage her sense of self?

Conservative efforts to ridicule the demand for curricula of diversity will not stifle this movement. What is perceived to be at stake is too basic: the emotional, psychic, and economic survival of children of color and future communities of color. Instead, conservative opposition will generate more demands. While state education departments have often been the primary targets of demands for curriculum revision, textbook publishers whose traditional histories and orthodox anthologies enshrine the Eurocentric canon are increasingly a focus of curriculum reform efforts. New strategies multiply. In New York City, many organizations and community activists are supporting a suit against the city's board of education to force revision of curricula to include genuine diversity. In Oakland, the city's school board has refused to use California's new history texts and is producing its own local versions, grade by grade. But considerable racial, class, and cultural distances separate constituencies working for restructuring and constituencies working for curricula of diversity. Restructuring advocates are predominantly white educators, while advocates of more pluralist curricula are predominantly people of color, often educators but also community activists, political leaders, scholars, and religious authorities. Though their goals are the same—to improve the education of all children and particularly those poor children and children of color badly served by our schools, these advocates approach schooling change so differently that often there is little awareness of shared goals.

Reflections

My own experience in education reform makes it difficult to separate these two agendas. I spent six years helping to run an alternative high school for dropouts in Newark and another six years directing an experimental college program for public sector workers and community activists in Jersey City. I have often asked myself what my students in both settings wanted from their schooling, to explore the interrelationships between these two approaches to schooling change. As best I can remember, my high school students wanted

- some means to explore, and begin to resolve, their gender and sexual identities as well as some ways to articulate and understand the complexities of their relationships with their peers of both genders;
- some means to explore their racial/ethnic and community identities and their relationships to the troubled city in which they lived and to the other racial and ethnic groups with whom they shared the city;
- some means to explore their family identities and the resulting dynamics, often conflicted, as well as the history that shaped those dynamics;

- some ways to think about why the conditions of daily life for themselves, their families, and the others they shared the city with were so difficult as well as some ways to think about what might improve those conditions;
- some ways to explore the various futures, particularly economic, that might become available to them;
- the skills and habits of mind that would allow them to inhabit a future they chose, and to continue these explorations on their own, once they completed schooling.

Again, as best I can recall, my college students wanted

- the skills necessary to advance in the settings they'd chosen to work in or to move into more advantageous settings;
- the disciplines necessary to better understand the worlds they moved through and the different groups with whom they interacted, politically, economically, and socially;
- the analytical categories to probe and solidify their identities and to situate themselves in a family, community, and racial/ethnic history;
- the critical categories to question and reshape the received wisdom that often marginalized them as well as the categories that would allow them to explore changing what limited them.

Though both my high school and college students were primarily people of color, each institution included a significant segment of working-class whites. Yet their aspirations didn't vary according to race or ethnicity. Moreover, almost all my high school and college students were "second chance" students; their initial schooling came far too close to defeating, rather than realizing, their aspirations. Yet, if what they wanted from their education is similar to the aspirations of poor students and students of color throughout the country, only massive school restructuring, brought about by the many revolutions Meier called for, could reshape U.S. schooling to realize those aspirations. My students were both determined and fortunate; too many students with similar aspirations never get a second chance.

New Alliances

Suppose everything reformers mean by school restructuring and everything activists mean by a curriculum of inclusion are necessary to reshape U.S. schooling to meet my students' aspirations. Suppose we need both a *pedagogy* of diversity and inclusion and a *curriculum* of diversity and inclusion to reshape U.S. schools to equitably meet the aspirations of all our students. Suppose reformers working for school restructuring and activists working for revision of curricula need each other's solutions to produce the scale of schooling change necessary to meet the needs and aspirations of the students for whom both groups are working.

Changing practice in classrooms, in school organization, in teacher preparation and support is not enough to bring about the scale of change we need. The content of what we teach must also change. But changing only the content of what we teach is also not enough to create the change required. How teachers work with students and other teachers, how students work with each other, the organization of the school building and the school day must also change to produce the effective teaching and learning we seek.

Both groups know this in practice. Examine classroom work in restructured schools and you will often find remarkable examples of reformulated curricula focusing on diversity and exploring a rich and accurate history of the school's students, families, and communities. Examine the pedagogy of a school committed to reformulating curriculum and you will often find inquiry-based instruction, peer tutoring, cooperative learning, team and interdisciplinary teaching, and mixed-ability grouping. Yet, politically, school restructurers and curricula activists often work separately for similar ends, divided by barriers of race, class, and culture.

Moreover, these separations reduce the chances of success for both groups. Though restructuring as *process* requires school-by-school transformation, policy supporting these initiatives (and the necessary funding) from state education departments, legislatures, and large school districts can significantly increase the pace of change. Therefore the Re:Learning component of the Coalition of Essential Schools, the School Development Program, and the Accelerated Schools Project have developed policy relationships with several states and districts. These relationships focus on changing the terms through which schools are funded, governed, and held accountable, to allow their teachers and administrators to focus far more intensively on building successful learning environments. Yet such relationships are always tenuous because they depend on the goodwill of educational and political decision-makers, because reformers' potential source of leverage, constituencies of support, are still relatively undeveloped.

Both national teachers unions, for example, strongly support school restructuring. But specific local teacher organizations may conclude that the necessities of collective bargaining and membership demands take precedence over support for restructuring efforts. Similarly, the rhetoric of national leaders of business and industry supports school restructuring. But the requirements of local production, tax-base considerations, and other economic and political calculations may limit business support for local restructuring efforts. Perhaps the most important potential constituencies for school reform are the parents and community members in districts failing to serve poor and disadvantaged students effectively. Yet school reform advocates have not managed, thus far, to reach these constituencies and mobilize them to support school restructuring. (See Fruchter, 1989, for an analysis of the gap between restructuring and empowerment that separates school reformers from many urban parents.)

Meanwhile, advocates of curricula of diversity and inclusion have begun to mobilize constituency support for curriculum revision. Though their parent and community bases have significant potential power, they face fierce resistance from defenders of the traditional canon and conservatives who insist that curriculum revision leads inevitably to barbarism. Without effective allies, the movement for curricula of diversity faces a long and grinding political struggle.

Conclusion

Let me conclude with some beginning thoughts about the possible politics of alliance between school restructuring and curriculum revision advocates. First, restructurers need to transcend their reluctance to support curriculum revision. The excesses, hyperbole, and occasional foolishness of curriculum revision advocates are no reason for silence or tentativeness. The damage done to all of us by the insistence on maintaining traditional Eurocentric curricula dwarfs whatever harm activists create in their zeal for revision. The fight for a genuine curriculum of diversity must not be defined as someone else's battle but as the inevitable, and necessary, complement to the restructuring of school organization and classroom instruction that together will bring about the changes *all our children* need.

Similarly, curriculum revision advocates need to consider not only the content but also the structure, processes, and practices of the schooling systems that damage all our children. Reformulating curriculum content without changing school organization or classroom instruction is unlikely to transform damage into proficiency. Finally, both groups must begin to talk across the divides of race, class, and culture that separate us, to examine what each considers successful programs, and to explore each other's visions.

Such explorations often occur in schools undergoing restructuring. (These explorations are immeasurably aided when teaching staffs include significant numbers of teachers of color and when schools make consistent efforts to involve parents and community representatives in school governance and policy.) Such explorations occur in parent organizing efforts focused on school improvement in districts throughout the country as well as in education reform and advocacy groups committed to helping parent constituencies improve their schools. (In New York City, the work of Educators for Social Responsibility, the Parents Coalition for Education, the American Social History Project, the *School Voices* newspaper, ACORN's education organizing, the Puerto Rican/Latino Education Roundtable, the Africana

Resource Center at Medgar Evers College, and the parent organizing of the Center for Collaborative Education all suggest potential directions.)

Such explorations are also developing into policy positions and broad-based campaigns by organizations such as the National Coalition of Education Activists (NCEA) and the National Coalition of Advocates for Students (NCAS). NCAS's *The Good Common School: Making the Vision Work for All Our Children* (1991) and the "Rethinking Columbus" special issue of the *Rethinking Schools* national school reform newspaper are current examples of how these two movements can come together.

These examples suggest how restructuring and curriculum diversity advocates might begin the difficult process of exploring alliances. We must reach out to engage one another because we need one another too desperately to remain separated. Nothing less than the future of U.S. schooling and the development of a genuinely pluralist democracy are at stake.

References

Finn, C. (1989). National standards: A plan for consensus. *Teachers College Record, 91*(1), 3-9.

Fruchter, N. (1989). Rethinking school reform. *Social Policy, 20*(1), 16-25.

William T. Grant Foundation. (1991). *Voices from the field: 30 Expert Opinions on America 2000.* Washington, DC: Author.

Greene, M. (1989). The question of standards. *Teachers College Record, 91*(1), 9-13.

Lightfoot, S. (1989). National standards and local portraits. *Teachers College Record, 91*(1), 14-17.

Meier, D. (1989). Comments on National Standards Symposium. *Teachers College Record, 91*(1), 25-27.

National Coalition of Advocates for Students. (1991). *The good common school: Making the vision work for all our children.* Boston: Author.

Rethinking Columbus. (1991). [Special issue]. *Rethinking Schools.* Milwaukee: Rethinking Schools Ltd.

Pignatelli's approach to the democratization of schools stresses the point that ongoing parent participation, including but not restricted to choice of schools, is critical to successful change. While school boards have traditionally been cited as a mechanism for parent influence, participation by parents in the selection of school board membership has been extremely low, thereby minimizing their role. He argues that the responsibility for bringing about such participation is largely an issue of educational leadership. While increased professionalization of the work force would be a significant school reform, what is also needed is a less hierarchic, more open organizational structure.

3. Reclaiming the School as a Democratic Site: Educational Leadership, Parent Participation, and School Restructuring

FRANK PIGNATELLI

Amidst talk of educational reform and restructuring of urban public schools in the United States, current mainstream thinking on the subject has remained steadfast in its belief that the work of educators is best expressed as a measure of greater

AUTHOR'S NOTE: This chapter is based on a speech given at Tokyo Metropolitan University, Tokyo, Japan, July 2, 1991. An earlier version appeared in *Proceedings of 1991 TMU International Seminars on Education and Economics.*

33

classroom efficiency by highly trained professionals. Along these lines, the move by New York City Schools' Chancellor Joseph A. Fernandez toward "democratizing" schools in New York City—what has been referred to as school-based management/shared decision making—remains largely an instrument to lift the heavy veil of educator as semiskilled worker and thereby raise the status of those who choose to remain in or enter the profession. Clearly, there is cause for concern among educational policymakers. For, unless the schools in large urban areas such as New York are transformed into more professional workplaces—workplaces that recognize the educator as responsible and worthy of the respect usually accorded to other professionals—it will become increasingly more difficult to ensure a steady supply of competent educators.

I argue here that further professionalization of the work force of public education will not be sufficient to sustain deep changes in the vast number of public schools in this city. What seems to be marginalized—indeed, forgotten—in the discussion of restructuring and school reform is a view of educators as leaders capable and willing to initiate, negotiate, and forge alliances with their counterparts in the community—the parents. Such efforts are rooted in, and take seriously, the Jeffersonian ideal of a literate, politically wise citizenry capable of safeguarding its own liberty. Put differently, such efforts recognize a fundamental sociopolitical concern educators are expected to address—namely, how to extend democratic habits of mind beyond the confines of the school. Expanding the role of educators this way is more than a strategy to democratize school governance and share power with "the other." It is also a way to legitimately and openly reinvigorate a vital conversation about what it means to be educated in, and for, a democratic culture. Hence the probability of effecting deep, systemic change in the way schools work may be more fully realized.

Awareness of the rights and responsibilities of parents is vital to ensure a healthy, responsive educational environment. The challenge for educators is to nurture and cultivate such involvements. Yet, working to realize these involvements—what Counts refers to as "the conscious and deliberate achievement of democracy" (Counts, 1932/1978, p. 37)—needs to be soberly embraced in the face of a popular and potentially far-reaching policy initiative gaining wider audiences of acceptance: the increasing reliance upon "the free enterprise logic of consumer choice and economic self-sufficiency" (Giroux & Aronowitz, 1985, p. 212; see also Chubb & Moe, 1990; Meier, 1991; Wells, 1991) to frame the reform of public education. So-called supply-side advocates offer a challenge to democratic, local governance. Consequently, serious questions are raised about how we define educational leadership.

Democratic Culture and the Public Schools

A vision of the common school as a public space that safeguards democratic culture and ensures its ongoing development runs deep throughout our history (Greene, 1965; Tyack & Hansot, 1982). Yet serious concerns about the tendency of schooling in the United States to reproduce economic inequality and sustain political indifference have been expressed (Apple, 1985; Bowles & Gintis, 1976). There is a troubling disjunction between an ennobling democratic vision of political life perpetuated by, and expected of, our public schools and the nagging, brute realities evidenced in the shabby quality of many schools (Kozol, 1991). It would seem, for example, that local school boards would provide an ideal opportunity to practice and nurture democratic habits. As an example of one earlier attempt to create more democratic schools, in 1969, after bitter feuding, a law was passed by the New York legislature that broke the New York City school system into 31 districts (the number of districts was later increased to 32). But, as Gittell (1981) reports, "The goal of increasing parental participation in policy-making was virtually ignored. The legislation largely preserved the primary areas of school policy-making—budgeting, personnel, and curriculum—as central functions to be conducted almost exclusively by professionals" (p. 182). It is not surprising therefore that, given the lack of responsibility delegated to community and parent constituencies, participation in school board elections in New York City remains at around 7% of the eligible voters. There are many who do not lose sleep over the "thin" quality of the political culture of our schools. Kirst reminds us that Finn, for example, a leading voice of conservative thinking in matters of school policy, called school boards a "dinosaur left over from the agrarian past" (Kirst, 1989, p. 74). Kirst sums up the decade of the 1980s as "an unprecedented attack" on school boards throughout the United States (1989, p. 74). At the same time, he cites this nation's lingering attachments:

> Many political observers believe the school board is in trouble and needs help. A national study by the Institute for Educational Leadership (IEL) found very strong support for the concept of a local school board as an institutional buffer from state and professional administrative control. School boards are deeply embedded in American political culture and appear to be here to stay, but the public does not necessarily support the school board in its own local community, rarely turns out for school board elections in greater numbers than 10-15% of the eligible electorate, and knows very little about the role and function of school boards. (Kirst, 1989, p. 74)

In the context of our current discussion, we might see the scenario Kirst sketches as a reflection of the anemic status of parents in the shaping of educational policy on the local level. It is also an indication of what happens in the absence of "strong versions of political life" (Barber, 1988, p. 18), when the school is viewed primarily as a provider of desperately needed services to parents, their children, their community (Epstein & Dauber, 1990, p. 17). In this regard, Mayor David Dinkins puts forward one aspect of his vision of what schools in New York City must aspire to become:

> Ultimately, I *believe* we must move to a system of community schools, where the physical school structure becomes a center for servicing a wide variety of social needs for both young people and adults after school hours, including adult literacy

and GED classes, health screening, recreation, employment training, and so forth. Providing this type of access to the building will help break down the psychological barriers that make many parents feel like interlopers in their children's schools. (Dinkins, 1990, p. 23)

There is much merit in what the mayor is saying. Confronted with the deadening effects and epidemic proportions of a host of social maladies—and the belief among most professionals who provide social services that these needs are interconnected and therefore require holistic intervention—common sense alone would indicate the wisdom of locating as many of these services as possible in or close to the neighborhood schools.

In the United States, schools have been responsive—some would argue, exceedingly vulnerable (Callahan, 1962)—to growing concerns of the public to remedy threats to the health (broadly defined) of the body politic. Despite its retreat beginning with the Reagan era (House, 1991), liberal, enlightened thinking, still quite prevalent in the "helping professions," assumes that the state bears primary responsibility to formulate and carry out social policy that fosters a more just and humane society. The concern, though, is that the integration, management, and delivery of these kinds of services to families may conflict with or diminish seeing the school as "a neighborhood institution" (Bowles & Gintis, 1976, p. 191; see also Covello, 1958) not only responsive to a local constituency but actively shaped and governed by it. Such efforts need to value and support the preparedness and willingness of those professionals who provide services to the schools not only to share power but to listen actively. Professionals need to remain attentive to the potentially collusive relationship between the work that they do and its effect as a form of social control.

By merely rallying the support of parents, motivating them, schools may be predetermining and prescribing the ancillary role they are expected to play. Institutionalizing/formalizing the role of parents in school governance is not enough to extricate parents from the status of client, to resist, as Lasch (1979/1991) puts it, "the ascendency of the 'helping professions' over the family"

(p. 228). Much would seem to rest on the will of school people (i.e., professionals) at all levels to actively support, and to provide for, the political education of parents and to encourage the ongoing development and training of parents as politically engaged citizens in the governance of their schools. Gutman reminds professionals of the risk of not choosing this as a responsibility, a project:

> Without the tumult of democratic politics, our educational institutions would not be governed by common values. We discover our common values partly through processes of democratic deliberation by which we agree upon the laws that govern our educational institutions. Take away the processes, and the educational institutions that remain cannot be properly called democratic. Take away the educational institutions, and the processes that remain cannot function democratically. . . . [And it is] "political education"—the cultivation of the virtues, knowledge, and the skills necessary for political participation—[that] has moral primacy over other purposes of public education in a democratic society. (Gutman, 1987, p. 287)

Given the vulnerability of schools to unmediated opinion, expressions of hostility, violations of property, and physical threat; given past and, no doubt, future incursions of clubhouse politics wherein schools serve as a source of employment for the loyal foot soldiers of local politicians; given, also, the ebb and flow and contested nature of bureaucratic regulation, contractual agreements, and the like—a commitment to educating for and participating in this admittedly tumultuous public space takes on ethical and moral dimensions. Maintaining (or assuming) neutrality in such a terrain is, at best, naive. Practically speaking, living in a "strong" democratic culture (Barber, 1988) requires that educators examine critically how their work challenges and offers an alternative to what remains, regrettably, as a corrosive norm, an embarrassing legacy of too many public schools and too many communities in urban America—"intellectual torpor and political passivity" (Lasch, 1979/1991, p. 130). It means recognizing that the political and the pedagogical are aspects of the same project.

The citizen/educator (or, put differently, the educator as political actor) operates in an environment where his or her professional status and officially recognized responsibilities can occlude opportunities to form coalitions with parents. As a member of a staff—as opposed to a community—the educator, him- or herself, is subjectively positioned (defined), hierarchically located, his or her actions regulated by the norms of his or her supervisors, union, colleagues. Where, one could ask, are the "gaps," the interstices that could provide educators with an opportunity to reach beyond their prescribed, regulated roles? The psychiatrist Robert Coles talks about how "the details of an individual life [can be] buried under the professional jargon" (1989, p. 17) and discovers in his early training the power of encouraging his patients to tell their own stories, of his growing interest "in the concrete details of a given person's narrative rather than in an aggressive formulation of her or his problems" (1989, p. 14). There is, I believe, an analogue here. When the educator only sees him- or herself as providing a service to members of a community "at risk," engaged in the business of diagnosis and remediation, he or she is situating him- or herself safely outside of the panoply of details that, if respected and encouraged to be told, form the stuff of sociopolitical life.

Parents and School Policy

An understanding of the role of parents in school governance needs to be situated within the broader cultural context. Giroux and Aronowitz comment upon how the public school is commonly regarded in the United States:

> For many people, schools occupy an important but paradoxical place between their daily experiences and their dreams of the future. In one sense, public education has represented one of the few possibilities for social and economic mobility. On the other hand, because of the many problems plaguing school systems, whether they be school violence, absenteeism, falling "standards," or the shrinking of economic resources, popular concern has shifted from the traditional emphasis on gaining

access to public education to a concern for shaping and controlling school policy. (Giroux & Aronowitz, 1985, p. 211)

To press this point further, popular concern must include deliberate strategies and a deep commitment to include the participation of *parents* in matters of school policy. It is fair to say that, in New York City, a *typical* assortment of responses by the majority of educators to such a suggestion would range from skepticism to outright resistance. It is important to explore why such resistance exists.

Categories do more than explain—much more. They construct social reality. They operate as "technologies of power" that move across institutions (Foucault, 1972/1980, p. 104). Thus the way educators name and speak about parents cannot avoid finding expression in the public space where school policy is shaped. The discourse employed in contested arenas both shapes and constructs the context. As Swadener reminds us, we need to be mindful of "the relative power of labels, including the label of being 'at risk,' and the ways in which words and discourse influence assumptions, policies, and opportunities" (1990, p. 20). The category, "at risk," Swadener notes, can reach beyond the student to his or her parents (1990, pp. 30-31). How, then, would educators think about parents in policymaking positions, given their "at-risk" status and given the ease with which they normalize such ways of speaking? In this kind of context, parents would be no more than a last hope effort to rescue a failed system. Rather than sustaining an invidious deficit model that merely tolerates the voices of parents and systematically trivializes their political education—specifically, in the realm of school governance—educators need to value and form their practice around Dewey's comment that "democracy must begin at home, and its home is the neighborly community" (Johnson, 1990, p. 10). In a country that espouses democratic values, our maturity as educators is marked by our ability to understand the necessity of extending democracy locally and acting upon that understanding.

Almost 25 years ago, educators in New York City missed a real opportunity for this kind of democracy in regard to the question of school governance (Gittell, 1981; Stein, 1971). Early on, any notion of real influence by parents dissipated rapidly under the growing influence of the teacher's union and the local political clubs (Gittell, 1981). There is a disabling perception of parent activism that I think complements the at-risk status; a legacy, I believe, from the community control struggles that erupted in 1968. It is the specter of defiant parents arguing passionately for their position, parents unschooled in the arts of compromise and unwilling to leverage power, unable to assess political realities (to play ball) and devise sophisticated political strategies in the face of formidable, extensively organized political machines.

With regard to parents, Connell (1989) suggests that, from the standpoint of strategy alone, it behooves them to engage in the "immensely complex process of negotiation and alliance." And, further, "the notion of community in the sense of neighborhood is too weak a base for democratizing whole educational systems" (1989, p. 128). This makes good tactical sense. It stresses the importance of understanding parents in matters of school governance and school politics as sophisticated, mature actors capable of effective deliberation and managing multiple alliances. And it suggests that educators need to work toward realizing such an understanding. Clearly, the perspectives of both Dewey and Connell need to be taken into account by educators willing to reframe what educational leadership means and to assume responsibility for initiating and sustaining the participation of parents.

Choice of Schools:
An Opportunity, Not a Panacea

I began this chapter talking about the growing attention being paid to the need to restructure schools in large urban areas like New York City. While I recognize some potential benefits of seeing educators as professionals—namely, a more stable, secure, and satisfied work force—I do not believe that democratizing initiatives that focus exclusively on raising status can sustain or guide deep reform of our public schools. Instead, policymakers need to distinguish between professionalization and leadership. The concept of leadership needs to be situated within a view of schooling as an opportunity to learn and practice democratic habits in an arena not restricted to the classroom. I want therefore to underscore the point Giroux and McLaren make about the importance of seeing the work of teachers (and, I would say, other educators) as "empowering for democracy." As they put it:

> It is one thing to argue that schools should become more democratic settings, but such a call is theoretically hollow if it isn't accompanied by an attempt to spell out the forms of knowledge, values, and social practices students will need in order to understand how a particular society works, where they are located in it, and what its more inequitable characteristics are. (Giroux & McLaren, 1988, p. 193)

But we should recall here, first, that the focus of educators cannot remain with the student alone and his or her positioning in the society. It must extend to the parent. Second, it must be admitted that instituting marketplace solutions (i.e., schools of choice) to calcified, failing systems of education is a compelling alternative and not only to conservatives like Chubb and Moe (1990), former Governor of Delaware, du Pont (Wells, 1991), Whittle (Shanker, 1991), and others.

While I acknowledge both the power and the possibility of marketplace initiatives to energize efforts to restructure our bloated, overly regulated public schools, I am concerned about the consequence of such thinking on our already sickly culture of democratic action and habits. The challenge for educators is to see their work as a commitment to this democratic tradition and to avoid confusing "the procedural nature of democracy" (Giroux & McLaren, 1988, p. 193) with effective action, substantive choices, and real alternatives. The way educators think about choice and the way they act upon their thinking is vitally important. Meier (1991), an educator that draws upon the Deweyan stream of U.S. progressive education, has also spoken about this point of introducing choice on a large scale throughout urban public schools. Most important, she and her growing number of colleagues throughout New York City have proven on a relatively small but growing scale that choice is not incompatible with cultivating democratic habits. As she sees it, "The argument over choice, unlike the one about vouchers, offers progressives an opportunity" (1991, p. 266). In her view, choice serves as a prerequisite, an opportunity to effect deep change in how schools work; it is not an end in itself. What is most promising in the work of Meier and her colleagues both in East Harlem (Community School District 4) and around the city is the kind of public schools that grow and are nourished as they rely upon a strategy of choice. "All of District 4's schools are small, largely self-governing and pedagogically innovative. They are schools with a focus, with staffs brought together around common ideas, free to shape a whole set of school parameters in accord with those ideas" (Meier, 1991, p. 266). In addition to ensuring an equal distribution of resources and a diverse student population, Meier underscores the point that the flow and quality of information about the schools to and among parents and educators is essential to a long-lived system of choice guided by progressive principles (Meier, 1991).

It is interesting to note that, in response to a new effort to create a chain of for-profit schools across the nation, also predicated upon the power and value of choice, Albert Shanker, president of the powerful American Federation of Teachers, takes the question of information a step further. He recommends that, to the extent school reform is colored by choice and marketplace machinations, "states should make sure parents have enough information to make good choices by passing legislation that requires private schools to meet the same testing and reporting standards as public schools" (Shanker, 1991, p. 7). While his primary concern is, understandably, the potentially disastrous consequences for public schools and public school teachers if the most active parents send their children to such private schools, the concern about the availability of information appears to be endemic to issues and systems of choice whether in the public or in the private school domain. But the significance of accurate, appropriate information among parents and between parents and educators cannot end at the point where the parent has exercised his or her choice of school, especially if the recognition that one has chosen intelligently is to be taken seriously. School governance needs to be mediated by responsible, ongoing working relationships with parents over matters as vital to the life of the school as budgeting, personnel, and curriculum. A needs assessment devised by the Professional Development Center at Bank Street College Graduate School to assess parent views in public schools in New York City is a case in point. In the analysis of responses to questions put to 56 parents at one school, Rosen and Jewell report that

> these parents revealed a commitment to helping effect change in needed directions through their expressed wish to become involved in school decision-making. At the same time they recognized that they needed a great deal of information in a wide range of areas to become active as informed participants in the important shift toward school-based management/shared decision-making. (Rosen & Jewell, 1991, p. 1)

Again, East Harlem's District 4 provides a strong case for including parents in the life of the school beyond the point of school selection for their children. Noting a change in leadership at the district level most recently, and subsequent unsuccessful efforts by this regime to dismantle the district's extensive program of school choice, Meier attributes the ability of schools of choice to endure "to the loyalty and ingenuity that choice and co-ownership together engender" (1991, p. 268). Habits of democracy, once inculcated and practiced, are hard to take back. They become that much more vital to the life of the school when participation is comprehensive and dynamic, not narrowly focused only on one decision. Snider (1991), quoting Seeley, makes a good point about parent involvement. Rather than understanding the involvement of parents as a measure of the number of positions allotted to them on school governing boards, he urges "a paradigm shift to a collaborative model." And he argues, convincingly, that

> the counting of votes is still within the existing bureaucratic model. If educators and parents agree that they need to work together, they will both end up with more de facto power than if they try to battle over who's going to have more votes on a governing council. (Snider, 1991, p. 13)

Agreeing with Seeley, I would encourage educators to recognize current school restructuring initiatives as an opportunity to rethink what it means to educate in, and for, a democratic society. This means working to create, in close collaboration with those most affected by what occurs in the schools, a democratic culture. At stake is whether the vision of the common school can be revived.

Jackson and Cooper (1989) make a similar argument. They take as their starting point what Epstein considers to be the most advanced form of parental involvement (type 5), which consists of

- parent involvement in governance and advocacy;
- decision-making role in groups like PTA/PTO, advisory groups, committees, ad hoc groups;
- advocacy for improved schooling, programs, support. (Jackson & Cooper, 1989, p. 265)

Jackson and Cooper contend that Epstein's five-tiered parental involvement construct has failed, for the most part, in urban inner city schools, for it rests on what they call the "'hierarchical approach'— one that depends on formal ('elected') parent leadership working routinely alongside the principal and school staff." In addition to placing parents in an ancillary role in predictable and controllable relationships with professional staff, it remains,

they believe, "too uncritical" (1989, pp. 265-266). Building upon
Epstein, they suggest the need to move *from* hierarchical participation and *along* two other lines: parents as consumers of education and "individual decision makers" who take advantage
of the opportunity to choose schools for their children, and parents as "social network members in self-help and school improvement" (1989, p. 264). In their analysis, the authors see the school
becoming the "center of [the] parent's life" (1989, p. 271).

Progressive educators have a rich tradition to draw from as
they move along these lines (Counts, 1932/1978; Covello, 1958;
Dewey, 1938). Indeed, they may also take some solace in the
fact that support for school choice and opposition to any talk
of centralizing school governance still finds expression in conservative circles despite a steady onslaught on the troubling
state of schooling in this country and their press for a national
curriculum (Hirsch, 1988; Smith, O'Day, & Cohen, 1990). The
opportunity for educators to reframe and embrace parental
participation is also an opportunity to effect deep change in the
culture of our schools.

References

Apple, M. W. (1985). *Education and power*. Boston: ARK Paper-
    backs.
Barber, B. (1988). *The conquest of politics: Liberal philosophy in
    democratic times*. Princeton, NJ: Princeton University Press.
Bowles, S., & Gintis, H. (1976). *Schooling in capitalist America:
    Educational reform and the contradictions of economic life*. New
    York: Basic Books.
Callahan, R. (1962). *Education and the cult of efficiency*. Chicago:
    University of Chicago Press.
Chubb, J. E., & Moe, T. M. (1990). *Politics, markets and America's
    schools*. Washington, DC: Brookings Institution.
Coles, R. (1989). *The call of stories: Teaching and the moral imagi-
    nation*. Boston: Houghton Mifflin.
Connell, R. W. (1989). Curriculum politics, hegemony, and
    strategies of social change. In H. A. Giroux & R. I. Simon

(Eds.), *Popular culture, schooling and everyday life*. Granby, MA: Bergin & Garvey.

Counts, G. S. (1978). *Dare the school build a new social order?* Carbondale: Southern Illinois University Press. (Original work published 1932)

Covello, L. (1958). *The heart is the teacher*. New York: McGraw-Hill.

Dewey, J. (1938). *Experience and education*. New York: Macmillan.

Dinkins, D. N. (1990). A master plan for restructuring education in New York City. *CSA Education Review, 23,* 20-25.

Epstein, J. L., & Dauber, S. L. (1990). *School programs and teacher practices of parental involvement in inner-city elementary and middle schools*. Washington, DC: Johns Hopkins University, Center for Research on Elementary and Middle Schools. (mimeo)

Foucault, M. (1980). Two lectures. In C. Gordon (Ed.), *Power/knowledge: Selected interviews and other writings, 1972-1977*. New York: Pantheon. (Original work published 1972)

Giroux, H. A., & Aronowitz, S. (1985). *Education under siege: The conservative, liberal and radical debate over schooling*. Granby, MA: Bergin & Garvey.

Giroux, H. A., & McLaren, P. (1988). Reproducing reproduction: The politics of tracking. In H. A. Giroux (Ed.), *Teachers as intellectuals: Toward a critical pedagogy of learning*. Granby, MA: Bergin & Garvey.

Gittell, M. (1981). School governance. In C. Brecher & R. Horton (Eds.), *City municipal priorities*. New York: Landmark, Allanheld and Osman.

Greene, M. (1965). *The public school and the private vision: A search for America in education and literature*. New York: Random House.

Gutman, A. (1987). *Democratic education*. Princeton, NJ: Princeton University Press.

Hirsch, E. D., Jr. (1988). *Cultural literacy: What every American needs to know*. New York: Vintage.

House, E. R. (1991). Big policy, little policy. *Educational Researcher, 20*(5), 21-26.

Jackson, B. L., & Cooper, B. S. (1989). Parent choice and empowerment: New roles for parents. *Urban Education, 24*(3), 263-286.

Johnson, T. W. (1990). Philosophy as education. *Educational Foundations, 4*(4), 5-16.

Kirst, M. W. (1989). Who should control the schools? Reassessing current policies. In T. J. Sergiovanni & J. H. Moore (Eds.), *Schooling for tomorrow: Directing reforms to issues that count.* Boston: Allyn & Bacon.

Kozol, J. (1991). *Savage inequalities: Children in America's schools.* New York: Crown.

Lasch, C. (1991). *The culture of narcissism: American life in an age of diminishing expectations.* New York: Norton. (Original work published 1979)

Meier, D. W. (1991, March 4). Choice can save public education. *The Nation,* p. 256.

Rosen, J. L., & Jewell, K. E. (1991). *Needs assessment of parents at [a public elementary school in New York City]: Analysis of questionnaires.* New York: Bank Street College of Education, Professional Development Center. (mimeo)

Shanker, A. (1991, May 27). Planning a national, for-profit chain: Whittle schools. *The New York Times,* Week in Review sec., p. 7.

Smith, M. S., O'Day, J., & Cohen, D. K. (1990, Winter). National curriculum American style: Can it be done? What might it look like? *American Educator,* pp. 10-17, 40-46.

Snider, W. (1991, February). Power sharing: Parental involvement in school rule has some teachers wary. *Teacher Magazine,* pp. 12-13.

Stein, A. (1971). Strategies for failure. *Harvard Educational Review, 41*(2), 158-204.

Swadener, E. B. (1990). Children and families "at risk": Etiology, critique, and alternative paradigms. *Educational Foundations, 4*(4), 17-40.

Tyack, D., & Hansot, E. (1982). *Managers of virtue: Public school leadership in America, 1820-1980.* New York: Basic Books.

Wells, A. S. (1991, February 27). A bold plan for choice in Delaware's schools. *The New York Times,* p. B11.

Similar to the previous chapter, Moscow's piece also focuses on parent involvement, in this case, the specific role of parents in the selection of principals in New York City. Recognizing the important leadership role played by the principal and the influence he or she can exert in affecting the nature and pace of school reform, the principal selection process is central to school democratization. Unlike in many other cities, in New York, principals are eligible for lifetime tenure in their schools after five years. Given the permanency of a school's administrative team, the selection process becomes a crucial opportunity for a school's community to voice its concerns and exert its influence. Moscow argues that the most current regulations of 1990, while an improvement, are still inadequate and suggests alternatives to assure more participation.

4. The Supervisory Selection Process in New York City: A Parent Activist Perspective

JON MOSCOW

Schooling is an important means of transmitting values and skills to the next generation. Therefore setting the educational agenda is inevitably an act of political and social power. Who sets the agenda, and how, has great implications for individual students and for society.

The issue of who controls schools has increased in significance as schools have come to play an increasingly critical role

---

AUTHOR'S NOTE: This chapter is an adaptation of the author's master's thesis.

in children's lives. The past century has seen a shift in responsibilities from families to social institutions such as the school as well as a shrinking of the family's domain. As Braverman (1974) writes:

> With the disappearance of farm and small-town life as the major arenas of child-rearing, the responsibility for the care and socialization of children has become increasingly institutionalized. The minimum requirements for "functioning" in a modern urban environment—both as workers and as consumers—are imparted to children in an institutional setting rather than in the family or the community. (p. 287)

Issues of governance, and the role to be played by parents, are very much on the table in urban school systems today, fueled by schools' failure to meet the cognitive and affective needs of large numbers of students. One focus for governance struggles has been the appointment of the principal, the school's educational leader. The Chicago school reform movement explicitly gives parent-dominated local school councils the power to hire and fire principals (Designs for Change, 1989). In a different political environment, strong parent participation in principal selection has been a key demand of New York's parent movement, reviving in strength for the first time since the defeat of community control in the late 1960s and early 1970s (Parents Coalition, 1990).

At the same time that parents have been seeking more power in principal selection as part of efforts to create more responsive and effective schools, another process has been taking place with the same goal. This has been the rise within public school systems of small schools with an educational vision based on preparing students to become active participants in a democratic society. With roots in the progressive tradition and the teacher professionalization movement, these schools, sometimes headed by a principal but more generally by a teacher-director, focus on creating collaborative school environments in place of traditional hierarchies.

In New York City, these progressive schools, usually called "option" or "alternative" schools, have put much thought into the relationship between staff and students. Staff-parent relations vary greatly from school to school, however, often as a function of the driving forces behind the founding of the school and the style and background of the director. Beyond the schools' relationships with individual parents, the option schools face many of the thorny issues of partnership in governance found in traditional schools. As in traditional schools, relations between the directors and organized parent bodies have frequently been strained.

In New York City, it is only recently that the parent role in principal, or director, selection has become a major issue in option schools. For years, there were relatively few such schools, mostly led by their founders. Parents were generally so happy that their children were in schools that "worked" that they hesitated to rock the boat. In addition, schools headed by directors rather than principals existed in an administrative limbo without an official selection process.

This situation has changed in the past few years. Many more option schools have sprung up in a wider range of community school districts, frequently at the initiative of parents. Directors are more mobile. As it is clear that option schools are here to stay, and that they are not exempt from many of the problems of traditional schools, parents are less worried about rocking the boat and more forceful in asserting a right to share in decision making. At the same time, principal selection procedures for traditional schools have become more precise, and alternative schools have been recognized by the system as a legitimate form of school. Finally, many of the leaders of the parent movement, and many progressive teachers, have their own children in the alternative schools and expect to have a say in their destinies.

The premise of this chapter is that a serious parent role in head-of-school selection is essential to selecting educational leaders for effective, responsive schools, whether traditional or alternative. Looking at New York City's selection procedures, I focus on some of the issues and pitfalls in achieving a sound process. In conclusion, I argue that alternative schools can and must take the lead in making collaborative selection processes work. In doing so, they will not only be strengthening themselves but creating an important model for all schools.

A Parent Activist Perspective

I come to this discussion from a parent activist perspective. As a parent who has taken part in several selection processes over the last 10 years, I have long been fascinated by the dynamics of selection. As cochair, and, now executive director, of the Parents Coalition for Education (PCE), I have seen those dynamics play out in many different situations.

PCE is an 8-year-old citywide parent organization composed of 30 parent associations and community organizations with a combined membership of more than 15,000. Its roots are in black, Puerto Rican, Dominican, Chinese, and multiracial groups, and active members range from parents who feel excluded from their parents association to parent school board members who form part of their board's majority.

During the past two years, we have taken the lead citywide in pressing for a more effective and more informed parent role in principal selection and have provided support to parents in schools throughout New York City. In doing so, we have become very aware of the enormous differences in outcome resulting from minor points in text or interpretation of regulations. We have seen the extraordinarily different practical effects of similar rules in different districts and schools, depending on the mix of educational, social, political, and personal forces. We have been conscious that inevitably all individuals—parents, teachers, administrators, board members—come to a selection process with a variety of agendas, some role related and some personal, as well as with very different sets of knowledge and experience.

We have struggled to figure out the characteristics of a selection process that can choose effective school leaders and the role of informed, effective parent participation in that selection. Given that principals are not selected in a vacuum, we have tried to look both at details of the process and at the larger institutional context within which it takes place. Based on these premises, what should the process look like?

Background to the Selection Process

The appointment of principals in New York City has long had an explicitly political side. In the recent past, a 1986 Bronx grand jury focused on principal and assistant principal selection in District 10; they found that the majority faction of the board had divided up assistant principal appointments on a patronage basis. In 1990, the Joint Commission on Integrity in the Public Schools, focusing on District 27 in Queens, detailed the political connections of the board members. Among its findings was that "the qualifications for assistant principal and principal have been set so low that ill-motivated board members have been free to select mediocre candidates for improper reasons" (p. ix).

Principal selection also has a long history of being central to parents' efforts to improve schools. It was a key issue in the community control movement of the 1960s in New York City (Rogers, 1968, pp. 366-370). In 1990 hearings held on proposed changes in selection procedures, PCE spoke about the then-existing process, known as "30-R" after the Chancellor's circular establishing it. Even though it was generally weak and unsatisfactory, PCE said: "The 30-R process is currently the only place in the school system in which professionals are required to pay any attention to the views of parents" (Parents Coalition, 1990).

Circular 30-R

Since the establishment of New York City's community school districts under the school decentralization law of the early 1970s, the principal appointment process has been governed by various versions of Chancellor's Circular 30. In 1977-1978, the chancellor issued Circular 30-R, which governed the process until 1990.

WITHDRAWN

SCCCC - LIBRARY
4601 Mid Rivers Mall Drive
St. Peters, MO 63376

Circular 30-R established an overall framework within which local districts could establish their own procedures (New York City Board of Education, 1977). The key points of the circular were as follows:

A Screening Committee was established as "an advisory committee to the Community School Board." Its function was to screen resumes, interview candidates, and make recommendations to the school board. For school-based positions, committee members included school board members, representatives of the parent association, and, for an assistant principal position, the principal. The community superintendent was a nonvoting member. Teachers and other school employees could be consulted but could not be voting members.

Selection criteria for positions were to be developed "in consultation with parents, staff, and others agreed upon by the Community School Board." Following elimination of candidates who did not meet minimum eligibility requirements, these criteria formed the basis for selecting candidates to be interviewed. Community school board members and the superintendent could submit names to the Screening Committee of candidates to be interviewed.

Following interviews, the Screening Committee submitted at least three names to the superintendent. The superintendent, in turn, submitted one or more names to the school board from among those *interviewed.* The key sentence here is this: "The names submitted to the Community School Board by the Community Superintendent *need not necessarily be the same as those submitted by the Screening Committee"* (emphasis added).

If the superintendent's recommendation(s) differed from the committee's, the superintendent was to meet with the committee "to discuss the Superintendent's action," prior to the submission of the name(s) to *the school board.* The school board had to choose from among the names recommended by the superintendent. If it refused, a meeting was to take place between the committee, the superintendent, and the board. If no agreement could be reached, the position was to be readvertised.

When Joseph A. Fernandez became chancellor in January 1990, he made revision of Circular-30 a top priority, issuing a draft revision on January 22. At the request of the Parents Coalition and other parent and advocacy groups, he held public hearings in March. Responding to virtually unanimous recommendations for a greater parent role, he modified the draft and issued Chancellor's Regulation C-30 on May 1, 1990 (New York City Public Schools, 1990).

Circular C-30

Circular C-30 differs sharply from 30-R. Instead of providing a broad framework, it mandates a single process for the entire city. The key points of the circular are as follows:

- The screening committee, now known also as the Level I committee, has been converted from an advisory body of the school board into a superintendent's committee.
- The voting members of the Level I committee are two teachers, six to ten parents from the school, and a supervisor (principal/assistant principal). The superintendent is the nonvoting chair, and school board members may be nonvoting members. The chancellor's office may appoint a nonvoting neutral observer.
- The Level I committee sets criteria, subject to the superintendent's approval, and conducts interviews. The superintendent, but not the school board members, may require the committee to interview up to two additional candidates.
- Following the interviews, the committee submits a minimum of five names to the superintendent, who submits two or more of these to the school board. Although the superintendent or school board may reject all the candidates, reopening portions of the process, they may not consider a candidate who has not been recommended by the screening committee.

The teachers on the committee are elected by the faculty in the school in an election conducted by the United Federation of Teachers chapter. The supervisor is elected by the members of the Council of Supervisors and Administrators (CSA) in the school. The parents are selected by the membership of the parents association (PA). According to the circular, they "should be representative of various groups in the school, e.g. Special Education and Bilingual Education."

The circular provides that efforts "must" be made to ensure that the committee be "appropriately representative in ethnicity and gender." Names of committee members, with an ethnic and gender breakdown, must be sent to the Office of Personnel for approval prior to the committee beginning work.

Issues

In some respects, C-30 clearly creates a more accountable process and is more favorable to parents than 30-R. It establishes a parent majority, chosen by the PA membership, and specifies that committee members must represent a variety of programs in the school. It requires efforts to ensure ethnic and gender diversity on the committee. Most notably, C-30 requires the finalists to be selected from among those recommended by the Level I committee.

The impact of these provisions is less clear in practice, however. Parents and other participants in schools that have gone through the C-30 process have reported back many problems. The following proposals are culled from this participant feedback and reflect both the existence of and possible solutions to major problems.

Proposal 1: Steps must be taken to ensure that parent representatives are democratically elected by a properly constituted parents association, following outreach to all parents. Committee selection continues to be a source of tremendous complaint and cynicism among parents. The minimum standards of the election process should be specified and enforced.

Among these standards should be basic assurances that the PA is properly constituted. PCE has recommended that PA bylaws, lists of officers, and election minutes and attendance sheets must be on file at school and district offices for *any* parent consultations to be valid.

All parents should be eligible to vote whether they have paid dues or not. Many parents choose not to pay dues for financial reasons, because of dissatisfaction with PA leadership, or for other reasons. In some PAs, control of the membership list and dues cutoff dates are used by the leadership to maintain dominance.

There should be specific minimum notification requirements and specifications for letting parents know about the meeting(s) at which parent committee members will be selected. It may, for example, make sense to require 10 days' notice and notification through the mail as well as through children. Notices should have to be in the major languages of parents and interpretation should be available at the meeting. Costs for the process should be borne by the school system.

These basic provisions would begin to respond to a reality in hundreds of schools, in which small groups of active PA members rely on and are dominated by the principal. Notices are sent perfunctorily and few people attend meetings. Bylaws and election records are obscurely documented and become issues at points of conflict.

Many of these issues go far beyond the details of the principal selection process, though the existence of independent, representative PAs is at the heart of parents' ability to participate meaningfully in the selection process. PCE has proposed radical revision of the board of education policy, "Parents Associations and the Schools," to create the conditions under which effective, independent PAs can flourish (Parents Coalition, 1992).

Proposal 2: The Level I committee should make three, rather than five, recommendations. A major complaint of parent committee members is that there are rarely, if ever, five "good candidates" for a position. Generally, there are no more than two or three. The requirement that the committee submit five names excessively dilutes the process. It has the effect of limiting parents' power to that of vetoing some candidates they consider completely unacceptable. PCE and other groups have urged that the minimum number of recommendations be reduced to three.

Proposal 3: Screening committee members need more opportunity to become familiar with candidates. Under current interpretations of C-30, the Level I committee is allowed only a single round of interviews (Division of Human Resources ruling in P.S. 6M selection, personal communication). In general, these tend to be short—20 minutes is not unusual. Level I committee members do not have an opportunity to conduct in-depth second-round interviews. They are not supposed to make site visits or to check references, all these tools being reserved for the superintendent.

A period of 20 minutes does not provide an adequate chance to get to know someone who could be the school's educational leader for decades. There is insufficient time to ask a wide range of questions, to follow up on answers, and to probe areas of particular interest. In addition, many people interview well but look very different on a site visit. Interviews cannot substitute for a chance to watch interactions with children, parents, and colleagues.

Parents and teachers who go together on site visits see and react to different things. Similarly, parents and teachers who check references may ask about different things and get different responses. The current process denies the committee access to these sources of knowledge.

Another effect of denying committee members the opportunity to go on site visits and to talk to the people listed as references is that the committee's educational knowledge remains limited. When the Bronx New School, an alternative, progressive school, was founded several years ago, parents and teachers on the director-search committee went on site visits together. The teachers showed parents things they were looking for in classrooms; the parents pointed out to teachers that some candidates responded to the visiting professionals and parents very differently; for example, some spoke only to the teachers, ignoring the parents (from personal conversations).

Proposal 4: Committee members need to be less isolated from their constituencies. A recurring complaint from parents, on committees and off, is that committee members need more interaction with and feedback from the parent body at large. Especially because few PAs have clearly defined educational philosophies, it is very difficult for a small group of parents to effectively represent the concerns and perspectives of the parent body. The isolation increases the likelihood of co-optation or intimidation by professionals on the committee as well as the possibility that small groups of parents will successfully push their own agenda, regardless of the wishes of the parent body as a whole.

Under Circular 30-R, one community school board in Brooklyn involved the whole parent body in portions of the selection and interview process. Board members reported that it increased the sense of community and the level of educational discussion and decreased the likelihood of a small group unfairly controlling the process. They have urged that they be allowed to reinstitute that procedure (from personal conversations). Complaints of isolation are sometimes countered with concerns about protecting candidates' privacy. It appears, however, that much more flexible procedures are possible without violating any legal rights of candidates.

Obviously, this issue is closely tied to the issue of an open process within an independent parents association. Mandates providing for open discussion by the PA membership of criteria and committee procedures would strengthen both the PA and the selection process. Similarly, there is no reason that committees cannot report back to the general PA membership on the variety of educational issues that are raised by interviews with candidates.

Proposal 5: Participants need more "training." Many parents identify lack of training as a serious problem. A parent member of a selection committee at a wealthy Upper East Side elementary school points out that even parents who routinely interview and hire professionals in their own jobs do not know how to interpret board of education resumes (from a personal conversation). A parent member of a Brooklyn school board argues that many parents have no framework for evaluating candidates on an educational basis, making them targets for manipulation by teachers, superintendents, and school board members (from a personal conversation).

I have put "training" in quotes because it seems to me that the issue has many levels and is closely related to the openness and depth of the process. One level is indeed being able to understand and interpret resumes. Another is understanding and having a vision of a principal's role. A third level involves truly being the representative of a constituency that has developed a coherent viewpoint. A fourth includes the opportunity to grow during the process itself, through such mechanisms as site visits and conversations with other committee members.

Proposal 6: C-30 should set minimum standards; the chancellor's office should monitor compliance with these; districts and schools should have maximum freedom to go beyond the standards. Circular 30-R provided a minimum framework; within it, some districts created structures that they felt were more democratic and effective than those created by Circular C-30. Many other districts took advantage of the lack of specificity to play political games. C-30 is clearly an improvement in mandating certain steps. There is no reason, however, that local bodies should be held back from doing more. In fact, such provision is the essence of Chancellor Fernandez's vision of school-based management/shared decision making.

Proposal 7: Principal selection must be viewed as one part of the process of improving educational leadership and schools. Principal selection does not exist in a vacuum. As outlined above, parent participation cannot be truly meaningful unless it is grounded in an active, democratic PA within a responsive governance system. Circular C-30 is one of several documents that together shape principal selection and governance as a whole. In New York, at the time of this writing, two of the most important of these are the Board of Education policy, "Parents Associations and the Schools," which is currently undergoing revision, and proposed new governance legislation in the state legislature, known informally as the "Marchi Bill," which would restructure the decentralized school system and, in its current form, strengthen parents' voice in school decision making. The Chicago school reform process raises another question. Among the many changes that were instituted was the hiring of principals on four-year renewable performance contracts (Designs for Change, 1989).

Currently, New York City principals go through a five-year probation period, followed by lifetime building tenure, except under extraordinary circumstances. If the C-30 process led to a four-year contract rather than to lifetime tenure, the stakes, the context, and the process itself would be radically different. A parent advocate recently pointed out in a personal conversation that most New York City principals have the job security of U.S. Supreme Court justices. He asked, "Can C-30 or any similar process bear that kind of weight?"

The Parents Coalition argues that the selection process cannot bear that weight. One set of problems are the procedural weaknesses. More fundamentally, PCE questions whether many principals can be expected to remain responsive and educationally dynamic leaders over a lifetime, in the absence of effective ongoing mechanisms for accountability. Unlike Supreme Court justices, principals do not operate in a national spotlight; in fact, most work with virtually no external attention. We believe that limited-term contracts will generate mechanisms for increased accountability.

Role of Progressive Schools

The most frustrating aspects of parent participation in C-30 processes are intangible. Parents at many schools confront a rigid, hierarchical bureaucracy that pays little respect to parents in the course of day-to-day life, especially when the parents are poor and are people of color. The administrative culture of the New York City Board of Education is conservative and filled with "old-boy networks." Procedural rules that are supposed to guarantee parents a say are frequently subverted. Even when they are followed, however, parents often end up feeling they have been part of some elaborate show with a predetermined outcome.

Alternative, progressive schools have their share of the barriers that separate professionals and parents. They have, however, shed many of the hierarchical aspects of school life. Because they are new, and challenge many of the traditional patterns of Board of Education life, they are less locked into the hierarchical culture. Because they have been formed in pursuit of a collaborative vision, many are potentially more open to experimenting with genuinely shared decision making between teachers, parents, and students. Because they are small, there is more possibility of personal access and interaction between staff and parents.

Thus alternative, progressive schools may be the schools that are most able to implement the spirit as well as the letter of the head-of-school selection process. They may lead the way in creating selection processes in which communities of adults, and, where possible, students, choose the best educational leaders for their schools.

References

Braverman, H. (1974). *Labor and monopoly capital.* New York: Monthly Review Press.

Designs for Change. (1989). *The Chicago school reform act: Highlights of Public Act 85-1418* (brochure). Chicago: Author.

Grand Jury of Bronx County. (1986). *Report of the March 1986 Bronx County Grand Jury: An inquiry into politics and the school system, politics in our school system: A corrupting influence.*

Presented by the Office of the District Attorney of Bronx County, New York.

Joint Commission on Integrity in the Public Schools, J. F. Gill, Chairman. (1990). *Findings and recommendations.* New York: Author.

New York City Board of Education. (1977). *Regulations governing the assignment and appointment of supervisors* (Special Circular 30-R, 1977-1978). New York: Author.

New York City Public Schools. (1990). *Regulation of the chancellor C-30: Regulation governing the selection, assignment and appointment of pedagogical supervisors and administrators.* New York: Author.

Parents Coalition for Education in New York City. (1990, March 14). *Testimony at the Chancellor's Public Hearing on Special Circular 30-R: Appointment of principals and other supervisors and administrators.* New York: Author.

Parents Coalition for Education in New York City. (1992, January). *Newsletter.* New York: Author.

Rogers, D. (1968). *110 Livingston Street: Politics and bureaucracy in the New York City school system.* New York: Random House.

With this case study of a single, progressively minded, alternative public high school, again in New York City, Born analyzes the work life changes that teachers experience as their school moves to a democratic, site-based-management/shared decision-making approach to organization and school governance. Born identifies factors that were present in the emerging professional culture of her school that allowed the process of school democratization to proceed. Her study demonstrates that, while most teachers have increased their involvement in issues around curriculum and pedagogy, climate, and personnel decisions in the context of this successful school democratization process, there are important variations in teacher perceptions.

5. Shared Leadership: A Study of Change at Middle College High School

TERRY BORN

In spring 1990, a group of teachers at Middle College High School, a New York City alternative high school for 500 students at risk of dropping out, was invited to meet with the principal and a representative from the Center for Urban Ethnography at the University of Pennsylvania. The center had been working in the school for several years doing qualitative research for the City University of New York. They evaluated collaborative programs between the City University and the New York City Board of Education. The teachers at the meeting were invited to consider framing research projects about their own practice. They were to be given training, coaching, and financial compensation, and their work was to be published. I chose to do a research project at that time, but it was neither the beginning nor the end of the story. My original topic was to be about the use of theater in teaching at-risk students. After several weeks of preparation, I lost interest in something I had lived with and thought about for almost 20 years and turned to site-based management/shared decision making (SBM/SDM), an issue that was emerging around the country and more specifically at Middle College itself. I was intrigued with the idea of how the process would work, how roles would have to shift, and how teachers would take to the benefits and burdens of greater responsibility. At Middle College, the staff had gradually begun to share responsibility and make policy from an internal need to reorganize time schedules. That expanded when we pulled together to establish a personnel committee and fought for a waiver from the Board of Education and the United Federation of Teachers to monitor the hiring of staff. As a staff, we chose to adopt SBM/SDM in the Chancellor's first initiative in 1990. The opportunity to do participatory research was related directly to the expanded teacher's role and afforded the school a vehicle by which to reflect on and evaluate the effect of the changes.

The National Commission on Excellence in Education's report, *A Nation at Risk: The Imperative for Educational Reform* (1983), called for greater teacher participation in the decision-making process of schools. One of many responses to that mandate came in Dade County, Florida, in 1987, when the superintendent, Joseph Fernandez, initiated site-based management and shared decision making in 33 public schools. In 1989, Dr. Fernandez assumed the chancellorship of the New York City Board of Education and introduced SBM/SDM into 85 schools in that city. Efforts in both cities have had mixed results.

A 3-year study of SBM in Dade County (Collins & Hanson, 1991) noted that, after a brief period of greater teacher participation, energy flagged and then fell. Teachers seemed to have been lifted from their former positions of powerlessness, but others, including administrators, students, parents, and community, were not involved in corresponding transformations of roles. It was stated that inconsistent and uneven involvement contributed to low teacher-principal rapport, feelings of lack of support for teacher-generated projects and policies, and growing disillusionment on the part of the staff (Collins & Hanson, 1991). The Office of Research, Evaluation and Accountability report (OREA, 1990), by the board of education in New York City, focused on the issue of teacher empowerment, but after one year the outcomes were unclear.

Though some schools have experienced frustration, bureaucratic snags, chaos, and outright failure, some have been successful. This chapter focuses on Middle College. The school occupies space and shares facilities with LaGuardia Community College. It has operated a highly successful SBM/SDM model since 1987. An earlier study conducted during the 1990-1991 school year concluded that shared decision making had successfully permeated the school culture, including decision by consensus, schoolwide charges implemented by teacher groups, an increase in parent and student involvement in the decision-making process, and identification of school/community-wide agendas such as peer support and alternative assessment. That study demonstrated that shared leadership was supported by the principal and that schoolwide morale was high (Born, 1991). Every teacher was functioning on one of three professional committees (personnel, curriculum, or climate). Time for planning and problem solving had been set aside, accommodating a variety of teacher concerns. A staff committee was conducting interviews and selecting new staff, and curriculum was and is being developed consensually by staff.

Vaill (1986) observed that within organizations too much change in a system can break down the shared purpose and identity of an organization. Certainly, Middle College was undergoing a period of transformation and redefinition. My observation of the process highlighted the difficulties that arise in the context of change. Administrators with clearly defined roles moved into roles that were ambiguous; teachers, who were accustomed to being given goals, were forced to create and justify goals for themselves and their peers. Change within the school leadership structure altered relationships and thrust some members into altered positions of authority. On the road to democratic governance of schools, the rules are up for grabs. The current study seeks to define the factors and the process that led to increased teacher participation and efficacy. How have teaching staff redefined their roles and taken positive action to improve the school community? It is the purpose of this study to try to understand the nature and implications of these changes.

Methodology

Two questionnaires were administered to 25 teachers at Middle College High School in September and December 1991, respectively. Of the participating staff, 60% returned the first questionnaires and 80% returned the second. The first questionnaire reflected the staff's involvement in decision making regarding their practice and school governance, while the second produced data on staff perception of their work. These data were combined with semistructured interviews of eight teachers and observations of four sessions each of SBM/SDM meetings, the Curriculum Committee, family meetings (guidance personnel and teachers talking about specific student problems), instructional meetings, and full staff meetings. Staff members also shared journals, reflections, and informal conversations with me in a spirit of collegial enterprise, collaborating in this research because of their own desire to understand the meaning of the changes under way.

Findings

Through attendance at more than 20 meetings, in my capacity of chair of the Curriculum Committee, as a member of the SBM team and leadership group, and as a researcher as well, I saw evidence that the talk was focused and that decisions were made by consensus. It appeared that meetings, which in the past had often been dominated by a few participants, now involved many speakers. Teachers who had been verbose, repetitious, or negative became much clearer and more considerate. The venting had given way to positive suggestions and support. Two or three of the staff who had always seemed arbitrarily negative continued to be so, and some who had never entered into the spirit of collegiality were no closer than before, in spite of concerted efforts made by staff to elicit change.

The committees were productive. The Curriculum Committee published a first draft of an alternative assessment manual with contributions from the entire staff. It established partnerships with several museums to provide staff, student, and parent training, and it initiated schoolwide curricular themes. The Parent Involvement Committee established forums for dialogue with a number of parents at three well-attended evening functions and elicited information to help plan for more joint, reciprocally beneficial experiences. The Climate Committee began disseminating information and motivating more students to apply for college scholarships, reorganized the end-of-cycle Events Day, and made an effort to bring students into the SBM process. The Personnel Committee began to define the issue of peer support, preparing to lead the school to develop its own peer support system.

Staff Participation in SBM/SDM: Changes Between 1990-1991 and 1991-1992

All of the teachers who returned the first questionnaire were involved in at least two committees, and the majority indicated increased concern about school issues and the desire to increase schoolwide participation. All the teachers indicated they had developed new and broader interests over the year. Most of those interests grew out of committee-generated projects such as scholarships, alternative assessment, or peer support. Others grew out of expanding opportunities for participation in the areas of budget and citywide school policies.

Interest in school issues was sparked directly from interaction with colleagues, interaction between staff and parents, personal reasons, and/or committee projects. Of the teachers who received the questionnaire, 75% indicated they had experienced a rise in professional self-concept, which was most often attributed to experiences in the classroom, professional committee work, and greater interaction with students about academic concerns.

Problems teachers cited were lack of compensation for extra work, time burdens caused by the responsibilities of committee work, conflicts between the visions of the administration and the committees, and the perceived remoteness of the 11-member SBM team from those who were not on it.

Responses to the second questionnaire on teachers' perceptions about their work indicated that, during the three months between administration of the first and second questionnaires, 50% of the teachers had become even more active in school issues (see Table 5.1). The majority felt they participated more in decision making, felt that there were more opportunities for expression of ideas and opinions, saw themselves as experiencing more success in the classroom, and felt increased professionalization through increased dialogue about teaching practice. One teacher felt completely the reverse on all of these issues, while a solid group remained middle-of-the-roaders.

Many teachers felt more fragmented, "exhausted," and no longer sure of their job definitions. These findings spoke directly to the issue of the internal changes that take place in an organization undergoing redefinition.

The surveys, when combined with the observations and interviews, delineated a paradox. Teachers were participating more as they served on committees, developed structures for staff development, questioned and experimented with issues of practice and made critical evaluations of one another, and established school policy. They were also, however, in conflict, confused about their jobs, and skeptical about the work. It is important therefore to consider the factors that make shared leadership

Table 5.1 Teachers' Perceptions About Their Work (25 teachers, 80% response)

	More Than Before SBM (percent)	Same as Before SBM (percent)	Less Than Before SBM (percent)
Participate in school issues	50	46.5	3.5
Active in decision-making opportunities	76.5	20	3.5
Opportunities for expression	66	30	3.5
Control over work	60	30	10
Classroom success	75	25	0
Colleagues listen to me more	85	0	15
Fragmented	65	0	35
Exhausted	75	25	0
Sure of one's job description	0	25	75

possible and successful in the school setting and to understand its interrelationship with individuals coping with change.

From these data and observations and from my prior research (Born, 1991), I identified five factors necessary for the evolution into a culture of shared leadership. They are (a) collegiality, (b) action, (c) reeducation, (d) voice, and (e) leadership. Interviews served to clarify the relationship of these five factors to the development of new identities for both the school community and the individuals within it.

Collegiality

Attempts to extend collegiality at Middle College led to conflict as well as to growth. The resource room teacher, isolated in "her" room in the corner of the building, with "her" kids and "her" IEPs, was a sharp contrast to the majority of the staff who said, "I feel people are listening to me in a different way," and to those who had never spoken at staff meetings previously and were suddenly participating, volunteering, and offering support to others. It appeared that, to increase participation, collegiality was essential but that with increased collaboration came an intensification of isolation for those who did not easily fit the "norm."

The collegiality at Middle College evolved as the result of deliberate planning. The staff had always been friendly but now personal collegiality had begun to incorporate a growing professional culture as well. Teachers increasingly talked about different phases of their work. This was due to the amount of work and number of responsibilities they were given, but it was also due to the opportunities that professionalization afforded them. This was nurtured by administrators who made the decision to expand team teaching at the school. The nature of the team-teaching experience forced teachers to bring the dialogue about practice into the open. At the time of the study, virtually every English and social studies teacher had been involved in at least one CORE program, most of the Science Department had been involved in a team, and the physical education teacher, art teacher, and several math teachers had also worked with colleagues.

The nature of collegiality also changed in interactions between the staff and students. Students and teachers who had always talked about personal issues in students' lives now talked about academic performance and ideas as well. Scholarship committees and debating clubs arose. A poetry club was formed by a group of students and teachers who enjoyed writing. After a year, the club included four teachers and 10 students who produced a monthly magazine, attended readings, solicited outside speakers, and provided an internship site (an external educational option). Teachers also worked with students on writing and math, without compensation.

Collaborative practice changed as well. As the staff began to work collaboratively with more people and with more than one group, they had more opportunities to dialogue, share, and learn from one another. Collaborative processes that had been successful in staff development and decision making were also demonstrated in classrooms, where formerly teacher-centered activities were more often replaced by group work, projects, and presentations that encouraged shared participation.

Fred, a well-liked math teacher who served as a committee chairperson, member of the SBM team, and part of a four-subject curriculum team, described his day as follows: "I'm always talking. I'm talking with the principal and with my colleagues. We talk about curriculum, classroom structure, etc., and I feel I have a say in that." In describing what a teacher interested in working at Middle College should be like, he said:

> I would say, the first thing I would look for is somebody who is competent in their subject area. The second thing I would look for is someone who is good with students. We work very closely with students. I would look for somebody I could get along with because we work very closely with our colleagues on various committees. I would look for somebody who is innovative and flexible. In our school they are constantly looking for assessment, for methods of teaching, people are very receptive to different ideas. A person who's not receptive can do their own thing, but if they're able to give us something new, that's great.

Doris, a former opera singer and a resource room teacher in her early 40s, stands as a direct contrast. If anything, SBM/SDM has served to emphasize her "difference" from the rest of the faculty. At Middle College, resource room students are mainstreamed but attend one resource room class per day and have House (official class) with other resource room students once a week. Doris shared special education responsibilities with two other teachers assigned to the hearing-impaired population. Her room was in the corner of the building. It was carpeted, housed three computers, textbooks, desks, chairs, a phone, and her office, and it had no view of the corridors or street.

Doris described herself, specifically, and only, as a resource room teacher. She defined that as one who "provides supplementary learning experiences for the learning disabled. I am a consistent person that's here for them. My relationship with them is a privilege. It frees them. They have underlying goals for learning, etc., and we have to live with RCTs [New York State tests]." Though Doris recognized her importance and loves the children, she was highly dissatisfied with the isolation of her job. She described her position as one where she's "sitting home doing the laundry. I know so few students; I feel my opinion is not worthy. I can't respond to curriculum, etc." Doris's isolation is further underscored in her identification of the area of schoolwork where her time was wasted. In instructional meetings, she said she felt like the school was moving but she was at a standstill. Not feeling part of the instructional flow, she regarded topics such as alternative assessment as inappropriate to her responsibilities as a resource room teacher. Doris was happy in her work as a teacher of the learning disabled but had come to see that she would like more diverse professional opportunities.

The SBM/SDM process allowed Doris to articulate a vision of what she would like in the future. It grew out of work that she began in the Climate Committee. She had begun to advise seniors applying for college scholarships. It enabled her to meet more students and help them achieve at a much higher level than she had been used to with the students she normally taught. She said:

> The school saves burn-out by Career Ed. [Career Ed is a teaching duty that requires teachers to supervise students in internships out in the field. Many teachers at Middle College avail themselves of this option for a period of three years, allowing them a different type of teaching-supervisory role.] I can never do anything like that. I want a senior house and to work on scholarship or teach a course through senior house in how to make it in college. I want to be away from my students. I get to know them well enough. I don't want to baby them anymore. I want to get to know more of the population. I would like to be the person who pursues all avenues so students can get scholarships. Now I have to neglect my kids in order to do that work. I'd like a mechanism so that I could avoid that.

Doris felt that SBM/SDM was a step in the right direction, but, at the time of our interview, she had not found her niche. Her physical separateness from others in the school makes collegiality more difficult, but Doris is not alone in her isolation. Others choose to be isolated to keep their autonomy or for reasons of insecurity or privacy.

Action

Research in Miami (Collins & Hanson, 1991) and New York (OREA, 1990) has demonstrated that SBM/SDM can gradually lose staff support through lack of implementation of shared decisions. Teachers who begin to work on a proposal or plan, make recommendations, or seek support will not continue to do so when they do not have firm support from administrators. In the last two years at Middle College High School, this has not been the case.

The Curriculum Committee's plan to engage the staff in alternative assessment practices has served to define the concept of "shared leadership." The project, expanding the repertoire of evaluation to include performance, portfolio, and exhibition as well as standardized tests, challenged the ability of a group of teachers to investigate and expand the practices of their colleagues and challenged each teacher to take a risk and try something new with his or her classes. When teachers were asked to spend time writing and sharing personal evaluation techniques among fellow staff members, the resistance was powerful. Teachers did not want to believe that the committee was serious. Some said they did not understand the assignment; others claimed they did not believe in the value of alternative assessment; still others used contractual issues to resist peers mandating work from one another. The principal and assistant principal stood behind the committee. Consultants were hired to help demonstrate the pedagogical value of the process and to work with individuals on their projects. The assistant principal spent time with teachers demonstrating that they were not being asked to give up their successful practice and shared his expertise to ease their stress. Teachers who were still conflicted about the extra work or by political implications were given time to work with leaders in the school. Finally, the principal demanded the work from everyone on the staff. Commitment to the teacher-driven task was always there.

For those teachers who complained of stress from extra work, additional counseling duties, and the confusion that results from change, a therapist was hired to run a teacher group once a month. That same counselor was brought in to work with the SBM team on group process and management. In response to the staff need for more time, the principal instituted a bimonthly hour and a half of personal staff development time, when no students were in the building and there were no meetings to attend. In response to a need expressed by one of the committee chairpersons who was frustrated in her efforts to organize, copy, and send out memos and minutes, and to file the paperwork, the principal allotted part of the SBM budget for secretarial services for the committees.

Reeducation

Dan Lortie's 1986 evaluation of the Dade County schools asked the question, "Teachers have changed over the last 20 years in average age, in amount of academic preparation and classroom experience . . . but what if the places in which they work have not changed? What if teachers, having invested more time, effort and money in their careers, find little acknowledgment of that investment within the schools and the school systems?" (Lortie, 1986, p. 570).

Through the SBM/SDM process, the faculty at Middle College became "learners" and, in that role shift, they changed the nature of the workplace. Learning occurred through staff development, collaborative planning, partnerships with institutions, conference attendance, opening of the school to outside visitors, teachers acting as staff trainers, and reading and writing about professional issues. The result has become a staff that is more knowledgeable and more sensitive to the learning process. It has made the school more dynamic but has also brought with it some problems.

When things are constantly growing, moving, and in flux, frustration, confusion, fragmentation, and disorganization result. The sacrificing of security, which is a basic human need, is the price we pay. Teachers have asked, "Who's in control here?" or "I've always done the history lesson this way. How can I shift gears at this point in my life?"

Barbara is a study in the reeducation process. A social studies teacher in her mid-40s, Barbara came from a traditional high school, where she taught for 10 years and was active in the United Federation of Teachers (UFT). She had been at Middle College for 10 years, teaching both history and career education. She claimed skepticism about SBM/SDM but was experiencing many changes in attitude concerning teacher activism and collaboration. Her paradoxical position on the issue of SBM and school leadership was not unusual.

Barbara defined her duties by saying, "I am a teacher. I am an attendance teacher. I am a guidance counselor. I am a social work committee person. I am chair of one of the committees [the Climate Committee]. I am at the point of feeling absolutely fragmented with all I am doing." When asked about how she felt about what she did, Barbara expressed frustration. In the course of any two hours, she can teach a class, meet a student and counsel him on scholarships, meet with her cochair about Climate Committee issues, and go back into the classroom. On her way out, she can run into the chapter chairperson of the UFT and meet with her. She said, "I feel like a crisis manager for myself. If things go right, I think it's in spite of me."

Returning to school after a long illness, Barbara was greeted with a new order. She had never taught social studies in a 70-minute block of time nor had she been part of the original SBM organization. Yet she was elected to the position of chair of one of the committees. Though an admitted skeptic about the process, she took the position in response to the trust and support of her colleagues, who considered her a fair and judicious spokesperson for the mainstream. In the first few months, she spent a lot of time trying to figure out the new system: Which seeming mandates, given by teachers to one another, were really mandates? Was the school really serious about alternative assessment? How was she going to reconcile her need to reflect, plan, and work things through in the culture of nonstop activity and diverse responsibilities that she faced? After 20 years of teaching, having developed a sense of personal self-esteem with regard to her teaching style and accomplishment, she was being asked to reexamine her practice, to take on new and unsought responsibilities, and to take risks. Her reaction was to recoil and say, "I get crazy if I change responsibilities. In that respect, I'm better off in a traditional school. There, I'm a teacher. Maybe every three months I get a building assignment, maybe every three months I'm an attendance teacher. You do less, and you have more time to focus on what you want to do as a teacher."

In the middle of the interview, Barbara began to speak in terms of the contradictions that revealed the effects of her ongoing reeducation. When asked about whether any of her work on the Climate Committee had negatively affected on her work in the classroom or the way in which she viewed students, she started to say the effect had been minimal. She admitted that working in one-to-one relationships with students on college scholarships had given her greater insights into who the students were. This was a sharp contrast to a previous response about her entry into a master's program in guidance. She had gotten straight As in all the courses and, when it came time to do her internship, she had dropped out. Her recent experiences with scholarship counseling, however, had provided an area of comfort, where guidance was crucial and nonthreatening.

The impact of the alternative assessment project (portfolios and exhibition as well as traditional testing), generated by the Curriculum Committee in the previous year, forced her to reevaluate her practice.

Things like assessment or House Curriculum become extra work until you find a need for it yourself. It can't be something that someone else wants. They can talk till they are blue in the face about how valuable it's going to be for you and it's going to be extra until you become intrigued by it yourself. I certainly felt that way about the assessment project.

By the end of the interview, she admitted that she was changing. "I never wanted control. I never wanted to be in charge. I never wanted to make decisions. . . . My autonomy is being threatened by wearing too many hats." When asked to define her role of teacher at Middle College, Barbara responded:

> I am a social studies teacher. I have an understanding of history. The kind of concepts they [students] need to make good decisions in life. I try to make them see the soap opera in history and I have developed a narrative approach because youngsters don't do homework. I set up the facts and I have the youngsters react to them. They don't have to know all the details because I'm going to tell them that. They have to make the decision. I give them the rest. I use primary sources, get them thinking and, hopefully, critically thinking. It is very much something where I'm generating and they are reacting to it. I'm beginning to see that the alternative assessment, which was something we had always done, but given up on because it was so time consuming that it was seen as something extra . . . interfering with the tests. Now I'm beginning to see the pedagogical foundation. I see this kid who I only knew as an intern and his eyes light up, and when I lose it in class, the kids step in and say, "relax!" I see how good it is for them. So now I'm caught in a worse quandary. In the past the structure was its fun, and we enjoyed it. It's better than the other stuff we do, but we can't do it. Now, I'm seeing we have to do it. It is valid. It is valuable. This thing presupposes a certain body of knowledge. It took me years to develop a narrative style, now I see I have to adapt an alternative style. How am I going to put this together? Probably for me, in the end, it will be a compromise. Elements will be woven into a narrative. It's tough at my age to be starting. You want to say, at a certain point, you've got it. Now I'm back at square one where I ask how do I allow for them to be partners and still meet the needs of the curriculum?

I asked her how what she was saying about the classroom also fits a paradigm of what is happening with administration. She responded, "It's giving up control."

This response became prophetic. As part of the alternative assessment project, Barbara engaged students in her first arts project: the creation of an American Quilt. When she spoke of the power of the American Quilt Project, she saw that power in the investment and shared involvement of the students. It was not merely Barbara's quilt project but the project of the class as a whole. When it was finished and mounted on the corridor wall, Barbara made a banner that read, "The American Quilt" and showed it to her students. They insisted that it should be "*Our* American Quilt.*"* She realized that, when she herself has no ideas, there is a good chance that a class member may have one; when she has forgotten the scissors, there is a possibility that someone in the room might have brought his or her own. Barbara was, in her own classroom, participating in an essential process of shared decision making.

Voice

In the study of Middle College teacher participation, individual voice became important. Professionalism requires self-esteem, which is fed by the feeling that one is being heard. As exemplified by the teacher who felt she was not worthy until the principal took her seriously, or the student who would not apply for a scholarship until teachers started to ask him to, people need to be encouraged to speak for their voices to emerge, for them to gain experience, and for them to make a difference.

Individual voice was still a problem at Middle College. Some teachers did not participate at meetings, attend functions, or express their views. Seven teachers did not return questionnaires, which might imply lack of investment in the process. The Hispanic population of the school (approximately 150 students, nearly one third of the school population) had no outlet, spokesperson, or advocate for their views. Only a handful of parents were actively involved in the decision-making process and few students attended staff meetings on a regular basis.

Marty, a 36-year-old teacher skeptical about SBM, had been a teacher at Middle College for seven years. He taught history, math, and science and was involved with several interdisciplinary programs. He had never taught in another high school but had taught science at the college level and had done anthropological studies in Africa. He organized student activities, was faculty adviser to the student government, and organized and managed freshman orientation.

Marty saw himself as a science teacher and coordinator of student government. When asked about other responsibilities he had at the school, he did not mention his work on the Climate Committee. When prodded about that part of his job, he replied,

> It is very peripheral. We meet with such infrequency [once a month] that there isn't enough time to get consistent policy going. I don't feel that the goals are defined. I think that of all the committees, it is the most amorphous. It could, potentially, be the most powerful one. How do you define *climate*? . . . It is very hard to be clear about climate.

On three occasions during the interview, he mentioned the lack of product from the Climate Committee as a frustration.

Marty sees his teacher role as satisfying. He indicated that he liked the ability within the school to follow any number of directions, the sense that you can "get the kids to explore areas that we, the faculty, are also interested in exploring." Though Marty did not see himself as a leader, he was pressing students into leadership roles and trying to make them more active participants in their education. When asked about what he would like to do differently, he spoke of integrating more hands-on work into his science classroom and making the student government more politically active. In his definition of a teacher's role, Marty, who rarely ventured an opinion in public, was articulate:

> In the worst of all possible times it's to keep a certain number of kids occupied for a certain amount of time so they won't cause havoc anywhere else. At the ultimate it is to enlighten people and have them look at the world in a different way. To ask them a question about something they never had questioned before or to make them see something they never

thought they'd see and, in my fantasy, it's having them spend the class looking at a drop of water and walking away saying, "I never thought it would look like that!"

Leadership

Leadership in successful SBM/SDM must be shared. Speaking of teacher management in schools, Conley, Schmidle, and Shedd (1988) state that managers who share leadership with their staff with the intent of "giving" power as a gift are, by and large, unsuccessful. They conclude that, to reap the benefits of shared leadership—that is, shared responsibility, a variety of points of view, and so on—managers must enter into the process with the notion that they are the receivers. Conley et al. cite evidence that, "in effective schools and other organizations, participation is associated, not only with positive changes in individual attitudes, but also with enhanced group and organizational effectiveness" (Conley et al., 1988, p. 276).

This was particularly true at Middle College, where, in 1986, the principal asked a group of teachers to form a personnel committee to hire staff and three years later brought the idea of alternative assessment to the Curriculum Committee. This sharing of vision and responsibility yielded a shared sense of investment and purpose. These activities were not solely the principal's agendas but the school's agendas.

As the principal was ready to share authority, there had to be teachers, like Valerie, who were ready to assume responsibility. Valerie, a social studies teacher, had been at the school for seven years. She was deeply involved in staff development and writing about the American Social History Project. She worked on a Vassar Summer School component at Middle College and served on both the Curriculum and the Personnel committees. At the time of the study, she was taking administration courses and saw herself as a school leader. Her described her role as being multifaceted:

I teach. I'm on the Personnel Committee. I collaborate. I think a lot about the Social History Project. I talk about it a lot. I used to be on the Curriculum Committee, so I think a lot about that. I spend a lot of time speaking to kids. I feel I'm on a mission with students and writing. I work closely with interns. . . . I have started working with Mario to learn video editing. I'm thinking about multicultural education.

Valerie was happy in her work. She did not feel burned out and she expressed exhilaration about her opportunities. She called herself a generalist and admitted that was what made her comfortable with the myriad committees, issues, and groups she was a part of in the course of a day. At the end of the previous year, Valerie opted to change committees to work on the issue of peer evaluation and support being examined by the Personnel Committee. She explained,

> It's an issue that I had thought about and now I have a formalized opportunity to work on and it's recognized. I'm very interested in peer evaluation and it's something that I would like to see in this school and for me to have it as my personal goal, with no formal network, or no formal structure to work through would be very frustrating. Now, it's an ongoing dialogue and I can understand why people have problems and I can speak to them.

Unlike some of her colleagues, Valerie felt that the system provided her with a good fit. She felt sorry for individuals who were struggling with the system and feeling that their needs were not being met. Valerie saw administrative duties as those activities that keep the machinery running smoothly. She believed administrators should be advocates for the people in the school. They need to be trainers or know where to get training for themselves. They must be the primary people in the school to set climate and tone.

She had difficulty separating the roles of teacher and administrator.

> I don't feel that's segregated right now. I don't think this or that is only what teachers do. I hope that it's a role that's evolving and I hope that I'm evolving with it. I could never

say that when I'm in the classroom is the only time I'm a teacher and that that's the only time teachers should teach. I think that in order to be well developed as a teacher, you have to take in more of the whole picture.

I can't segment myself to only look at a kid's academic development. I don't want to do that. I don't know how to do that. And I also can't say I have nothing to do with anything outside the classroom. I get upset when I see things happening and I want to be a part of figuring out how not to have those things happen or make the decisions that will help.

Conclusions

Valerie wished everyone could feel as good about SBM as she did, but some staff members would much prefer to teach their classes and go home. Some, like Doris, were caught in the middle, wanting to be a part of it all yet unable to find an entry point. It would be unrealistic to believe that any school could be populated with 40 to 100 teachers who did as much as Valerie did in one day or to believe that any school could house a staff of teachers who thought about nothing but pedagogical issues, a student body that was purely intellectual, or an administration that never wanted or needed to have the final say. Within any staff, there are many different types of people who have strengths and weaknesses, needs and talents, personal realities and interests. An effective leader can work with committed teachers to synthesize these elements so that people share responsibilities according to ability, availability, and readiness.

The process of adjusting to the need to change and grow requires complementary shifts in teachers' roles. Barbara's story points to two possible starting points: The school can begin changes in areas where teachers are comfortable or can begin with those issues with which teachers identify. The shift in teachers' role redefines the school as a learning community as opposed to a place where children are the only ones who learn. It implies that the end of education cannot be finite and that everyone is involved in the process of being educated. It is necessary to honor the potential and voice of each member of the community, by continuing to nurture him or her, while receiving the services of their expertise.

The committee structure allows talk to occur. In groups of 10, it is more likely that reticent members, like Marty, will be heard and that more members will feel comfortable to speak. Choice and variety are also important when expanding the teachers' role. At Middle College, the alternative assessment project enabled teachers and students to participate in more hands-on performance-based activities that are shared with the entire school community and that allow both the teachers and the students avenues in which to speak in their personal, diverse languages of art, music, dance, science, and so on.

The process by which leadership becomes shared is that of dialogue. Through the practice of dialogue, leadership moves from autocratic to democratic. Because of ongoing professional development, opportunities for dialogue in practice were provided by the restructured school day, and, especially because of the clearly shared school mission, that dialogue usually led to action at Middle College.

Moreover, dialogue requires listening. Speaking of her current role as chair of the Personnel Committee and UFT chapter chairperson, a teacher who was never considered a leader claimed, "I changed when the principal started *listening* to me. I didn't see myself as a leader until she did." The principal must listen to her or his staff to hear complaints and ideas, information, and opinions. It is also imperative, if shared leadership is the goal, to listen to what the staff needs and is ready to accept.

The demands of SBM are difficult and risky. Moving teachers into the area of decision making makes them accountable for decisions and practices that traditionally are the responsibility of administrators. It exposes educators to practices that were not part of their training.

As the playing field broadens, questions arise. How much of a role can or should parents and students take in policymaking in schools? How can they be positively incorporated into the process and how can they be educated in order to feel comfortable? Will staff be willing or able to adjust to this type of involvement and scrutiny by members of the community, who, previously, had not played active roles in school change?

Also of concern is the question of what is given up as more responsibility and variety are thrust into the already crowded day of the average teacher. Barbara says she is confused by all her hats, has no time to reflect and perfect her strategies as a teacher. She fears her class performance is the price she must pay as she walks the tightrope of redefinition and added responsibility. Will students be the ultimate beneficiaries? Is instructional quality being traded for power?

These questions are crucial as researchers evaluate the impact of change. No radical movement within a system can be carried out without losses. The results at Middle College took place over six years, with consistent administrative support, within the constraints of a small faculty who had worked together for many years. It was a slow progression of compromises. As teachers change their roles, the rules by which they operate, and their relationships to the school community at large, how can they be guided through the compromises of style, technique, and redefinition that will be necessary? The paradigms set by this small school show that it is possible.

References

Born, T. (1991). SBM/SDM at Middle College High School: The first six months. In *An evaluation of the CUNY/NYC Board of Education collaborative programs* (pp. 52-64). Philadelphia: University of Pennsylvania.

Collins, R. A., & Hanson, M. K. (1991). *Summative evaluation report: SBM/SDM project 1987-1988 through 1989-1990*. Miami: Dade County Public Schools, Office of Educational Accountability.

Conley, S. C., Schmidle, T., & Shedd, J. B. (1988). Teacher management. *Teachers College Record, 90*(2), 259-280.

Lortie, D. C. (1986). Teacher status in Dade County. *Phi Delta Kappan, 4*, 568-575.

National Commission on Excellence in Education. (1983). *A nation at risk: The imperative for educational reform.* Washington, DC: Government Printing Office.

OREA Report. (1990). *Toward SBM/SDM: A research perspective.* New York: New York City Board of Education.

Vaill, P. B. (1986). The purposing of high-performing systems. In T. J. Sergiovanni & J. E. Corbally (Eds.), *Leadership and organizational culture.* Chicago: University of Illinois Press.

Also an analysis of the process and importance of school democratization, Levine's study focuses on one kindergarten/first-grade inner-city classroom. The chapter emphasizes the social and cultural knowledges and personal experiences that the children, representing a range of classes, ethnicities, and cultures, bring to the start of their schooling. Because the sociocultural context is always in the making, emergent, Levine contends that the role of the teacher in the construction of the classroom as a public sphere is crucial. Focusing on the classroom discourse surrounding mostly story reading and other school activities, Levine highlights how a gifted, progressive teacher enables his children to use their background experiences and knowledge to prosper and learn.

6. "Who Says?" Learning to Value Diversity in School

LINDA LEVINE

I have moved from thinking primarily about the individual child to a much more ecological perspective, heeding Gregory Bateson's warning that to focus on one spot in the web is to miss the nature of its interconnectedness.

Yonemura (1986, p. 478)

AUTHOR'S NOTE: I am grateful to several anonymous reviewers for insightful comments and assistance on earlier drafts of this chapter. The recommendation that I note community-specific preferences for oral versus print traditions was especially helpful. My warmest thanks to the young teacher featured in this study, the director of the school, all their colleagues, and the children who benefit from their collaborative efforts.

87

Missing from the prevailing discourse on educational reform, with its stress on producing a more internationally competitive labor force, is the notion of school as a critical site for advancing democracy. Those who view excellence and equity as mutually exclusive tend to indict progressive education as responsible for our declining status in the community of nations (see Meier, 1984; Mitchell & Weiler, 1991, for cogent responses to such attacks).

In the current climate, too little attention is paid to those progressive theorists who envision school as a "public sphere" (Giroux, 1987) that offers opportunities for young people and adults to participate in a crucial "dialogue across differences" (Burbules & Rice, 1991). Both prospective and in-service teachers need to know that such democratic dialogues in public schools are not only theoretically possible but are now being enacted—albeit far too infrequently.

To learn more about ways in which teachers can help advance a democratic dialogue, I chose to conduct ethnographic research in an alternative urban public school. This chapter, based on that research conducted during the 1985-1986 academic year, supports Giroux and McLaren's view that "schooling should promote forms of morality and sociality in which students learn to encounter and engage social differences and diverse points of view" (Giroux & McLaren, 1986, p. 225).

Classroom Discourse

Discourse and other forms of classroom communication continue to engage the attention of critical theorists concerned with equity in U.S. schools. Since the early 1970s, we have learned a great deal about the power of teacher-mediated exchanges, how they reflect and help shape children's emergent understanding of themselves and others in this society. As Au and Jordan (1981), Fine (1987), Gumperz and Hernandez-Chavez (1972), Labov (1972), Michaels (1981), Philips (1972/1985), and others have shown, different "ways with words" (Heath, 1983) have had much to do with the uncertain welcome too many of our children find in school.

Rejecting "deficit" theories proposed by some researchers in the 1960s (e.g., Bereiter & Engelmann, 1966; Deutsch, 1963) to explain widespread school failure among children who are not members of the white middle class, the social scientists cited in the previous paragraph conducted naturalistic research showing how communicative competence acquired out of school—if different from mainstream practices—can be misconstrued as deficiency in school settings. As these studies reveal, teachers who have not learned to examine cultural preconceptions that underlie their own expectations, who do not recognize or honor what children learn in different communities, are likely to encounter resistance. These studies explore encounters between children of (currently) marginal communities (e.g., Native American, Latino, Native Hawaiian, black or white working class) and mainstream teachers whose deeply rooted middle-class beliefs and practices lead them to ignore or unwittingly discredit different "funds of knowledge" (Moll & Greenberg, 1990) that students bring with them. (For more on this topic, see Payne & Bennett, 1977, on the "middle-class aura" in public schools.)

It is important to note, however, that these theorists offer more than description and critique of existing practices, more than an intractable set of givens that preclude change. Based on empirical studies of communication in community and school settings, their work suggests ways in which teachers and students can become more responsive and effective in their interactions with one another.

A caveat here: There is always the danger, in discussions about culture, of reinforcing stereotypes by ignoring both intracultural variation and cross-cultural similarity. We all recognize the increasing cultural complexity and accelerating social change that characterize our cities and classrooms (Labov, 1982; Schieffelin & Eisenberg, 1984). As Scollon and Scollon (1981) point out, "in most cases where cultural and communicative pluralism exists, it exists in abundance" (p. 201). While multicultural exchanges may reveal and even exacerbate inaccurate assumptions about oneself and others, they also offer new opportunities for enhancing cross-cultural understanding. In culturally diverse classroom settings, much of what happens depends on the teacher's role as mediator and guide.

We cannot, in any event, assume a one-to-one correspondence between race or class or gender and culture but must investigate what these factors come to mean in particular cases. In the meantime, it is worth noting that one's identity and affiliations have as much to do with individual aspirations and available options as with community of origin. As Barth (1969) noted in a classic work, we need to describe and make sense of social life in terms of its dynamism and "emergent forms" rather than relying on "categorical ascriptions."

When I began my ethnographic study in an East Harlem alternative public school during the 1985-1986 academic year (Levine, 1988), an early finding was that almost two thirds of the children in the target classroom that year were members of biracial or interethnic families. Further exploration yielded similar data for other classrooms and evidence of an increasing trend in this direction during the school's brief history. While all classrooms remained ethnically diverse, and one third of the students continued to be from white middle-class families, the "originally intended ratio of one third Black, one third Latino and one third other" (E. Rosenfeld, personal communication, 1985) was no longer in evidence. (The school staff, by design, is also culturally diverse.)

This chapter, based on that study, suggests that we may need to revise earlier notions of "culturally responsive education" (Cazden & Leggett, 1981). It is proposed that teachers in ethnically diverse classrooms, under rapidly changing social conditions, are understandably reluctant to ascribe identity and predict student behavior on community of origin; they will need, however, to continue guiding student discourse so as to encourage a more inclusive, truly democratic negotiation of meanings. What we might reasonably expect, given collegial and broader social context support for this strategy, is for teachers to recognize and mediate intercultural conflict, where it occurs, in ways that validate a wide range of student voices and perspectives. This would not mean, of course, an end to learning about community-specific practices but greater attention to the social meanings students and teachers attach to the different choices available to them.

The Teacher's Interpretive Dilemma: Gatekeeping Versus Advocacy

Almost daily, as Erickson (1979) reminds us, there are "decision points" at which conflicting assumptions and worldviews underlying behavior become apparent in classroom discourse. When these occur, teachers have choices to make; whether to ignore them, make light of them, attempt to dismiss them, or address them as learning/teaching occasions is a complex matter. Too often, mainstream educators respond to student beliefs and practices different from their own by reasserting prevailing school standards and foreclosing further discussion. While it is essential to clarify classroom rules and teacher expectations, teachers need to reconsider the balance they maintain between gatekeeping and advocacy. Too seldom are such moments viewed as opportunities for joint exploration and negotiation of meanings, as a stimulus for democratic public dialogue. The potential of such occasions, as Giroux (1987) argues persuasively, deserves greater attention from teachers. He urges progressive educators not to miss those opportunities for "moral discourse" and reminds them that too many have "conceded the high ground to a view of schooling and society that is fundamentally incapable of defining a notion of the public good. Lost is the ability to define a democratic vision" (Giroux, 1987, p. 10). What occurs in our classrooms on a daily basis, as Fine (1987), Giroux (1987), and Cazden (1988) have all emphasized, has ethical as well as political consequences for the future of this society.

Methodology for the Study

Data sources for the ethnographic study on which this chapter is based include field notes from participant-observation both in and outside of a K-1 classroom, transcribed audiotapes of classroom discourse (with increasing focus, as the year progressed, on story reading), open-ended interviews with teachers, administrators, and parents, and examination of site documents and the material culture. Although I had intended to investigate interethnic exchanges around the writing process, interpretive conflicts around the ritual of "story reading" proved a richer source of data and led to a redirected focus for the study.

The Wrong Kind?

Consider the following exchange. The time is early October. In a K-1 classroom that is both socioculturally and socioeconomically diverse, a young black teacher, George,[1] is reading *Peter and the Wolf* to his children in the combined "reading/meeting" area. He shows the class an illustration that depicts Peter and the hunter leading the captured wolf away. Peter is pointing a gun at the wolf. Please note that names, in all of the discourse samples below, have been changed to protect the identities of the participants. Also, the use of *WMC* (white, middle class), *BWC* (black, working class), and *LWC* (Latino, working class), in the discourse samples that follow, refers to the way in which caregivers spoke about their children. As noted earlier in this chapter, cultural identification in this classroom is a far more complex matter. One further note: Discourse samples are drawn from transcriptions of naturally occurring conversations in George's classroom and elsewhere in the school. I cannot claim that children would respond similarly or differently in other settings. It is important to note, however, that each discourse sample signals an interactional pattern that the investigator found over time in the target classroom. Viewed in comparative perspective with data from other ethnographic classroom studies, this teacher's approach is not the conventional one.

Corey: (WMC child, points, calls out) That's the wrong kind of gun!

George: (the teacher, looks up) What? What's wrong with it?

Corey: It's supposed to have a ball and a string on the end. The ball pops out of the gun.

Mickey: (BWC child, looks at Corey)*Who* says? Who?

Corey: (smiles indulgently at Mickey) I have the book at home and we read it lots of times. That's (points again to book) the wrong kind of gun!

George: It may look *different* from *your* book at home, Corey, but that doesn't mean it's "wrong" and the other one is "right."

It is noteworthy that Corey, age 5, does not say: "It looks different from the picture in my book at home." Instead, he presents himself as an authority (e.g., "I have the book at home" and "It's supposed to have a ball and a string on the end" and "That's the wrong kind of gun"). His response may well, of course, reflect the "print-reliant" approach to knowledge documented in studies of middle-class families in this society (e.g., Cochran-Smith, 1983; Heath, 1983). It is crucial, however, to note the potential impact of such comments in socioculturally and socioeconomically mixed classrooms where young children are learning lessons about the value placed on what they and others bring to school. As Schieffelin and Eisenberg (1984) point out, socialization into a white middle-class family in this society carries with it a high degree of assurance about status. When Mickey, a child from a black working-class family, attempts to challenge him ("*Who* says?"), Corey publicly reasserts his authority. His assumptions and declarations about the way "it's supposed" to be reveal his conviction that what he has learned at home is "right" and that other versions are surely "wrong." He has learned to cite references to past experience (i.e., "we read it lots of times") in support of his claims. His demeanor and language leave little doubt that he has learned and expects to be taken seriously as a conversational partner (see Gleason & Weintraub, 1978).

Far more, of course, than informational content is at stake in such exchanges. As Hymes (1972) states eloquently, what happens in classrooms has much to do with "what we think of each other and ourselves" (p. xxxiii). In this classroom, Mickey and Corey—and all the other children listening and watching—are learning a great deal about ways in which authority can be negotiated and shared rather than preempted and are beginning to extend their understanding of what counts as legitimate knowledge. The teacher, George, might have responded simply, "Well, this is a different book," but that would not have called Corey's assumptions into question. Adding "That doesn't mean it's 'wrong' and the other one is 'right,' " advances the notion that one illustrator's version, or one child's interpretation, is no more automatically valid or deserving of respect than another's. In a society where difference is too often misconstrued as deficit, this point needs to be made explicit.

Note that George waits to serve as "mediator" (Vygotsky, 1978) until after an interpretive conflict has arisen. His response exemplifies what Vygotsky referred to as teaching in the "zone of proximal development"; this teacher recognizes the propitious moment and mode for assisting his children to move beyond what they can accomplish independently. Doing so reveals George's understanding that young children learn best from concrete examples. A didactic, decontextualized lesson about respect for others would be far less effective. (Contrast this, for example, with the school library event described later in this chapter.) Seeing and hearing what prompts their teacher's response as well as what ensues is essential to their learning about diverse ways of representation. One might argue, of course, that, by intervening earlier, George could have avoided a conflict with potential for reinforcing Corey's authority at the expense of Mickey's. But believing that similar conflicts are likely to occur out of his hearing, he takes this opportunity to offer guidance. As the discourse sample illustrates, all of those present experience an exchange that, in microcosm, reflects the all too familiar social dynamics of the larger society: The middle-class child, even at an early age, confidently claims access to greater knowledge, dismissing challenges from others. What makes the crucial difference here is that the expected outcome is altered by the teacher's equitable intervention. Thus everyone present hears and sees that "official" versions of stories—or of social relations—are open to question, that they can be differently construed and constructed.

It is evident that this teacher does not ignore student conflicts over interpretation. It deserves notice, however, that the kind of mediation he offers not only encourages interpretive freedom but also specifies its limits. No one is to be put down or dismissed. While a variety of perspectives and ways of presenting them are recognized and encouraged, children may not, in his classroom, deride what others think and know.

Reading With the Group:
Rotating Leadership in the Interpretation of Texts

What happens over time as children have opportunities to assume leadership in the dialogue around interpretation of texts? The next portion of this chapter, highlighting a student-centered ritual known as "reading with the group," suggests ways in which teachers can help students begin to appreciate the diverse "funds of knowledge" (Moll & Greenberg, 1990) available in their classroom.

Some background is called for here. Early in the fall, George had initiated a daily routine called "reading time" at the start of the morning session. For 20 minutes or so, every child—alone or with others—was involved with books. Activities included turning pages and reading a story silently or aloud (either from pictures or by decoding the print), comparing several versions of the same story with a peer, arguing about whether or not a sequence of events made sense, collaborating in the reading of different parts of a story (which often meant adding "pieces" of their own), and explaining "how you hold your place when you forgot to show a picture and have to go back and do it."

Some first graders and one kindergarten child were also learning word-attack skills and sentence building via the Breakthrough program at another time during the school day. It was noticeable at morning "reading time" as well as during "reading with the group" that the children involved with the Breakthrough program were far more concerned than those who were not about fidelity to the text in their own and others' readings ("Is that exactly what it says?") This is consistent with Taylor's (1983) finding that, as children gain competency in reading, they become increasingly concerned about precision of form in their own written language.

By December, as the children gained greater confidence in their ability to communicate what they were learning about and from books, George offered them rotating responsibility to assume leadership in "reading with the group" at midmorning. What this meant in practice was a chance to sit in the teacher's chair, to share a written story (orally interpreting a sequence of pictures or print) with one's classmates, and to field questions as they arose. It should be emphasized that this did not require an ability to decode print, although a number of first graders and one kindergarten child were beginning to do this. (These children usually "read" more slowly than the others.) "Reading with the group" offered each child an opportunity, at whatever level of communicative competence she or he had attained, to display and experience different ways of telling as a part of preparation for literacy.

Each child's turn to do this was preceded by a private discussion with the teacher about the choice of story as well as opportunities, as needed, to practice (with the teacher, student teacher, and/or peers). As was true of the teacher-directed story-reading time described above (*Peter and the Wolf*), this child-centered event always took place in the combined "meeting/reading" area just below the windows. The location for this ritual was significant: The locally valued link between oral and literate modes of communication was reflected in the organization of the material culture; there were no separate locations for group "reading" and group "meeting." Entering this dual-function space in the classroom, it was common for children to pick up books and hold them while the child designated as "reader" had the floor.

Every child, whatever the level of his or her literacy understandings and skills, was encouraged to select a book of personal interest and to share it in this way with peers and adults. More specifically, "reading to the group" meant a chance to learn about and encourage locally appropriate behavior around print materials, to use and show pictures in order to tell a story aloud to the group, and to invite and answer questions from the audience. Emergent decoding skills, as they appeared, were treated as the next stage in an expected progression, not as a demarcation between "good" and "poor" readers in this inter-age K-1 classroom. Equally important, all of the children were being exposed to various ways of telling, what Cochran-Smith (1983) has called different ways of "taking from books." Black dialect, code-switching between Spanish and English, ebulliently invented words like "swabbin'" for "swimming," monotone word-calling, and more fluent standard English delivery (with or without attention to print)—all were welcome in the "reading with the group" ritual.

During this activity, the children in George's class learned to assume greater responsibility for hearing and valuing one another's voices. Deriving mutual benefit from learning about diverse out-of-school experiences, each was expanding his or her "communicative repertoire" (Hymes, 1972) in ways that have enormous potential for improving social life in a multicultural society. "Reading with the group," in short, was a ritual event in which the "narrative rights" (Cazden & Hymes, 1980) of children from different communities were being honored, whatever their origin. My data strongly suggest that story reading in this classroom, whether teacher or child led, entailed setting the stage for more democratic meanings and uses of literacy.

This is not to suggest that such events were conflict-free. As the *Peter and the Wolf* example indicates, social interactions around story reading in school tend to expose and reinforce notions about self and others that students bring with them from different communities in a diverse and stratified society. Teacher intervention at strategic "decision points" (Erickson, 1979) is essential. As Michaels's study of "sharing-time" (1981) and Heath's (1983) exploration of cross-cultural communication in U.S. classrooms have both demonstrated, teachers need to become more knowledgeable about out-of-awareness factors that have a negative impact on classroom life—and to revise school rituals that tend to benefit some children over others.

Learning in the Library

In the interest of exploring that issue further, I want to contrast two episodes of story reading that George's children participated in during the same week. One occurred in the school library, the other in their classroom a day later. (The reader should note that, to understand classroom interactions and events in a broader school context, I accompanied this group of children wherever they were scheduled to go: such as to "sing" with other classes, on trips to museums and special exhibits outside the school, into the yard for recess, to the assembly, the lunchroom, and the school library.)

The following is a detailed account, reconstructed from handwritten field notes, of one visit with George's class to the school library. There were four alternative schools housed in one large building. One library served them all. The librarian, a white middle-aged former classroom teacher, was employed by the *building* principal and was not a member of the alternative school staff. George was absent on the morning that his children, accompanied by a student teacher and by me, made their first visit to the school library.

Entering a cavernous room, George's children saw three straight rows of chairs facing a desk rather than the rug-and-circle arrangement they were used to. The librarian, perched on her desk, greeted the children and asked them to "take chairs as quickly as possible." Some but not all seemed to understand that instruction. "Good for you!" responded the librarian to those who did. When two others picked up chairs and began to move them closer to her, the librarian said, "No, put them back where they belong."

The students who knew what she meant told the others what to do. This exchange followed:

Librarian: Soon we are going to go over to the tables.
Martin: (calling out) You said we could take out books today!
Librarian: Now let's remember to raise our hands.

She then held up two books she said were "about helping" and someone uttered an "Oh-h-h-h" sound of disapproval. It was followed by a chorus of "Oh-h-h's." One child said, pointing to a book called *Swimmy* by Lionni, "We read *that* book too many times!" Brightly, the librarian answered, "Sometimes I read a book *I* like over and over and over." When a second child called out: "What's the other book?" she responded with another question: "Who can raise a hand—one at a time?"

This last reminder that rules had been violated seemed to act as a bar to further challenges from the children. They sat, uncharacteristically quiet, while she read both books to them. Sepi forgot himself momentarily and called out (pointing): "That one 'posed to be the eye!" and was brought back into line by Jamie, who muttered irritably, "We *know* that." Tomas, at the back of the group, looked restless (fiddling with something small and swinging his feet against the chair) and uncomprehending; it was hard for him to follow the stories in English. At the end, the librarian summed up the moral lesson of each book: "In the first story, all the birds helped the cat; in the second story Swimmy helped the other fish." Completing these stories of interdependence, she looked up and smiled. The children, after a brief pause, clapped.

As we were about to leave, I stopped to talk with her briefly. Hearing that I was engaged in a study, she volunteered: "You know, these kids interrupt me more. They're much more verbal than kids in Ms. M.'s class. It would be hard for me to be with this group alone. There's much more to do." I thought, but did not say, that these children also must feel they had "much more to do," that is, restrain their enthusiasm, decipher and follow new interactional rules, remember to forget the old ones, balance that agenda simultaneously with attempts to take care of one another and make sense of the stories.

This librarian's interactions with the children of the K-1 class recalled classroom encounters Michaels (1981) has aptly characterized as promoting "differential access to literacy." During the 35 minutes spent there, it was apparent how easily opportunities to encourage and validate a wider range of student voices could be missed, how gatekeeping, at each perceptible "decision point," could easily take precedence over advocacy.

More Learning in the Classroom: "Reading With the Group"

"Reading with the group" in the K-1 classroom involved some risk taking, not only for the child assuming temporary leadership of the activity but also for a teacher committed to treating conflict as an opportunity to discuss the meaning of differences. George's children occasionally attributed others' views to ignorance ("You dumb!") or themselves felt inadequate for beliefs and practices discrepant from those of the mainstream. Such conflicts were marked by visible evidence of mistrust, such as skeptical or threatening facial expressions, stances, or gestures. At such moments, George's intervention was vital to restoring a fruitful climate for social interaction.

As the following example illustrates, a frequent trigger for such conflicts was, again, argument over the truth and/or value of a text.

Martin, a black child from a working-class family, chose *The Gingerbread Man* as his selection to read with the group. On "his" day, seated in the teacher's chair with light from the windows behind him, he faced the other children, George, and me—all seated in a semicircle around him on the rug and on benches. I was sitting opposite George, on a bench between two children, recording the event on audiotape and taking contextual notes.

Martin looked up, apparently "taking in" the scene. Then slowly, deliberately, he stretched out his legs and, with eyes lowered, holding the book, he crossed his arms in a gesture we had all seen George assume many times. His posture said, "I'm waiting. I'll read when you show me you are ready." Like an experienced actor, Martin added an element of his own, a rhythmic toe tapping that added amusingly to his portrayal of the patient but watchful teacher. A few seconds later, again imitating George, he said: "O-kayyy!" Looking up suddenly, he directed his gaze all around the group, then began to read. All of the children were quiet.

My field notes say:

> Martin has an extraordinary delivery style. He's only five—but he knows when to slow down or speed up, knows how and when to change pace so as to make the narrative even more suspenseful. He "reads" the story fluently from the pictures, occasionally supplying alliteration that lends added drama to his performance. He remembers, most of the time, to turn the book so his classmates can see the picture. When he forgets and they call out to remind him, he smiles and leans forward indulgently to accommodate them. He is "in charge" and exuding confidence in this role.

Martin has reached the point in the story where the crafty fox is swimming across the river with the Gingerbread Man on his back:

Martin:	So they was swabbin' and swabbin' across the river. (pauses, looks around, sits back)
Children:	(several lean forward)
Betsy:	(WMC child, calls out to George) Is that what it says?
Martin:	(looks up at George)
George:	(does not answer, continues looking at Martin)
Martin:	(resumes reading, reaches a page that depicts the fox arriving alone at the river bank) So the Gingerbread Man fell into the water!
Charlie:	(WMC child, raises his hand)
George:	Yes, Charlie?
Charlie:	That's not what happened. The fox ate the Gingerbread Man.
Martin:	(makes a face, lowers his head, drops the book)
Children:	(whispers, laughter)

George: (moves over to stand near Martin, shows the picture
               in question to the group, waits a moment, then, to
               Charlie) Look. (then to the group) Look at the picture.
               All we see here is the fox in the water alone. There are
               different ways to understand this picture, different
               ways to read the story. Martin's doing it his way.
               When it's your turn to read, you can read it *your* way.
               (hands book back to Martin and returns to his seat)
Martin: (lifts his head, continues reading)

Schieffelin (personal communication, 1987) has observed
that "no one owns a story or has exclusive rights to its telling."
As we know, folk tales are retold and rewritten and illustrated
over time in ways that reflect and reinforce belief-and-practice
systems in different places at different times. In a pluralist
society, children deserve to know which forms of communication and representation are most used and valued by those from
their own and from others' communities. It might be helpful,
for example, for teachers to explain that some groups have
traditionally placed greater value on the oral tradition than
have others (see Heath, 1983; Ward, 1971, on language acquisition and socialization in a black working-class community and,
similarly, Michaels, 1981). All our children need to learn that
stories are social constructions that can be, and often are, differently organized by others.

The book illustration Martin refers to is an ambiguous one, open
to diverse interpretations. Note that George treats Martin's oral
reading as a performance, rewards him for originality and for
engaging his audience, that is, responding as adults and other
caregivers often do with young children in black communities.
This exchange around story reading is strikingly different from
the event in the library described above. In this classroom,
gatekeeping (Erickson & Shultz, 1982) does not take priority over
advocacy. Although the conventional version of the story has the
fox eat the Gingerbread Man, this one leaves room for alternative readings and meanings. George does not discredit either
child's version of the story. He makes clear there is room for both
versions and insists that children treat one another with respect.

In a larger sense, of course, George is helping children deconstruct the "official" story about schooling: that is, that one standard is to be valued and rewarded above all others. In this classroom, Martin's dramatic flair, his range and flexibility with nonverbal as well as verbal communication skills, imaginative use of language, and logical interpretation of a picture are given the credit they deserve. Charlie and Martin and all the others present are learning that different preschool experiences should not entitle children to special privilege or prevent their voices from being heard.

Students Making Room for Students

A critical measure of effective teaching is the way in which students demonstrate "internalization" (Vygotsky, 1978) and application of lessons learned. In George's classroom, it was increasingly evident by January that children were playing an active role in helping to construct the particular kind of context into which they were being socialized (Wentworth, 1980).

One example reveals how a child with limited proficiency in English is encouraged to use the resources he brings with him and, consequently, is drawn more easily into classroom life. It concerns two children in the K-1 classroom, Carolina (a 6-year-old girl) and Tomas (a 5-year-old boy). What follows is intended to provide a sense of the context that enabled this boy to progress from the margins toward full participation.

From my field notes:

Been thinking about Carolina. She's pretty comfortable with both Spanish and English—can use one or the other exclusively, as the situation requires, or she can code-switch. One day I saw her sitting at one end of a table watching and listening to a small group of children and the student teacher do a rendition of a "rap record." She was smiling and moving along with them and I wondered if she understood the fast-paced black dialect I couldn't decipher at all. "No," she admitted matter-of-factly when I asked her, "but I like it."

Another day I saw Carolina rush in when Tomas was being scapegoated by several classmates. His limited English proficiency was a problem because, unable to make his needs known, he often resorted to pulling or hitting other children. Early in the year, I heard one child say "Go 'way Tomas!" Another said: "You a bother!" Carolina said to the first child, "He's just trying to play," and to the other "Don't be mean to him. He can't help it." I hadn't yet observed her own direct interactions with Tomas, but this incident prompted me to take a closer look.

I had seen Ida, a school aide, pull Tomas closer to her in the school library when the librarian read stories to the children in English. I thought then, and Ida later confirmed, that she was providing a whispered Spanish translation. I had a sense that Carolina, too, was helping Tomas bridge two cultures and I wanted to find out more about how she did this.

On October 15, the large standing sandbox was opened. George assigned Tomas, Carolina, and Nan (also a Spanish speaker) to work together and I watched Tomas timidly follow the girls there. Looking back at him, Carolina said softly *"Venga, Tomas/*Come on" and he did.

My field notes say:

> They're pouring sand into and through several containers, seeming to enjoy the way it sifts or pours, depending on what they use. Nan works silently while Carolina describes what she is doing, each time in Spanish then in English. Tomas, like Nan, is sifting and pouring without speaking. Several moments pass. Needing to get to another part of the sand table, Carolina smiles, says *"Con permiso, Tomas"* as she moves behind and past him. He smiles back at her. Each time she speaks to Tomas during the remainder of the time at the sand table, she uses Spanish first, then repeats the message in English.

Notice in the transcription of an audiotaped discourse sample reproduced below the complex communicative task she has taken on. Not only is she helping Tomas directly to understand and participate in the sand activity, but she is also attempting, simultaneously, to evoke a sympathetic response toward Tomas from me, the Anglo observer:

Carolina: To-mas, *'pera te*/wait (then to me) That's his name in Spanish.

Linda: What? What is it in Spanish?

Carolina (smiles at Tomas, sing-song) To-mas, To-mas.

Linda: Ah (imitating her) To-mas.

Carolina: (to Tomas, demonstrating how to use a funnel) *Asi, tu puedes*/That's how you make a bi-ig thing over there. (points with a spoon)

Tomas: (to me, pointing to tape recorder) What da?

Linda: (to Tomas) A tape recorder.

Carolina: (to Tomas, returning him to their activity) A bi-ig thing. That's why we taking this sand over there.

Tomas: (to Carolina) No *need* no sand deah! (pushes it in another direction)

Carolina: *'Pera*/wait. (to Tomas) Gimmee a little sand for a minute, I'm making a cake for you.

Tomas: (giggles, then dumps a large container of sand in front of Carolina)

Carolina (grins) NOOOO! Then it's gonna be all together. (all three children work quietly and separately on "cakes")

This exchange was striking for a number of reasons. First, Tomas's attention span was noticeably greater than at other times I had observed him. Aware of Tomas's discomfort about his lack of English proficiency, George provided an opportunity for him to work and communicate in a context where he is most likely to be understood and supported, one in which he can risk taking new steps. Because Carolina feels free in this classroom to provide the assistance he needs, Tomas has needed peer support to gain meaningful access to the language, curriculum, and social context of his classroom. In this brief exchange, Tomas can be seen sharing materials, working collaboratively, showing resilience, laughing and teasing along with the others, able to sustain concentration on both gross- and fine-motor activities, integrating the verbal and nonverbal aspects of a new learning experience. More secure because of Carolina's availability to help him, Tomas not only ventures a full sentence in English but even dares to disagree with her. ("No need no sand deah!") At one point, he touches the tape recorder and asks me: "What da?" As I say, "Tape recorder, Tomas," I realize it is the first time he has asked me a question. Carolina is beaming. The following field-note entries are included to provide a brief chronology of Tomas's progress during that first semester:

> October 22, a.m. After meeting, the student teacher calls me over excitedly to hear Tomas "reading" to Charlie and Jim. He has some of the conventions—first time I've seen this: Turns pages, shows kids the pictures, says "Shhh!" when they get noisy. He's using brief phrases, not sentences, but kids are listening, interacting with him. So he's getting a sense of audience.

> October 22, p.m. After lunch I note that boys are teasing Tomas again. His past reputation is still a problem, even though he's doing better . . . so my day begins and ends with Tomas.

> November 14: Tomas and Jim sit with their arms over each others' shoulders at meeting. Can't get over the change in Tomas now—a regular member of the group. George tells me a previously scheduled Family Meeting has been canceled because of Tomas's progress.

> I see him in the "airplanes" reading group with Margaret, Carlo, and Kit. George says, "When kids are interested in the same thing, I put them together." I notice there's no mention of reading levels.

On November 19, Tomas, Selim, and Charlie are at the water table. I observe and audiotape the following interaction:

Charlie:	(to George) George. Come look at what Tomas is making! (Tomas has blown bubbles through a tube, managed to surround a submerged small boat with a structure resembling a geodetic dome.)
Tomas:	(to Selim) You do i dat! (You do it like that!)
Selim:	(to Linda) Look at mine!

Tomas:	(to Linda) Look at mine! (Several other children approach the water table.)
Charlie:	(to Kit) Tomas's is much bigger. (accidentally sprays Tomas with water)
Tomas:	(to Charlie) STOP! (then continues to blow bubbles through the plastic tube)
Betsy:	(comes over to look) Wow! Looks like all of 'em are connected now.

Tomas continued to make progress in the classroom, although keeping up with conversation was often difficult. At appropriate times, George provided a respite by suggesting activities in which the level of communicative complexity (in English) was reduced. On the other hand, there were new challenges. The resource room teacher/poet in residence introduced Tomas to poetry during the second semester by encouraging him to "explore" an orange. Hesitant at first, he soon plunged into learning experiences like this one with energy and evident pleasure. At the end of the school year, Tomas moved on with his peers to the next grade.

Conclusion

My findings suggest that the "culturally responsive education" Cazden and Leggett (1981) advocate may be more a matter of greater interpretive freedom—of recognizing, making room for, and building on whatever verbal and nonverbal resources children bring and acquire over time (what Schieffelin & Ochs, 1987, call "communicative accommodation") than a narrower focus on why and how children from specific marginal communities are likely to encounter difficulty in school. Too frequently, access to data on community-specific practices provides a rationale for insisting that classroom teachers need only become more explicit about their expectations. Meier (1984) states the broader challenge of pluralism: "The heart of the democratic dilemma is how to make the formal culture accessible to all without requiring renunciation of a student's own culture" (p. 68).

This chapter advances the view that children's conflicts over the authority of texts are crucial "decision points" (Erickson, 1979) for teachers. It suggests that the adult "mediation" (Vygotsky, 1978) provided on such occasions can do much to help children question and move beyond currently prevailing notions about dominant and subordinate cultures within the United States. I have proposed that the ways in which teachers guide classroom discourse, particularly around story reading, may serve either to reinforce prevailing attitudes and practices or to explain and celebrate what diversity and interdependence can mean. This approach to multicultural education derives from and is responsive to the dynamics of social life. For that reason, it is far more likely than a grafted-on multicultural curriculum to engage children in helping to create and maintain a truly democratic dialogue.

Note

1. "George" and other members of that faculty have served as cooperating teachers since 1987 for the Venture: Urban Education and Urban Education Semester programs, inspiring many liberal arts undergraduates who now plan to enter the profession. They share the view that an emphasis on community and collaboration is a key factor in their ongoing success with urban children from a wide range of backgrounds.

References

Au, K., & Jordan, K. (1981). Teaching reading to Hawaiian children: Finding a culturally appropriate solution. In H. Trueba, G. Guthrie, & K. Au (Eds.), *Culture and the bilingual classroom*. Rowley, MA: Newbury House.

Barth, F. (Ed.). (1969). Introduction. In *Ethnic groups and boundaries*. Boston: Little, Brown.

Bereiter, C., & Engelmann, S. (1966). *Teaching disadvantaged children in the preschool*. Englewood Cliffs, NJ: Prentice-Hall.

Burbules, N. C., & Rice, S. (1991). Dialogue across differences: Continuing the conversation. *Harvard Educational Review, 61* (4), 393-416.

Cazden, C. B. (1988). *Classroom discourse.* Cambridge: Cambridge University Press.

Cazden, C. B., & Hymes, D. H. (1980). Narrative thinking and storytelling rights: A folklorist's clue to a critique of education. In D. H. Hymes (Ed.), *Language in education: Ethnolinguistic essays* (Language and Ethnography series). Washington, DC: Center for Applied Linguistics.

Cazden, C. B., & Leggett, E. L. (1981). Culturally responsive education: Recommendations for achieving Lau remedies II. In H. Trueba, G. Guthrie, & K. Au (Eds.), *Culture and the bilingual classroom.* Rowley, MA: Newbury House.

Cochran-Smith, M. (1983). *The making of a reader.* Norwood, NJ: Ablex.

Deutsch, M. (1963). The disadvantaged child and the learning process. In A. H. Passow (Ed.), *Education in depressed areas.* New York: Teachers College Press.

Erickson, F. (1979). Mere ethnography: Some problems in its use in educational practice. *Anthropology and Education Quarterly, 10*(3), 182-188.

Erickson, F., & Shultz, J. (1982). *The counselor as gatekeeper.* New York: Academic Press.

Fine, M. (1987). Silencing in public schools: Nurturing the possibility of voice in an improbable context. *Language Arts, 64,* 157-174.

Giroux, H. (1987). Schooling and the politics of ethics: Beyond liberal and conservative discourses. *Journal of Education, 169* (2), 9-33.

Giroux, H., & McLaren, P. (1986). Teacher education and the politics of engagement: The case for democratic schooling. *Harvard Educational Review, 56*(3), 213-238.

Gleason, J. B., & Weintraub, S. (1978). Input language and the acquisition of communicative competence. In K. Nelson (Ed.), *Children's language* (Vol. 1). New York: Gardner.

Gumperz, J. J., & Hernandez-Chavez, E. (1972). Bilingualism, bidialectalism and classroom interaction. In C. Cazden, V. John, & D. H. Hymes (Eds.), *Functions of language in the classroom.* New York: Teachers College Press.

Heath, S. B. (1983). *Ways with words: Language, life and work in communities and classrooms.* Cambridge: Cambridge University Press.

Hymes, D. H. (1972). Introduction. In C. Cazden, V. John, & D. H. Hymes (Eds.), *Functions of language in the classroom.* New York: Teachers College Press.

Labov, W. (1972). The logic of non-standard English. In P. P. Giglioli (Ed.), *Language and social context.* Harmondsworth, United Kingdom: Penguin.

Levine, L. (1988). *Everyone else . . . including me: Learning to value diversity in school.* Unpublished doctoral dissertation, University of Pennsylvania, Philadelphia.

Meier, D. (1984, Winter). "Getting tough" in the schools: A critique of the conservative prescription. *Dissent,* pp. 61-70.

Michaels, S. (1981). "Sharing time": Children's narrative styles and differential access to literacy. *Language in Society, 10*(3), 423-442.

Mitchell, C., & Weiler, K. (Eds.). (1991). *Rewriting literacy: Culture and the discourse of the other* (Critical Studies in Education and Culture series). New York: Bergin & Garvey.

Moll, L. C., & Greenberg, J. B. (1990). Creating zones of possibilities: Combining social contexts for instruction. In L. C. Moll (Ed.), *Vygotsky and education.* Cambridge, UK: Cambridge University Press.

Payne, C., & Bennett, C. (1977). "Middle-class aura" in public schools. *Teacher Educator, 13*(1), 16-26.

Philips, S. (1985). Participant structures and communicative competence: Warm Springs children in community and classroom. In C. Cazden, V. John, & D. H. Hymes (Eds.), *Functions of language in the classroom.* New York: Teachers College Press. (Original work published 1972)

Schieffelin, B. B., & Eisenberg, A. (1984). Cultural variation in conversation. In R. Schiefelbusch & J. Packer (Eds.), *The acquisition of communicative competence.* Baltimore, MD: University Park Press.

Schieffelin, B. B., & Ochs, E. (1987). Language socialization. *Annual Review of Anthropology, 15,* 163-191.

Scollon, R., & Scollon, S. B. K. (1981). *Narrative, literacy and face in interethnic communication: Vol. 7. Advances in discourse processes* (R. Freedle, Ed.). Norwood, NJ: Ablex.

Taylor, D. (1983). *Family literacy*. Exeter, NH: Heinemann Educational.

Vygotsky, L. S. (1978). *Mind in society* (M. Cole, V. J. Steiner, S. Scribner, & E. Souberman, Eds.). Cambridge, MA: Harvard University Press.

Ward, M. (1971). *Them children: A study in language learning*. New York: Holt, Rinehart & Winston.

Wentworth, W. (1980). *Context and understanding: An inquiry into socialization theory*. New York: Elsevier.

Yonemura, M. (1986). Empowerment and teacher education. *Harvard Educational Review, 56*(4), 473-480.

Francis-Okongwu and Pflaum also use the perspective of social and cultural diversity, and they apply it to teacher preparation. Focusing on different educational outcomes, they note the influence of race, class, culture, and ethnicity. Drawing upon several strands of research that attempt to explain such school outcomes as well as studies that provide evidence of structures that demonstrate the role schools play in social reproduction, the authors propose new goals and strategies to be used in preparing teachers for today's schools. These goals and strategies are suggested as the means by which teachers may be prepared to effectively teach all students.

7. Diversity in Education: Implications for Teacher Preparation

ANNE FRANCIS-OKONGWU
SUSANNA W. PFLAUM

When significant changes and shifts in curriculum and instruction occur in teacher preparation, the potential exists for particular and long-term impact on society. Teacher candidates, especially those in undergraduate teacher preparation programs, acquire subject matter knowledge and also, unlike those in other professions, learn about the structure of the disciplines and approaches to their professional work. What curriculum and what instruction they experience influence what and how they will teach. As the persons beyond the family who are uniquely charged with the responsibility of enculturation

(Goodlad, 1990), teachers are the major actors in the process of cultural and social reproduction. Students in teacher preparation programs will transmit the values, attitudes, and patterns of interaction in their work with individuals and groups. They will interpret for their students what are the negative and positive sanctions of various orientations and behaviors of the wider society. What happens in their studies in college is critical to the society at large. And, of course, who they are and what educational and cultural histories they come to college with are the lenses through which college experiences are understood.

It is from this perspective, the interaction of individual and group experience with the college academic experience, that implications for teacher preparation programs may be developed. For, in most programs, the students represent a wide range of elementary school, secondary school, and college backgrounds, come from very different socioeconomic backgrounds, hold a range of expectations about being teachers, and come from different racial, language, and cultural backgrounds. Such differences are related to their roles as teachers. (As an example of how such differences in teacher background are perceived, we note that the media present the Teach for America teachers as making a sacrifice; on the other hand, the graduates of urban public institutions may be seen as moving toward logical career roles.) Professional programs can reflect and incorporate these differences and be enriched by them. In this chapter, we suggest goals for revitalizing teacher preparation programs and provide illustrative strategies.

This discussion is divided into three parts. In the first, theoretical structures are examined, particularly with reference to the outcomes of schooling for students from different socioeconomic, racial, language, and cultural backgrounds. In the second, concerns about the organization and content of programs designed to prepare prospective teachers for contemporary schools are raised. Finally, drawing upon our own teaching experiences, we offer some concepts that appear to be useful in addressing the issue of the preparation of differentially prepared college students pursuing careers in education.

The Problem of Differential Academic Outcomes

Over the past three decades, considerable research has yielded valuable insights into the multifaceted problem of differential academic outcomes of U.S. students. Voices stressing different and unequal genetic endowments among racial groups (Jensen, 1969) are not taken very seriously today, and the overwhelming majority of researchers focus, instead, on the importance of community and school environments as well as broader socioeconomic and cultural forces in shaping the different degrees of academic success among U.S. students. Thus the central issues in the current debate revolve around disagreements about the causal weight to be given to three critical domains of experience that shape the contours of academic outcomes: (a) family and community environment; (b) the school environment, including teachers, peers, administrators, and other school personnel; and (c) overarching social, economic, and political forces and the ways in which they continue to structure race, class, and gender relations in our social institutions, in this instance, schools.

Since the 1960s, attention to variables within each of these domains of experience, and in combination, has proven useful in refining our understanding of the complex ways in which all three of these domains of experience interact to determine academic outcomes of students. The domains of race and class are the focus of the discussion of this research as illustrated through selected studies over the past three decades.

Several strands of research illustrate the different theories proposed to explain school success and failure. In an effort to explore the causes of differential academic achievement among groups of children in the United States, several studies during the early 1960s developed what became known as the cultural deficit approach (Deutsch, 1964; Deutsch & Brown, 1964; John & Goldstein, 1964). Focusing on the family and community, these researchers identified school failure among the poor as caused by family structure, attitudes, values, and culture as contrasted with mainstream middle-class American worldviews and behavior. These writings suggested that family organization and the behavior of the poor reflected adaptations to socioeconomic factors. Moreover, in opposition to the cultural deficit theory, ethnographic research generated during the 1960s demonstrated that neither culture nor class should be treated as a variable in which individual behavior is uniform. Rather, this work demonstrated that variations in attitude and life-style among people occur within socioeconomic categories as they do among people belonging to the same culture. Such variations were seen to be reflected in differences in child-rearing patterns as well (Jeffers, 1967; Leibow, 1967; Lewis, 1967; Stack, 1974).

An important shift of inquiry into causes of low academic achievement occurred in the 1970s and 1980s as the research focus moved away from the individual, the family, and the community to include the study of schooling and the implications of overarching social, economic, and political structures. The studies that emerged during this period focused on the process of schooling and variations in student experiences within schools serving different socioeconomic, racial, and cultural groups (Anyon, 1981; Erickson, 1987; Leacock, 1969; Rist, 1970; Shannon, 1985). In this work, close attention is given to several important factors: differential verbal and nonverbal interactional patterns between teachers and students, fundamental differences in curriculum content and curriculum use resulting in differing learning experiences, and academic knowledge and outcomes for students.

This issue is partially addressed by the ethnographies of researchers using a social reproduction theoretical perspective (Leacock, 1969; Rist, 1970; among others) and those stressing conflicting cultural interactional patterns, or cultural mismatch, between teachers and students (Delpit, 1990; Heath, 1983; Phillips and Ong, in Erickson, 1987). Despite the differences in theoretical perspective, both approaches conclude that differential verbal and nonverbal interactional patterns between teachers and students result in differing learning experiences and outcomes for students. Social reproduction theorists such as Anyon (1981) and Rist (1970) demonstrate that, within one classroom, one school, one district, one city, students may experience fundamentally different schooling. Therefore the role that schools play in the reproduction of social inequality leads to differential placement in occupational and social structures. Schools as social institutions are linked with the wider social structure of which they are a part. A focus on social class highlights social inequalities; understanding the processes sensitizes educators to their own role.

Another approach during the 1970s and 1980s took a cultural relativist perspective and focused on the ways in which cultural difference in language use and communication styles between teachers and students from nondominant families and communities negatively influences the academic outcomes of students (Heath, 1983). For example, Heath's work demonstrated how linguistic patterns and communication styles are central to the representation of understanding of others. When the kind of preferred talk, interactions, organization of time, materials, and space differed from the expectations of teachers, children and teachers alike became confused, and learning suffered. For students whose teachers have different patterns of language and communication, the patterns of language may be understood as indicative of academic problems rather than as representations of the frameworks of understanding. Yet language is more than words; it is a product of an individual's experience and learning within the context of family and community and thus serves as the medium of representation of understandings and knowledge. When teachers came to understand their own and their students' communication styles, as those with whom Heath worked did, helpful teaching and learning strategies emerged.

These two kinds of study converge on several key issues. First, the patterns of verbal and nonverbal interaction between teachers and students provide valuable insights into how interactional patterns may negatively influence the academic success of students. Second, language use influences teachers' perceptions of students' academic potential. Third, in most instances, teachers are unaware of the ways in which their interactional patterns with students may inhibit the academic success of some of the children in their classrooms. Finally, it is important to sensitize teachers to cultural difference rather than cultural deficiency. These notions are critical in the training of teachers in enriching understanding of the complex interaction of class, culture, language, race, and ethnic variables in determining the academic outcomes of students.

It is important to recognize the wide range of diversity within socioeconomic, cultural, and racial groups (Gordon, 1991). Without adequate attention to the types of variations within groups and the relationship of these differences to academic performance, it becomes impossible to explain individual variations in academic outcomes and, more important, to develop adequate strategies of intervention to meet student needs.

The cultural relativist perspective may be problematic in another way. Researchers who focus solely on cultural differences may overlook the social, political, economic, and historical contexts in which schools operate (Erickson, 1987; Foley, 1991; Ogbu, 1981). They may thereby ignore the tension existing between the U.S. ideology of equality and the structures of inequality based on class, race, and gender. While free public schooling is projected as the "equalizer," cultural clashes in language use and in patterns of participation occur that favor the dominance of Euro-American language and culture. Inclusion of analysis of the participatory structures between dominant and minority group cultures such as Native Americans, African Americans, and Mexican Americans provides an important explanatory dimension in the understanding of the tenaciousness of educational issues (Phillips in Foley, 1991; Weinberg, 1977). A comprehensive understanding of differential academic achievement and attainment requires the integration of race, class, culture, and gender relations in analysis of the problem.

In this regard, the importance of class location in the question of differential academic experience is clear from Anyon's (1981) discussion. Anyon studied five New Jersey public schools serving different socioeconomic groups. Using the perspective of social class and school knowledge and attending to the perceptions of teachers of the academic and occupational possibilities of their students, to students' perceptions about their own academic and professional possibilities, to differences in the physical environments and tones of these schools, and to curriculum content and curriculum use, Anyon demonstrated that, although there was a fairly standardized public curriculum in these schools, there were substantial differences among these schools in each of these areas, resulting in qualitative and quantitative differences in the level and types of education. For example, children of working-class parents learned very little social information and "little or no conceptual or critical understanding of the world or their place in it" (p. 32). For these students, the emphasis was on mechanical behaviors. On the other hand, in the two schools serving upper-middle-class and upper-class children, students were expected to be able to acquire critical thinking processes and problem-solving strategies and, as a result, developed a fundamentally different knowledge base. Comments by teachers in these schools reflected the congruence of teaching and their predictions of their students' future lives.

Rist's (1970) work considered the variables of class as well. In contrast to the study of class variation among whites in Anyon, however, Rist's study examines class effects within the context of a black teacher working with black youngsters. The kindergarten teacher in the Rist classroom responded differentially, by class, to her students even before formal academic instruction began or any achievement testing had occurred. Rist demonstrates the tenacity of class in schooling. Some of the teacher's students learned behaviors of deference; others of power and affirmation. Through the inadvertent social reproduction of that classroom, students internalized feelings that would influence their learning.

But not all schooling that reproduces class is inadvertent. Studies of the schooling that upper-class children receive (Baltzell, 1964, 1979; Cookson & Persell, 1985) illustrate how, at elite private day and boarding schools, their teachers, the parents, and school administrators are keenly aware of the process of social reproduction and seek to ensure the power and entitlement of their class, even to the selection of teachers and consideration of their background.

In these elite classrooms, students not only experience small class size, creative use of materials, and, often, innovative curriculum, they experience the benefits of attention to their role in their own knowledge search. In the words of such an educator:

> Because of the way in which we ask questions and they write about their work, students also learn that their ideas and experiences are central in their learning process. With the emphasis on the process of searching as well as what is learned, students also gain a sense that it is relevant to think about where ideas come from, how they grow and change and how ideas continue to develop. (Bishoff, 1990, p. 10)

Such a student-focused approach to learning is illustrated in the Cookson and Persell (1985) study of elite boarding schools. The creation of excitement in the process of inquiry and learning is a common experience for children being prepared for leadership roles and for roles in knowledge generation. The authors point out that, at preparatory schools, education is a "cottage industry" where learning experiences are "handcrafted," that, although learning for these students might not always be easy or fun, it is generally not equated with pain or failure either.

These descriptions of the contrast between the schooling of middle- and upper-class children differ from that experienced by poor children. There are three critical differences: teachers' preparation of the future roles of their students in society, teachers' understanding of the relationship between self-confidence and learning and efforts to develop in students the confidence to risk while learning, and the demystification of the process of knowledge generation (Anyon, 1981; Bishoff, 1990; Winograd, 1991). The recent report by Kozol (1991) constitutes a vivid description of how material and human resources are differentially provided in schools according to class. Both the teachers and the students Kozol quotes are aware of the effect of resource differentiation on student outcomes. In schools serving (in many cases, not serving) lower-class students, however, teachers do not perceive their role as instrumental; instead, like their students, they feel the effects of inequities as beyond their control.

Clearly, those involved in education need to have a more explicit understanding of how schools and teaching perpetuate group distinctions. Teachers need to be sensitive to and understanding of variation in communication as they interact with students of diverse class, race, and language. Moreover, the institutions that prepare teachers need to examine how they are structured to alter the pattern of social reproduction. (Although not addressed directly here, ethnicity and gender are important factors to be included in the development of new teachers.)

Preparation for Teaching

Understanding differential preparation is important to students pursuing careers in education. They need to understand not only the roles of language, communication, and participation but also the content of the curriculum and instruction experienced by students from different socioeconomic groups. Students entering schools of education, as is true of all students, bring to their studies the crystallization of their academic and personal histories. They present various levels of preparation for the challenges of a four-year college or graduate school curriculum. Teacher candidates enter preparation programs for a variety of reasons and with different ideas about what it means to be a successful teacher, what constitutes a positive learning environment, and what represents positive outcomes for children. Today, the task of teacher preparation programs is to prepare teachers for schools that promote excellence and that prepare all students, regardless of race, ethnicity, class, or gender, to be successful in competitive, complex workplaces, to be thoughtful participants in the civic arena, and to experience full personal development.

Accomplishment of this task presents a challenge to the faculties of schools of education. Faculty members need to define more clearly what is meant by "excellence" and how excellence is manifested in schools. They must also demonstrate through their own teaching how to effectively engage students from diverse educational and personal backgrounds. Through their own teaching examples, they must demonstrate to prospective teachers that what is being asked of the teachers of today is, indeed, possible.

Goodlad (1990) recently criticized teacher education programs for not enabling teacher candidates to learn actively, to experience a variety of schools in which to practice, in short, to have ample opportunity to structure their own knowledge of schools, teaching, children, and learning. We propose that there are significant gaps in experience that may contribute to problems in teacher preparation, gaps that need to be closed to enable teacher candidates to acquire the knowledge, sensitivity, and explicit behaviors to be in a position to alter the process of social reproduction that inhibits real equity in the outcomes of schooling.

To represent an approach to teacher preparation that responds to the criticisms raised above, we want to point out that we are situated both in different institutions and in different roles and are engaged in a process of struggle with the development of strategies to enable students preparing to be teachers to meet the challenges of a rapidly changing society. As Gordon (1991) states, the future in which new teachers will be working is one in which it is not possible to predict what technological changes, what work lives, what social relationships within and across groups will be. Experiencing ourselves in contexts in which ever-increasing rapidity of change is occurring in every sphere of national and international life, we need to look to the likelihood of this momentum continuing as qualitative and quantitative transformations occur in all aspects of experience. Those of us involved in teacher education need to go beyond the superficial rhetoric for change to try to imagine how to prepare teachers given changes in the organization of economic, political, and social forces, such as increased poverty among children, changes in desegregation rulings, and increased violence. Just viewing group and individual hostility in the context of economic downturns in these times suggests that the new teachers currently in teacher preparation programs will experience new and dynamic periods of multidimensional change and more difficult and complex contexts in which to teach.

We come to this task with different perspectives. One of us is an anthropologist-social worker; the other, an educator. One of us teaches would-be teachers and practicing teachers in an urban public institution; the other is a dean of an urban private graduate school who has had considerable public higher education experience. One of us is African American; the other, white. We do share common understanding of the problems and goals, and we have struggled with these difficult issues for some time, including the period in which we team taught. While we agree on the discussion presented here, we have each learned from the other and come to the recommendations through considerable dialogue.

A fundamental question underlies the structure of the formulation of a more responsive teacher preparation program: *How do overarching social structures of inequity coalesce and interact to shape the individual's experience of academic success or failure?* The variables to be considered in examining disparities in academic outcomes must include race, class, gender, culture, and ethnicity in both their internal and their external dimensions. By *internal*, we mean the way in which these variables are personally experienced; the *external* is the response to these differences by the wider society and its institutions encountered by each individual in the process of daily living. It is critical that, in preparing teachers to teach all children well, it is recognized that what must occur is a "profound shift in the direction of daily practice and its symbolism, away from hegemonic practice and toward transformative practice" (Erickson, 1987, p. 355). At the least, transformative practice means that teachers must be able to examine the macro- and microenvironments in which students live and understand how to help them negotiate through their experiences in school, family, community, and society.

First, we identify what ought to be the major goals of a revitalized educational program. Each of the following goals, of course, requires considerable individual and collective reflection (Perry, 1992). Goal delineation is a long and continuing process; the actual goals for an individual institution will, of course, vary according to the persons involved. We hope that working consensus will be reached and will be continually reviewed and reaffirmed as newcomers bring new insights and knowledge to the process. The outcome of revitalized teacher preparation ought to result in teachers who are prepared to criticize those policies, practices, and negative perceptions of the students they teach that inhibit full educational opportunity. Moreover, these teachers ought to be able to act on their beliefs on behalf of their students. The following goals represent a process; full attainment for the teachers preparing today would take considerable time, support, personal effort, and ingenuity.

1. Teachers need to understand the complexities of the issues surrounding differential academic achievement. They must explore the ways in which race, class, gender, culture, and ethnicity interact to influence educational outcomes.

2. Teachers need to learn techniques for observation based on inquiry, on observation, that stimulate new questions and new hypotheses. They need to listen so that they hear the varied, sometimes contradictory, messages their students speak. They need to delve into the reasons for some students' silence. They need to engage in dialogue about difficult matters: homelessness, divorce, AIDS. Teachers must be able to respect the points of view and represented experience of students and their parents even if it conflicts with the teachers' perceptions.

3. Teachers need to have had a significant experience in a cultural context that differs from their own. From the perspective of another context, they can reflect critically on the familiar. They need, then, to be able to converse effectively with the

families of their students, whatever their racial, class, or cultural backgrounds.

4. For teachers to read and hear voices of those from different life experiences, they need, during their period of preparation, to study the history of different groups. They need, as well, to critically examine different frameworks within and across academic disciplines so that, as they build their own constructed knowledge, they are able to understand how people come to have quite different understandings of the same phenomena.

5. Knowing, through explicit discussion, the parameters of the wide fundamental changes through which society is moving, changes involving intergroup relationships, the reconstruction of work, economic shifts, and civic participation, teachers need to understand that what is important is for their students to acquire transferable skills. The acquisition of strong skills in literacy, in mathematics, in the social sciences, in the sciences, and in aesthetics is a right for all students, but such skills are not sufficient. Teachers need to be able to engage students in problem solving in many different situations so that they are prepared to adapt to a changing world.

6. Teachers need to be able to be exploratory, active learners themselves in relationship to their teaching. That is, when classroom activities do not bring about desired outcomes, teachers need to be able to reconceptualize the problem and develop new strategies.

7. Teachers need to have experienced, initially vicariously, but later directly, demonstrable successes in the teaching of children from a variety of social, economic, and educational settings.

8. Teachers need to develop an understanding of their "potential" as reproducers of social structures and decide whether their preferred approach is to be reconstructors.

This list represents the complexity and difficulty facing schools of education, for few would say that their graduates leave with such skills. But, for us, not one of these goals could be eliminated. Of course, in the process of developing goals for individual institutions, there will be considerable change. Our goals would be difficult to reach, as would be true of any set of goal statements that reflect the complexities resulting from use of a multidimensional view of social influences.

Strategies in Teacher Preparation

To initiate the process, the faculty, together with practicing teachers who enact these principles in their teaching, need to cooperatively develop curriculum that affects courses, fieldwork, readings, dialogue, knowledge base, and practice. It is important that a collaborative endeavor of this magnitude is only enriched by the diversity of participants. Moving with these goal statements are some strategies we hope are useful.

1. For teachers to understand how race, ethnicity, class, gender, and culture affect educational outcomes, they must experience differences themselves. A good way to start is for teachers and students to explore their own educational histories and how their experiences interact with each of these variables. We used a process we call educational paths (Francis-Okongwu & Pflaum, 1991). This exercise, conducted the first day of class, involved students introducing themselves by sharing the most memorable precollege educational incident and the ways in which their race, class, ethnicity, culture, or gender had shaped the contours of their schooling. Later, after that session, the content of the students' experiences became the exemplars for course concepts. This exercise helped students see the interaction of these forces in their own lives and in the lives of their fellow classmates. Second, the activity sensitized them to the wide variation in school experiences of which they were not formerly aware. It also sensitized them to the difficulties that arise when assumptions are made about these factors on the experience of others. And, as anyone who teaches knows, adult students do make assumptions about one another, too often based on little knowledge. The exercise is a helpful introduction to shared study of current and historical differential academic achievement.

2. The use of inquiry based on observation and on listening to others is not new; in fact, it is an essential part of the curriculum

at one of our colleges. For this to occur powerfully in the collegiate experience, course instructors need to be able to analytically observe and hear their own students. It is important that persons preparing to teach closely examine at least two students, one of a different social background and one of a similar background. The observations should include classroom learning experiences, interaction of the individual with others, and interaction in other contexts outside of school. Challenged by the course instructor and by fellow students, the observations need to lead to understanding of how the child perceives his or her world as well as how the observer's lenses may influence interpretations. Using perceptions gained from shared observations while in collegiate study, teachers in practice will be better prepared to understand children's interactions, silences, conflicting behaviors, and responses and will seek to consult with other professionals to validate interpretations.

Prospective teachers often discuss the significance of societal problems on schoolchildren; in the safety of the college classroom, adults can talk of the effects of homelessness, of divorce, of AIDS, of substance abuse on the lives of students. More challenging is the realization of such insights in real work with students. In-depth discussions with and observations of professionals who successfully work with children and their families in such circumstances need to be part of programs in teacher preparation. In their own work, teachers need to become proficient at allowing students and parents to express various perceptions of social ills, for perceptions differ according to people's experiences. To be effective, teachers need to support one another in their efforts to allow the "unspeakable" to become permissible talk between teacher and student. When drug sales occur outside of the school, when a family member has died of AIDS, when a parent is imprisoned, children's observations and pain need to be acknowledged, and structures are required to support students through difficult times.

3. Strongly recommended is the development of arrangements for students preparing to teach to experience another culture. In the context of fieldwork connected with program

requirements, at least one school placement and one noneducational setting in conjunction with coursework should be with children from cultures and social classes different than their own. This requires individual tailoring of assignments to students according to their own status and their experiences. Reflective discussions with other students will enrich the learnings that result. At one of our colleges, all students meet weekly with five other students and a faculty adviser for the purpose of integrating experience with ongoing learning.

Part of the experience in working with students of a different culture requires developing relationships with their families or caretakers. At one of our colleges, a course on parent involvement requires that graduate students (who are teachers) use their individual classrooms as the laboratory for testing and developing strategies for involving parents in their classroom activities. In cases where parent and teachers did not share the same language, for example, students were challenged to provide communications by using children, colleagues, and so on. They made themselves available to discuss a wide range of issues of concern to the parents by coming to school earlier, by staying later, by telephoning, and by establishing cooperative baby-sitting arrangements so parents could attend school meetings and workshops to understand school practices. The students develop a model from this work for parental involvement. In this way, teachers are helped to move with parents into the community to use community resources and to cooperatively enrich the education of their students.

4. Ideally, students who are preparing to teach come to their study of education with familiarity with at least one discipline in depth and, furthermore, with the experience of contrasting frameworks within that discipline. In fact, recent changes in requirements for teachers (e.g., New York State) include the requirement of a major in a liberal art or science. We hope that, as programs in the arts and sciences in undergraduate study expand to abandon the extreme forms of Euro-American focus and move toward the inclusion of the histories of other groups, students preparing to teach will have a broader base from

which to explore differences among individuals. Within the study of the United States, for example, the histories of African Americans, Native Americans, Mexican Americans, and others need to be included. Where the students in teacher preparation programs represent these, and other groups, and where the discourse is dynamic, other peoples' histories become concrete and valid.

5. It is critical that prospective teachers learn about the significant differences among schools, particularly in regard to academic outcomes. No longer can we afford to prepare teachers for one type of school setting, the imagined ideal school of some past time. To acquire greater understanding of diversity, prospective teachers need to hear from others, including fellow students, about the impact of early experience and differential schooling on later learning. They need to read and discuss the critical literature in education and related disciplines. They need to read and discuss the news, including critical readings of *Education Week*. They need to consider not only mainstream educational news and issues but also community changes and issues. Such readings will inform their knowledge while in teacher preparation programs and, as the practice becomes habitual, will inform their teaching practice as well.

In the different content areas, specialists need to explore with prospective teachers the perception many students have that traditional lines of study are beyond their reach. For example, teachers need to understand the educational advantages and occupational status of those with specialized knowledge versus those without such knowledge. Moreover, they need to learn about innovative programs that have opened access to this knowledge to those traditionally excluded. In mathematics, for example, Triesman's (1983) direct work and Berry's strong observations (1985) with college students in the United States and children in Southern Africa, respectively, illustrate the success of new ways of empowering students. Experts from the different disciplines can help teachers understand how to make the knowledge base more accessible. By understanding the disciplines and the cross-discipline connections, teachers can develop effective strategies for approaching problems in different areas. Methods courses, then, can become the contexts for problem solving.

6. Teachers are inquiring, active learners when they are challenged to seek new approaches to difficult problems while in preparation programs and later as they meet the academic needs of their students. In the process, they can integrate their theoretical and practical learning, create new syntheses, and, also, produce new knowledge. Called "inquiry" or "reflective" teaching, methods for combining readings, observations, and careful review of the outcomes of different teaching strategies provide the framework for effective teaching. Case studies may be used in the college classroom; observations of good practice in the field are also important. In this regard, "challenge" is the key. There needs to be, from faculty working closely with each teacher in the field, an optimism about success and the expectation that any teaching experiences can be reconfigured in new ways with different resources, materials, and strategies of instruction to produce different outcomes.

7. For teachers to experience successful teaching of children in various educational settings, they need, first, to observe practicing teachers whose students achieve academic empowerment in contexts in which too often there is academic failure, such as inner-city schools populated by the children of the poor. Prospective teachers need to see experienced teachers successfully shift their approach when learning does not progress until their students experience success. They need to be able to recognize, analyze, and articulate the flexible adaptations teachers make as they use different strategies to promote successful learning. They need, in the process of their preparation, to take on the challenge of working with a difficult-to-teach student and, with faculty guidance, to achieve success. This can occur in connection with tutoring required in courses in reading difficulties. Such practice is enriched as students work in pairs or teams and share their regular written reflections about their specific work with tutees. In this way, students learn to incorporate a range of perspectives in their search for success for all students.

8. For teachers to be able to make reasoned choices about their role vis-à-vis society, they must have a vision of a preferred society. Ideally, teachers, concerned as they must be about educational inequities, ought to believe what Freire asserted, that the current time is not to be accepted in place of the "preferred future" (Freire, 1972). Teachers need to look at what they are doing, and their own and their students' learning, and how these interrelated processes are building toward or inhibiting success.

Teachers should be required, as part of their preparation, to prepare a written formulation of what type of society they hope to help create. This formulation needs to consider issues such as the tax base for school support, the placement of teachers in schools in regard to race and ethnicity, the distribution of resources within districts and between districts, the verbal and nonverbal messages in educational environments, the perceptions of teachers as to their students' educational and occupation attainments, the relationships between schools and communities.

The above comments represent what we imagine will be a continued discussion. Certainly, even to begin to achieve these goals, much greater support for prospective and practicing teachers is needed. We reflect the discussion of those we cite, as well as others, and hope this piece represents an invitation to a continuing conversation.

References

Anyon, J. (1981). Social class and school knowledge. *Curriculum Inquiry, 11*, 2-42.

Baltzell, D. E. (1964). *The Protestant establishment: Aristocracy and caste in America.* New York: Random House.

Baltzell, D. E. (1979). *Philadelphia gentlemen: The making of a national upper class.* Philadelphia: University of Pennsylvania Press.

Berry, J. W. (1985). Learning mathematics in a second language: Some cross-cultural issues. *For the Learning of Mathematics, 5*, 18-22.

Bishoff, B. (1990). Searching for answers. *The Friends Select Journal, 2*(2), 8-10.

Cookson, P. W., & Persell, C. H. (1985). *Preparing for power: America's elite boarding schools.* New York: Basic Books.

Delpit, L. (1990). Language diversity and learning. In *New perspectives on talk and learning* (pp. 247-266). Urbana, IL: National Council of Teachers of English.

Deutsch, C. (1964). Auditory discrimination and learning: Social factors. *Merrill Palmer Quarterly, 10,* 277-296.

Deutsch, M., & Brown, B. (1964). Social influences in Negro-white intelligence differences. *Journal of Social Issues, 20,* 24-35.

Erickson, F. (1987). Transformation and school success: The politics and culture of educational achievement. *Anthropology and Education Quarterly, 18,* 335-356.

Foley, D. E. (1991). Reconsidering anthropological explanations of ethnic school failure. *Anthropology and Education Quarterly, 22,* 60-86.

Francis-Okongwu, A., & Pflaum, S. W. (1991). The importance of including scholarship by people of color in teacher preparation. *Transforming Anthropology, 2,* 25-27.

Freire, P. (1972). *Cultural action for freedom.* Baltimore: Penguin Education.

Goodlad, J. (1990). *Teachers for our nation's schools.* San Francisco: Jossey-Bass.

Gordon, E. W. (1991). Human diversity and pluralism. *Educational Psychologist, 26,* 99-108.

Heath, S. B. (1983). *Ways with words: Language, life, and work in communities and classrooms.* New York: Cambridge University Press.

Jeffers, C. (1967). *Living poor: A participant observer study of choices and priorities.* Ann Arbor, MI: Ann Arbor Publishers.

Jensen, A. R. (1969). How much can we boost IQ and scholastic achievement? *Harvard Educational Review, 39,* 1-123.

John, V., & Goldstein, L. (1964). The social context of language acquisitions. *Merrill Palmer Quarterly, 10,* 265-275.

Kozol, J. (1991). *Savage inequities: Children in America's schools.* New York: Crown.

Leacock, E. B. (1969). *Teaching and learning in city schools: A comparative study.* New York: Basic Books.

Leibow, E. (1967). *Talley's corner.* Boston: Little, Brown.

Lewis, H. (1967). Culture, class, and family life among low income urban Negroes. In A. M. Ross & H. Hill (Eds.), *Employment, race and poverty*. New York: Harcourt.

Ogbu, J. (1981). *Minority education and caste: The American system in cross-cultural perspective*. New York: Academic Press.

Perry, T. (1992, January 28). Presentation at the Bank Street College of Education.

Rist, R. C. (1970). Student social class and teacher expectations: The self-fulfilling prophecy in ghetto education. *Harvard Educational Review, 4*, 411-451.

Shannon, P. (1985). Reading instruction and social class. *Language Arts, 72*, 604-613.

Stack, C. B. (1974). *All our kin: Strategies for survival in a black community*. New York: Harper.

Triesman, P. U. (1983). Improving the performance of minority students in college-level mathematics. *Innovation Abstracts, 5*, 17.

Weinberg, M. (1977). *A chance to learn: The history of race and education in the United States*. New York: Cambridge University Press.

Winograd, W. (1991). Confidence and learning: Exploring the education of the whole child for the whole life. *The Friends Select Journal, 3*, 2-5.

The author vividly chronicles the beginnings of the progressive, parent-controlled East Harlem Block Schools from 1965 to 1968. At the Block Schools, low-income parents worked closely with middle-class professionals to develop an approach to early childhood education that was child centered, progressive, and attuned to the culture of the children and their families. The process of building the schools unleashed energies that transformed people's lives and influenced public policy, in East Harlem and beyond. The story demonstrates the power of parents and professionals working toward shared goals in a climate of mutual respect.

8. Education, Equity, and Community: Lessons From the East Harlem Block Schools

TOM RODERICK

In the summer of 1966, Anna Rivera was running a candy store on a tenement block in East Harlem and living with her husband, her two young children, and her nephew in a tiny apartment separated from the store by a curtain. Running the store suited her better than the factory work she'd done after dropping out

AUTHOR'S NOTE: Thanks to all of those who gave freely of their time for the interviews on which this chapter is based (see note 1). Thanks also to those who made helpful suggestions on earlier versions of the manuscript: Norm Fruchter, Rosie Gueits, Hayes Jacobs, Sonia Medina, Antonia Perez, Maxine Phillips, Anna Rivera, Dorothy Stoneman, and Tony Ward. This chapter was adapted from a larger project that the author has partially completed: a full-length book that tells the story of the East Harlem Block Schools.

of high school, but still she felt trapped. "I was a very quiet, withdrawn, alone kind of person," she recalls. "I didn't have any close friends. I was really heavy, and felt very ashamed of myself. I thought I had nothing to offer."

Then one day, while shopping, Anna saw a sign advertising the East Harlem Block Schools. She had no idea that by enrolling her son she was beginning a new life. Within a few years, she would become a teacher, loved and respected by her students. In her work with adults and children, she would earn a reputation as a wise and trusted counselor. After receiving her B.A. degree in 1978, she would become director of the Block Schools' College Program.

At the Block Schools, Anna found excellent schools for her children, teachers who listened to parents, work she enjoyed, professional counseling, and many other things. But, most important, she found community. "Looking back," she says. "I can see that I needed a body of people real bad. My parents were in Puerto Rico. I had no family here except my own. So I attached myself to the schools."

How can schools best serve children from poor and low-income neighborhoods? How can parents be effectively involved in their children's education? How can schools become communities where people of different racial and class backgrounds work together effectively? The experience of the East Harlem Block Schools has much to say to these questions. In this chapter, based on extensive interviews with the Block Schools' founders,[1] I share some aspects of the first two years of the Block Schools' story, and make some observations about its significance.

The East Harlem Block Nurseries began in 1965, the happy result of two marriages and much luck. One marriage had joined Carmen Maristany, a young Puerto Rican woman with four children, and Tony Ward, a young Anglo community organizer. The other brought together two worlds: the radical social vision of the 1960s and the traditional culture of 111th Street between Park and Madison avenues, an "urban village" in the heart of New York City's Spanish Harlem.

Today, the block is a desolate landscape of crumbling tenements and rubble-strewn vacant lots. But, as recently as 1960,
it was home for 3,000 people. Carmen Maristany was born on
the block in 1938, one of eight children in a family where only
Spanish was spoken. When she was 12 years old, her father
died, leaving her mother to raise the family on a meager pen-
sion. Like many of the block's residents, Carmen tended to
confine her life to the block and the close community it offered.
"I had never taken a subway ride until I started high school,"
Carmen admits. "My first train trip at age 14—and I was petri-
fied!" After graduating from high school, Carmen got married.
By 1960, her marriage had dissolved; she and her four young
children were living with her mother; and she was working as
a counselor in a children's shelter.

At this time, the American Friends Service Committee (AFSC)
was operating its "East Harlem Project" out of a building at 94
East 111th Street. The project drew a number of young middle-
class social activists who lived and worked in the neighborhood. One of those young people was Tony Ward.

Tony had grown up in New York City, become a Quaker
during high school, been active in disarmament and civil rights
organizations in college, and after graduation had worked for
a year in South America. As part of his work with AFSC, he
developed a tutoring program on 111th Street that served 120
children. As part of the tutoring program, he also started a
summer school and camp.

Tony and Carmen were married in 1962. Through their in-
volvement in community affairs, they became friends with
Vivianna Munoz, the daughter of a former governor of Puerto
Rico. Vivianna brought together a group of people, including
Carmen, to discuss the idea of starting a baby-sitting co-op on
105th Street. Gradually, the concept evolved into the idea of a
storefront nursery run by parents. In April 1965, Vivianna
submitted a proposal for the project to the federal Office of
Economic Opportunity ("War on Poverty"). Because of
Vivianna's connections at Aspira, an influential Puerto Rican

organization, funding was virtually assured. But Vivianna's original group had dwindled to the point where there was no one to follow through. The venture was on the verge of collapse when Vivianna asked Carmen and Tony if they would take over.

Carmen was both excited and hesitant. She had never done anything like this before. On the other hand, she was intrigued by the concept of parent control. "I used to go to the public schools, and ask the teachers to do more for my kids," she explains.

> They were polite, but I got no results. Then I married Tony, and the whole thing changed. I became one of their peers because they were talking to Tony, who was one of their peers. They became very concerned and started to expect more of the kids. They'd call home. They'd tell us about this special program and that special program. I always felt frustrated if my mother had to go to the school for my kids because she just didn't get the respect. I wanted to see a school where none of that nonsense would happen, a place where the teachers would be people *we* had invited.

Finally, Carmen decided to go ahead. She knocked on doors, inviting her friends and neighbors from 111th Street to get involved. By June, she had found nine people who seemed interested, and she invited them to a meeting. Those who attended this first meeting included Sonia Medina, who lived next door to Carmen's mother; Connie Arevalo, Carmen's closest childhood friend and godmother of her children; Rosie Gueits, an acquaintance of Connie's; Florence Ali, Carmen's sister; and Tony.

Carmen approached the meeting with trepidation. But, far from agonizing over whether to make a commitment, the group plunged right into discussing what the school would be like and what to do first. "There was so much to be learned," recalls Sonia. "All of a sudden we were going to start something new, and we didn't know how. I had to remind people that we didn't have space, we didn't have money, we didn't have staff, and we didn't have the children. Only enthusiasm kept people in the program."

There was one rather sharp exchange, which Sonia triggered by making what she thought was an innocent suggestion: "Do you want the children to have uniforms?" she asked. "You know, like a little dress a child may wear and they're all alike so you don't know who's the child that's got money, and who's the chi—"

"*Ay dios mio!*" Connie burst in. "You must be crazy! I went to Catholic School for eight years with uniforms, the same blouse and jumper for eight years! There's no way I'm gonna have my two sons dressed alike, and no way I'm gonna wash the same pants and shirts—for eight more years!"

"By uniforms," Sonia explained, "I mean dungarees or a little corduroy dress—something comfortable and washable—so that children won't suffer if their parents can't afford to get them clothes as nice as someone else's."

But, in the end, the other women agreed with Connie. "We want our school to be different," Connie argued, expressing the feelings of many. "We want to treat our kids on an individual basis. How can we do that if they all look the same?"

When the controversy about uniforms had run its course, the women went on to such matters as where to begin looking for space, how to recruit children, and how to let people in the neighborhood know. Rosie admits that they went into a number of other topics as well, which had nothing to do with starting a school.

When the meeting finally ended around 11 p.m., Carmen wasn't sure if she had somehow managed to assemble a group of unusually daring and energetic people or if they just didn't know what they were getting themselves into. But one thing was clear: Their enthusiasm went beyond her highest expectations. That evening, the East Harlem Block Schools were born.

On June 18, word arrived that the grant had been approved: $65,000 for a five-month period beginning August 1 to establish two nurseries. Through a highly unusual convergence of circumstances, a group of young Puerto Rican mothers from a crowded tenement block in East Harlem would have the opportunity to create their own schools.

Their first order of business was to hire an executive director. Assuming the role of parent to the fledgling organization, Aspira recommended several Puerto Rican professionals as candidates for the position. The parents met and talked with these people but decided, over the strenuous objections of Aspira's director, to hire Tony. Tony had a degree in education and was fluent in Spanish. The parents knew him from the tutoring program and summer camp. "We appreciate the help you gave us in getting the proposal approved," Sonia told Aspira's director. "But that proposal says very clearly that our school is parent controlled. *Our* decisions and *our* procedures will make the difference." In making this decision, the group of neighbors coalesced into a board of directors. As Sonia put it: "After we hired Tony, that's when we began to get serious."

Having phased out the East Harlem Project, the AFSC agreed to let the Block Nurseries use the brownstone at 94 East 111th Street. With that as a base, Tony and the parents set about the myriad tasks involved in creating a school from scratch.

A major challenge was to find space. The brownstone provided a place for meetings and an office, but classrooms were another matter. Although East Harlem had recently acquired several new high-rise projects, most of the buildings in the neighborhood were decrepit tenements. It would be difficult to find space that could be made adequate for children at a reasonable cost. As a first step, the parents fanned out over East Harlem to see what was available.

By September, Tony had begun the process of recruiting and hiring professional staff. "Even before we started," Tony observes,

> It was clear to me that there had to be a balance of forces. On the one hand, the professionals came with a whole load of class and racial prejudices—attitudes that caused all kinds of problems if they got into full control. That was true no matter how nice they were as people. On the other hand, the parents, left to their own devices, really couldn't come up with a great educational program. They needed people who were skilled as educators—and highly skilled.

Tony set up a process by which he did an initial screening and the parents did the final interviewing and selection. Decision making was by consensus, with all encouraged to talk and express their views.

The matter of hiring parent staff was awkward because the only parents involved so far were the board members. Tony ended up simply telling the board members at one of their meetings that, if they wanted jobs in the schools, they could have them.

"When Tony said we could work for the schools, we were in a state of shock," explains Sonia. "None of us was expecting anything for ourselves." But most of them jumped at the chance. Rosie's reaction was typical: "I knew this was what I wanted to do. It didn't bother me, being a housewife. I just felt maybe this would be a change of pace: Let me get out there and do something! The idea grabbed me immediately." And so Sonia, Rosie, and Florence went on staff as assistant teachers; Connie, now board chairperson, was hired as clerk-typist.

In October and November, the staff took part in a three-week training program orchestrated by Tony. A child psychologist from Bank Street College coordinated a week-long series of lectures and workshops on child development, room arrangement, equipment, art, and children's literature. The week gave the staff an introduction to Bank Street's philosophy, which appealed to Tony because of its attention to all aspects of a child's development, emotional as well as intellectual.

During the next two weeks, the staff made visits to some of the best progressive independent schools in the city. From their experiences and observations, the parents got ideas for their schools, though what they learned would have come as a shock to staff at the exclusive private schools they visited. Recalls Rosie:

We noticed that in a lot of those places, you didn't feel comfortable. You felt funny, you felt out of place. And another thing. It was cold at the time. Sonia used to say, "There's no coffee in this place. People don't offer you a cup of coffee." So we said, "Okay, the first thing we're going to do when we open up our school is to make sure that we have coffee. Even if we don't have the money for donuts, we're going to have coffee, and a place where people can sit down and stay for a while and talk." We said we'd try to keep a smile on our faces regardless of how we were feeling. And we said, "Our school will be different from those other schools. It will be a place where everybody—kids, parents, and even people who aren't parents in the school—can feel at home."

Finding children for the nurseries presented no problem. The parents wanted to reach the children who needed a nursery school most. And so, armed with masking tape and flyers, they went into the tenements, plastering up notices and knocking on doors.

The canvassing proved to be an eye-opener for the parents. "We were shocked at some of the things we saw going on in families," says Connie.

> Some of the people really opened up to us. They told us all kinds of personal things—about their health problems, about what they were going through with their husbands, and about how desperate they felt sometimes with their children. And the saddest thing was that they thought they just had to sit and take it. They had no one to talk to, no place to go.

Like the school visits, the experience of canvassing played an important role in shaping the schools. "We'd come back to the office after a day of canvassing," Connie remembers, "and we'd talk about what happened. Right away, we saw that we couldn't just have a nursery for children. We realized that we had to figure out a way to help the whole family. We weren't sure exactly *how* at first. But we knew we had to find a way."

November arrived, with only two possible classroom spaces. One was a storefront on 106th Street in Franklin Plaza, a middle-income co-op, and the other, not available till February, was a storefront on Madison Avenue in Taft Houses, a low-income project.

Finally, during the last week of November, the co-op board approved the Block Nurseries application. One Block Nursery had a home at last. Elated as he was, Tony also felt uneasy. The bareness of the two huge rooms reminded him of the gloomy fact that had been obscured by the desperate scramble to find some place—any place—to house the school: It would take thousands of dollars to make the former stores into decent places for children. Where would the money come from?

He had already raised the matter with the board. Like him, they could see no choice but to take the spaces if the program was to open at all. If we have to do it, their attitude had been, we have to do it. We'll worry later about the consequences. They'll have a harder time shutting us down if we are running and have children than if we have nothing and are asking. And so they decided: "Damn the torpedoes, and full steam ahead!"

Everyone pitched in to do the painting and repairing that would make the space livable, temporarily. On December 28, 1965, three days before the initial five-month grant would run out, the first Block Nursery opened its doors. It opened not because it was ready to open but because the parents and staff just could not bear to put it off any longer. As Carmen said, "I kept expecting more things to happen so that the school would open, and then, all of a sudden, it just opened!"

Connie has a vivid memory of that first day. "We all got there early," she says.

> Everything was spic and span. I was so nervous that my hands were cold. I couldn't believe it was finally the moment to greet new parents and children into our school.
>
> Everyone was fighting to get the first kid. The kids looked so cute and nice. As they came in, we'd say "hello" and start to talk to them. We greeted the parents too, and offered them coffee. I was proud that people were calling me "Mrs. Arevalo," even though as soon as they'd say it, I'd tell them, "Call me Connie. We use first names here."
>
> When I saw everything running so smoothly, when I saw that it was gonna work and our dream was coming true, tears started to come down. I remember Rosie coming over and the two of us hugging and kissing each other. We had a wonderful feeling of accomplishing something, of doing something beyond ourselves.

In February 1966, the second Block Nursery opened in the
storefront in the Taft Houses on Madison Avenue. Just eight
months after receiving their grant award letter, Tony and the
parents had their entire program in operation. But to do that,
they had, as Tony put it, "broken every rule in the book."

Most fateful was the matter of the "revolving funds," $36,000 in
cash advances from OEO that Tony and the board decided to
spend to pay for necessary renovations, although it greatly ex-
ceeded the amount in their budget. They did this to get out of
a catch-22 situation: They were convinced that OEO officials
would not approve these expenditures, which were, however,
necessary to get the centers licensed. "We decided to go ahead
and do it," says Tony, "and deal with the problem when it came
up, by which time we'd have some reputation and some political clout. That's how things worked out, though much, *much*
more painfully than we might have hoped."

In fact, Tony and the parents spent little time brooding over
the decision. "Although I was spending large sums of money,"
Tony admits, "I probably didn't have more than an average of
ten minutes a week to consider how I was doing it." The
question of how the bills got paid was trivial compared with
the challenge of creating excellent schools for the children.

*October 1966—a park in Franklin Plaza behind the 106th Street
nursery:* Lois Goldfrank, teacher of the 5-year-olds, is playing
monster with a half a dozen boys and girls. The children taunt
the "monster" and then run away screaming as Lois hunches her
shoulders, growls, and stalks off after them. "That's all for now,"
Lois says finally. A graduate of Bryn Mawr with a master's degree
from Bank Street College, Lois is in her second year of teaching.
She sits down panting on the bench, and a stocky 5-year-old boy
runs up to her, his brown corduroy winter coat flapping open.

"Teacher, look what I found!" he cries.

"Oh Wayne, those are crab apples," Lois says, looking at the
small green fruit in his hand.

"Are they alive?"

"No. Once they fall off the tree, they're dead."

"But if I put them on the tree again, they'll be alive, won't they?"

"Why don't we try it and see what happens? Where's the tree?"

Wayne grabs his teacher's hand and pulls her to the spot where he had found the crab apples. A few minutes later, Lois, Wayne, and two survivors from the monster game go inside to get some tape.

So begins a month-long exploration of living and dying in the 5-year-olds' classroom. Using tape, the children fasten the fruit back onto the tree. Checking every day, they find that the tiny apples become brown and rotten. Meanwhile, Lois and the children are talking about living things, dead things, and things that have never been alive. Looking around the classroom, they sort objects into categories. "What about chairs?" someone asks. The wood is dead. But can you say that a chair is dead when as a chair it's never been alive? The question provokes a lively discussion. Several days later, a little girl brings in a dried-up starfish. When she puts it in the water, it starts to move. Is it alive? To find out, the children devise a series of tests.

"It was like a web," Lois explains. "One thing led to another. Starting from Wayne's question, we explored an important scientific concept, tried our hands at scientific investigation, learned new words, and got practice putting things into categories."

Rest time in the 106th Street nursery: Today is Lois's turn to put the children to sleep. Florence Ali and Antonia Perez, parent assistant teachers in the 5-year-olds' class, are sitting on a couch in the parents' lounge, meeting with Millie Rabinow, the Block Schools' mental health consultant. Half an hour into the meeting, Millie asks, "Wasn't Lois supposed to join us?"

"Oh!" Antonia exclaims. "We forgot all about her!"

At that moment, the door to the classroom opens and out comes a flustered, red-faced Lois. "I can't do it," she says with a sigh. "Nothing works. I no sooner get one to sleep than another pops up."

"We forgot all about you," Florence says grinning. "Why didn't you tell us sooner you were having a hard time?" Florence walks over to the classroom, and looks into the darkened room. *"Baja la cabeza y trata de dormirte,"* she says in a calm, firm tone. The buzz of conversation stops. Two boys hiding behind a bookcase go to their cots. Three minutes later, Florence joins Lois, Antonia, and Millie for the rest of the meeting.

The morning work period is in full swing. Skyscrapers are rising in the block area where Lois is working with six children. A lavish, if imaginary, breakfast is being prepared in the dollhouse corner. The rabbit is earning its carrots, enduring its daily round of cuddles and strokes. Florence is with three children who are playing with water, using funnels, tubes, and containers of many shapes and sizes. And Antonia is simply bewildered.

It's all so different than what the 30-year-old mother of three ever did when she was in school. The jobs she held after dropping out of high school—assembler in a toy factory, mail clerk—certainly didn't prepare her for this either. And, in her family, she was always "the stupid one, the ignorant one."

"Toni, draw me a picture of a doll," whines Karen, a chubby girl with big brown eyes and two pigtails of straight dark-brown hair. Antonia makes an outline of a doll for Karen. "Now you color it in," she says, smiling.

As Karen sets to work, Antonia feels a light tapping on her shoulder. It is Florence. "Can I talk with you for a minute?" she asks.

"Sure," says Antonia, standing up. "What did I do now?" They walk a few steps away from the table, and Florence whispers, "Don't do their drawings for them. If you do, they'll try to copy your drawing. If it doesn't come out the same, they'll get frustrated, and say they can't draw. So let them try to do it themselves."

Antonia is still thinking about what Florence has said when Lois comes up to her. "Toni, would you watch the block area for a few minutes? I'll be right back."

The children's work is impressive. Two elaborate buildings, over four feet high, are nearing completion. Then Antonia notices Nuncio, a short little boy, working by himself. While she watches, he tries twice to start a building. Both times it comes tumbling down. When, on the third try, a wall of the building collapses once again, Nuncio angrily pushes the whole building down and starts kicking the rubble.

Antonia freezes. What to do? She knows why his building is falling, and she wants to help. But should she? Suddenly, she hears a quiet voice behind her. It is Alice Graves, educational director of the 106th Street nursery. "Go ahead, Toni," Alice says. "Go over and give him a hand." Antonia goes over and shows Nuncio how to place the blocks so that they won't fall.

During the two-year period from 1966 to 1968, the Block Nurseries, aided by adequate funding and relative freedom from bureaucratic interference, created an excellent educational program for young children. Each of the schools' six classrooms had unique characteristics, but common to all was a distinctive "Block Nurseries approach" to early childhood education. That approach—combining the progressive ideas of middle-class professionals with the special talents and strengths of parents from East Harlem—jelled within a year after the nurseries opened. Its features come through clearly in the recollections of Lois, Florence, and Antonia, who worked together with the 5-year-olds at the 106th Street nursery during the school year 1966-1967.

Lois focused primarily on curriculum, and the center of the curriculum was the block area. The block area took up a quarter of the classroom and extended into the dollhouse corner so that girls as well as boys would get involved. In the beginning, she would get down on the floor with the children and help them build. By talking with them about their buildings, appreciating their work, and providing accessories, she engaged their interest and showed them the possibilities. "It wasn't long before they were building really fantastic hotels and apartment buildings," she recalls. "We'd put signs on the buildings and save them for a week, which was amazing when you consider that some of the constructions were six feet high."

Working with the children in the block area, Lois developed a number of projects based on the concept of the "web." For example, a study of the fire department included going to the local fire station, creating an electrified "fire board" for the children's block city, using raincoats and rubber boots in the dress-up area, playing fire fighter on the playground, reading books, and dictating stories about fire fighters.

Antonia's primary challenge as a first-year teacher was to know when to intervene in children's activities and when not to. "Being a mother, I had a tendency to do everything for them," she admits. "I had to learn to step aside, and to let them be creative."

It helped that she had good models. "I learned from seeing how Lois talked with kids and what she did with them," Antonia recalls.

> I was impressed by the way she'd sit on the floor with them. At first, I thought it was strange. But then I asked myself, "Why do I always have to be above them? Why not come down to their level sometimes?" I loosened up and started to play with them more. I learned better ways of dealing with children. I was very rough with my own kids before I got involved with the Block Nurseries. After I started teaching, I began to understand children better. I learned that, when you discipline a child, you have to say why. If you tell a child to sit down for ten minutes, you've got to explain the reason. If you don't, he won't know any better the next time. It's the same thing when a kid gets mad at another kid and hits him. You stop the fight, but you let them talk it out.

Antonia doesn't remember any disagreements with Lois over the curriculum. "At first I had my doubts about water play," she admits:

> But then I saw how it was helping the kids in measuring. I would always ask, "Why are we doing this?" and Lois would always give me an explanation. She encouraged me too. She'd say, "Toni, if you want to try something, tell Florence and me, and we'll help you." That really got me to try my own things.

Her greatest contribution that first year came from the fact that, although all three of the teachers spoke Spanish, she had the best command of the language. "Most of the kids in the class were Spanish speaking," she says.

> Their parents wanted them to learn English because they'd soon be going to first grade. So teaching them English was one of our main goals. But we didn't have a structured program.
>
> When we noticed that some kids weren't following the stories Lois was reading, I started taking a group of kids to another part of the room and reading them stories in Spanish. Or if I didn't have a Spanish book, I'd use an English book and translate it into Spanish as I want along.
>
> We put up signs around the room in Spanish and English—blocks, *bloques*; sink, *lavado*; and so on—and we sang Spanish songs. Those are some of the things we used to do. The kids picked up English very fast.

In contrast to Antonia, who spent much of the year struggling with self-doubt and insecurity, Florence was perfectly clear about what should happen in a classroom and did not hesitate to say so. "I battled with Lois Goldfrank," Florence says,

> and we got very close. Lois had to realize that she couldn't teach the kids middle-class education. It didn't make any sense to stand up there and talk about daddy when some of the children had never seen daddy. I felt, "No. We don't even discuss daddy. We discuss mom and where mom is coming from and how to stabilize mom." I'd grown up in the neighborhood. I knew what the problems were, because I was one of the examples. I'd grown up without a father, and I didn't have a "father image." Lois couldn't tell me that I didn't live the way I did. She had her master's degree, and there I was, without a high school diploma, saying things like, "Why do you let Wayne treat you that way?"
>
> "Well, he's a very angry boy, and he needs a place to let that anger out."
>
> "Come on now, Lois. When you say things like that, you're coming from Boston [Lois's hometown]. I was born and raised here, and I know it's not right for him to hit you and curse at you that way."

We just battled until she saw the need of what I was saying. One day she came to me, and said, "How do *you* think
we should deal with Wayne?" We discussed it, and finally
she agreed with me. "I'll be real clear that he can let his anger
out by screaming or hitting a pillow if he wants to," she said,
"but I won't let him hit me."

I could see that she wasn't coming from Boston. So I said,
"Okay, that's cool. Let's try it." And it worked.

And so the Block Nurseries developed a child-centered progressive approach to education, attuned to the culture of the
children and their families. On a daily basis, this was negotiated
in discussions among the professional teacher and the parent
teachers in each class. Though each adult had different strengths,
the three worked together on an equal basis. Every day, after the
children left at 3 p.m., they met to plan the next day's activities.
Issues about curriculum and ways of dealing with children
were hashed out, and the parents took substantial responsibility. Professional teachers were expected to provide leadership,
but their influence depended on their powers of persuasion and
the effectiveness of their work with the children, not on the
prerogatives of their role. Nor did the professionals jealously
guard their expertise; they shared it with the parent teachers as
the parents shared theirs with the professionals. The result was
that the children in each class got the full benefit of the talents,
skills, and wisdom of all three teachers.

The Block Nurseries' embrace of progressive approaches had
much to do with the influence of Alice Graves, who started as
a teacher and soon became educational director of the 106th
Street nursery. At their first meeting, the founding group had
agreed that their schools would be different, that children would
be respected as individuals. Tony had made it clear from the
beginning that he supported a progressive philosophy.

To make the philosophy their own, though, the parents had
to see it working in *their* school, with *their* children. That's
where Alice's role was pivotal. "I felt the classrooms should be
a certain way," Tony acknowledges. "Alice showed they could
be *superb* that way."

If professionals took the lead in shaping the Block Nurseries' educational philosophy, it was parents who developed the other key dimension of the Block Nurseries' program: parent involvement.

Eduardo has recently entered the 3-year-old class at the Madison Avenue nursery and is having great difficulty adjusting. Barbara, one of his teachers, has suggested that he be allowed to bring his favorite teddy bear to school to help him feel more comfortable. His mother is open to the idea, but his father, Sam, has flatly refused, saying it's too childish. Barbara turns to Lydia Rios, the parent coordinator, for help. "Oh yes," says Lydia, "I've known Sam for a long time. I'll see what I can do."

Through a phone call, Lydia is able to get Sam to agree to a meeting. After school, Lydia, Barbara, and Sam sit down on tiny children's chairs in the classroom and discuss Eduardo's teddy bear. "My son almost died at birth," says Sam, a husky man with short, curly black hair.

> He was born fighting for his life, and if he is going to make it in this world, he's going to have to keep right on fighting. That's why I tell my wife she's got to stop babying him. I don't want him to go soft on me. He's not a baby anymore. It's time for him to grow up.

"Sam," Lydia says, smiling, "with you for a father, he'll be a fighter all right! You don't need to worry about that!" Sam laughs. "We're not saying you should baby him," she goes on. "But don't forget he's only three. This is the first time he's been away from home. Lots of kids bring a favorite toy with them when they first start school. It makes them feel more at home."

By the end of the 45-minute meeting, Lydia has managed to persuade Sam to allow his son to take the teddy bear to school and not to belittle him for "childish" behavior. As Barbara has anticipated, the security provided by the teddy bear helps the boy make a successful adjustment to school.

The parent coordinators played a key role in developing the Block Nurseries' program. Though the entire staff shared responsibility for drawing in and working with parents, the parent coordinators were the central figures in the process.

The job of parent coordinator had not been included in the original conception of the Block Nurseries. But, in the canvassing she did to recruit children, Connie Arevalo had seen the importance of finding ways to support parents. Though she was hired as a clerk-typist, everyone soon recognized Connie's effectiveness with parents. By following her natural inclinations, she was creating a new job that was obviously needed. In January, not long after the opening of the 106th Street nursery, Connie left her position as clerk-typist to become "parent coordinator."

When poor health forced Connie to resign in the fall of 1966, the board decided to replace her with two people. Lydia Rios became parent coordinator of the Madison nursery, and Rosie Gueits, of the 106th Street center. Their work illustrates the variety of roles played by the parent coordinators. Both began by setting a distinctive tone. "When you walked into the nursery, it was like a family," says Carmen Gonzalez, a parent, describing the 106th Street center. "They'd greet you. After you took your child to the classroom, you could come out, have a cup of coffee, and talk for a while. If you were lonely or had any problems, you could just drop by and people would be there to listen."

To a casual observer, the daily activities of parents in the centers could hardly have looked more ordinary—just some women hanging out. But, for the women, many of whom had felt trapped and isolated through most their married lives, "hanging out" at the Block Nurseries was one of the first steps in a process that would change their lives. And, in spite of how natural it looked, it didn't just happen.

The parent coordinators created an inviting space for parents, made sure the coffee was ready, chatted with parents informally, thought of jobs around the school that needed doing, and enlisted parents' help. But, most important, they fostered an atmosphere of people caring about each other. "Rosie was a very friendly person who you could go to and talk about your problems without being turned down," recalls Carmen Gonzalez.

> She was a person who felt for your hurt. She was always eager to help. If I had a problem with Welfare, she'd call. If I had a problem at the clinic and she had to go with me, she would. After a while we started talking about our lives, about what it had been like growing up. That's when we found out we'd both lived in a home. Rosie became my friend, and she will always be my friend.

More than anything else, it was the opportunity to care and to be cared about that deepened the involvement of Carmen and other women in the nurseries.

Rosie and Lydia developed the confidence and skill to take on these challenges and help troubled families because of the support and supervision of Millie Rabinow, the Block Nurseries' mental health consultant. Rosie gives Millie credit for teaching her to be an effective counselor. "She made you feel that everything you did was right, that you weren't stupid," Rosie observes.

> Like me now, I had only completed high school. And yet, when I was with her, I was able to talk about all kinds of things and give her answers and even advice. The main thing she taught me was how to listen to people, to listen to both sides before coming to a conclusion. She helped me be more under-standing. "Things will work out," she'd say, "if you want them to work out, and you believe they're going to work out, and you have patience."

This ends our account of the first two years of the East Harlem Block Schools. But the ripples issuing from the meeting Carmen gathered in the summer of 1965 have spread far beyond 111th Street and are spreading still. This chapter touches only on the beginnings of a vital community organization with a rich 27-year history. Other chapters in the story include

- the Block Nurseries' struggle for survival when they lost their an-tipoverty funding in 1968 and their successful negotiations to be-come the first parent-controlled day-care centers in New York City;

- the Block Nurseries' challenging of Division of Day Care policies, which were undermining the integrity of their program, and helping to lead a citywide movement that achieved major reforms in the city's day-care program during 1968 to 1973;
- the creation of the East Harlem Block Elementary School, which began as a first-grade class in a storefront in 1967 and continues as an alternative public school in Community School District 4;
- the development of a college program in which many Block Schools' parents received high school equivalency diplomas and more than 20 went on to earn their bachelor's degrees; and
- the development since 1978 of the Youth Action Program, which spawned an array of substantial youth-run community improvement projects, organized and led a citywide coalition that persuaded the city government to fund new youth employment programs for 30,000 young people, and launched the national YouthBuild Coalition, which now has 295 member organizations in 42 states advocating for federal funding to employ young people in housing rehabilitation for the homeless.

What can we learn from this account of the Block Schools' early history? What stands out as we reflect on this story?

Perhaps most striking is the tremendous amount of creative, loving human energy released by the parents' getting the opportunity to create schools for their children. People stuck in dead-end jobs or in suffocating family situations discovered their considerable talents and unleashed them for the benefit of their children and their community.

Another thing that comes through clearly is the primacy of "respect," a concept as central for Block Schools' parents as "freedom" was for many other activists during the 1960s. Respect began with being listened to, but it went further than that; it meant that parents and professionals had equal status. By making parents feel welcome, by encouraging them to "hang out," and by asking them to volunteer in classrooms or serve on the board of directors, the schools were telling parents, "We need you." There is no higher form of respect than that.

Respect was highly valued by the parents because of the injuries they had suffered from race and class discrimination. Anna Rivera describes such an incident:

I didn't get close to people easily, especially teachers. But in ninth grade, I got very close with a Miss Ehrhart. One day I sat down with her, and told her I wanted to become a teacher. "Oh Anna," she said. "I don't recommend that *you* become a teacher. You're not too strong in academics, and you fly off the handle too easily. Since you're good with your hands, why don't you try to be a beautician or something? But in any case it's nothing to worry about. You'll be getting married, and you won't be working anyway."

Miss Ehrhart's advice to Anna is just one example of how our institutions ignore the dreams of poor people and narrowly circumscribe their lives. Most of the Block Schools' parents tell similar stories, and many go on to say that at the Block Schools they had their first experiences of really being listened to, of having their ideas taken seriously.

The idea of respect was directly linked to the idea of parent control. Although neighborhood people had the majority of staff positions at the Block Schools, the parents knew they needed professionals. And yet, professionals had been responsible for some of their deepest hurts. The parents knew they must not be subordinate to professionals, or the oppression would continue. Even an official school policy of equal status for parents and professionals would not be sufficient, for deeply ingrained class attitudes would likely come into play, causing even the most aware professionals to tend to take over while causing the parents to tend to allow that to happen. The solution was to *reverse* the usual power relationships. Instead of professionals being in the dominant position, as is usually the case, the parents would be in charge. The aim was not to enable parents to boss professionals around but to bring the relationships between parents and professionals as close to equality as possible.

Parent control did not guarantee that the parents would be treated with respect, any more than a constitution providing for elections ensures democracy. But the Block Schools were dedicated to the proposition that governance by the parents would set the stage for a productive collaboration between parents and professionals.

Respect was the foundation for the development of "community," the other key concept at the Block Schools. Anna refers to it when she says she "needed a group of people real bad." Most of the parents express it by saying that "the Block Schools were a family." Community was the web of relationships that grew up out of the common work of building the schools. No one planned it or anticipated it. It just happened. But it turned out to be what made the difference for people. People caring about other people over a long period of time—that was what ultimately changed people's lives, that was the essence of the Block Schools.

Low-income people in our society are often viewed by middle-class professionals as deviants or failures who have pathologies that need to be treated or "remediated." The Block Schools' community was based on a very different point of view: namely, that poor people living in East Harlem are members of an oppressed community and that the most appropriate role for middle-class professionals is to help people develop leadership so that they can take charge of their own lives and achieve justice for themselves and their communities. We tend to associate politics with pulling a lever in a voting machine on election day. But politics permeates everything we do. Our institutions, including schools, reflect the power relationships in society and operate so as to reinforce them. In her book *Personal Politics*, Sara Evans (1979) describes how "consciousness raising groups" helped launch the women's movement by providing what she calls "free social space." The Block Schools have done something very similar: They have been a place where low-income people could be free to some extent from the oppressive conditions of the larger society and could experience new possibilities for themselves.

This is quite different than using "services" provided by huge bureaucracies, the more usual recourse for low-income people. If bureaucratized services are able to fill people's needs at all, they often do so in ways that are demeaning. At best, they offer survival. Only small personal institutions like the Block Schools can offer a sense of meaning and purpose in life, high expectations, and caring over a long period of time. Those qualities go far beyond survival; they lead to personal growth and, in the case of the Block Schools, to social change.

A lesson from the Block Schools' story is that progressive educators have much to offer people from low-income communities. The progressive tradition has a wealth of ideas and teaching strategies that are useful in the struggle for justice. But the context in which we offer ourselves and our approaches is all important. Our ideas will have lasting impact only if they are freely chosen. We must not impose our views but cultivate a climate of mutual respect where real dialogue is possible. This is not easy. Because of the pervasiveness of racial and class prejudice, we will need to create ways of governance that hold ourselves and our colleagues to high standards of respect. And, even in the most favorable settings, we will have to be vigilant to prevent our relationships from being undermined in subtle and not so subtle ways. We will be most successful if we can stay flexible, maintain a commitment to listen more than we talk, and live the humility that comes from knowing that we will, in all probability, learn more than we will teach.

Note

1. The chapter is based on extensive interviews conducted by the author during the period from 1977 to 1982 with these members of the Block Schools community: Florence Ali, Connie Arevalo, Lois Goldfrank, Carmen Gonzalez, Alice Graves, Joe Gueits, Rosie Gueits, Sonia Medina, Antonia Perez, Lydia Rios, Anna Rivera, Barbara Slemmer, Dorothy Stoneman, Carmen (Maristany) Ward, and Tony Ward.

Reference

Evans, S. (1979). *Personal politics: The roots of women's liberation in the civil rights movement and the new left.* New York: Vintage, Random House.

Kleinman looks at a unique alliance between a private university and the New York City public school system. The Speyer School, a five-year experiment begun in the mid-1930s, was an attempt to apply tenets of progressive education to an ethnically diverse, working-class population of children. While the author identifies several positive consequences of this collaboration, he also notes the inability of the large school system to use the experiment for widespread change.

9. P.S. 500 (Speyer School): An Early Experiment in Urban Alternative Public Education

JOSEPH KLEINMAN

For 15 years, I worked as a teacher, dean, and assistant director in several inner-city New York City alternative public schools. During that time, I often experienced the dilemmas and tensions that arose, as we, the staff, tried to incorporate progressive educational philosophy and techniques within the school curriculum and design. In the course of listening to the arguments that grew out of our innumerable staff and administrative meetings, often I found that I tended to consider our struggle as unique.

My love of history inspired me to examine the efforts of earlier educators who tried to integrate progressive education within a public school context. In the process, I learned that many of the problems experienced in creating a cohesive and successful school environment were also part of the historical experience. The records of experiences with progressive education in public schools shed light on current conditions and raise questions important today in planning for more effective schools in the future.

During the 1930s, high truancy rates, the challenges of educating the children of a growing foreign-language-speaking immigrant population, along with the exigencies of a national depression, encouraged educators at the New York City Board of Education to seek alternatives to the widely used traditional methods. One alternative was progressive education. In 1935, to test progressive education in a practical context, then schools' superintendent, Dr. Harold Campbell, launched several experimental programs throughout the city (Board of Education, City of New York, 1941).

One such experimental program was P.S. 500/Speyer School, which opened in 1935 and included grades 3 through 8. It was a particularly unique experiment because it combined the efforts of the board of education with support from Columbia Teachers College, a major center of progressive education. Teachers College had begun a new program, "Advanced Education," and was searching for a school site in which educators who were part of the program could apply their theories; the Speyer School offered such an opportunity (Hollingworth, 1936).

Designed specifically to be an experimental school for an identified five-year period, the Speyer School, located in Harlem, drew students from around the city as well as from the largely working-class homes and families on home relief who lived in the neighborhood. Its goal was to serve two distinct populations—gifted and slow learners—who were not doing well in traditional settings (Featherstone, 1938).

In applying progressive education theory, Speyer School educators encountered several complex issues: cultural pluralism, grouping students, testing, curriculum, school and community, and professional development. In the process of dealing with these complex issues, Speyer School educators made choices, choices that revealed the inconsistencies and ambiguities inherent in the tenets of progressive ideology.

Many of these inconsistencies and ambiguities continue to pose important questions concerning the nature and purpose of progressive schooling: How does one create an effective school that reflects a commitment to equality in a society that is hierarchical and fragmented? How does one empower students and promote cooperation in an increasingly atomized world? How does one provide equal opportunity in education for a mass number of children with varying skills and abilities? In the case of the Speyer School, the attempt to resolve these questions found progressive educators caught between contradictory positions.

Cultural Pluralism

One of the complex issues is the role of cultural pluralism and diversity in a school. For example, how does an inner-city school composed of mostly one racial or ethnic group address the cultural diversity of U.S. society? Even when the school includes an ethnically diverse student population, the issue of cultural pluralism is multifaceted. The question of class and the ways in which individuals of different ethnic groups and of different classes may connect with each other increases the complexity surrounding cultural pluralism (Banks, 1983).

Another issue that concerns progressive educators involves the role of multiculturalism in education. Multicultural education has different meanings and uses for different people. For the educators who favor integration, multicultural education is a tool to teach minority children the tenets of U.S. culture and better help them assimilate into U.S. society. Others see multicultural education as a way to create a school community that recognizes the rich diversity of people and cultures that constitute our society (Banks, 1983). When thinking about multiculturalism, educators often find themselves in a position of using multicultural education both ways—for integration as well as strengthening ethnic identity.

Both ethnic diversity and multicultural education concerned the Speyer School planners. For example, the Speyer School student recruitment policy rested on the progressive belief that a school should reflect the heterogeneity and ethnic diversity of U.S. society. Therefore the school's students included African Americans, Austrians, British West Indians, Chinese, Dutch, English, French, Germans, Greeks, Hungarians, Italians, Mexicans, Rumanians, Spanish, and Swedes (Board of Education, 1941). The greatest degree of cultural diversity, however, showed itself in the population of the gifted learners. Leta Hollingworth, school director and prominent faculty member at Teachers College, chose children purposefully from throughout the New York City area who would represent the heterogeneity of the city. Not only did she select students who would exemplify diversity in this way, Hollingworth accepted an equal number of boys and girls, thereby portraying giftedness as occurring regardless of race, ethnicity, and gender. This refuted the widely held notion that boys were naturally more gifted than girls (Kerr, 1990). In contrast, there is no evidence in the record of a similar effort to create a heterogeneous student body among the slow learners. While racially mixed and including boys and girls, these slow-learning students came exclusively from the local neighborhood and were economically poor.

Speyer School staff also used multicultural awareness and appreciation to achieve several goals: to broaden children's exposure, to strengthen student personal identity, and to encourage tolerance. For the Speyer School staff, ethnic and racial diversity in recruitment and curriculum were held in high regard. They were tools to be used to combat prejudice and discrimination. Paradoxically, they were also used in the service of social control. Speyer School staff used diversity and multicultural education to forge even more securely the bonds of commonality among people as a way to promote assimilation and lessen societal tension and turbulence. They hoped that, by celebrating ethnic pluralism, they would reduce group tensions and prevent truancy, both of which were considered factors in retarding assimilation (Montralto, 1981). Whether parents agreed with the Speyer School's definition and use of multiculturalism remains one of many unanswered questions.

Grouping Students

While progressive educators agree that their goal is to treat each child as an individual, most educators, especially those handling large classes with students of diverse abilities, find the need to group students. The whole issue of grouping comes under question as these educators search for meaningful criteria upon which to base grouping decisions. Are teacher evaluations a valid basis for grouping—given the fact that, by definition, these evaluations are determined solely by the teacher? In certain public alternative schools today, students are evaluated based on a parent-child interview. In this instance as well, how heavily do ethnic, gender, and class issues weigh upon an educator's decisions?

Assuming that criteria for grouping have been established, additional questions arise regarding integration of separate groups. Should students be heterogeneously or homogeneously grouped? If, for example, intellectual ability forms the basis for grouping, teachers must consider the expectations they bring to the teaching of their students. If educators treat student groups differently, can such differences in treatment be considered discriminatory, even if the intent of the educator is to provide the most effective means they believe of educating a particular group of children?

The issue of grouping persists today. In the case of the Speyer School, however, educators and planners clearly favored homogeneity. In fact, Hollingworth spoke out against heterogeneity, claiming that heterogenous grouping connoted a notion of an equality of capacity that was unscientific and ultimately undemocratic because it prevented each individual member of society from developing according to his or her ability. She believed that heterogeneity caused a number of emotional and social problems for children on either extreme (Tolan, 1990).

Hollingworth based this belief on observations she made regarding inadequacies in the education many children received. In the case of the intellectually gifted child, for example, the typical approach was acceleration, resulting in widespread age differences among students in a single classroom and social isolation and potential anger toward authority. Also, younger gifted students were too often subject to physical and verbal abuse by older classmates who felt envious and intimidated by the intellectual superiority of the younger child. As for the slow learner, the traditionally trained public school teacher did not rely upon a specialized curriculum, and, as a result, these students felt frustrated by their inability to keep up with the rest of the class (Silverman, 1990).

While Hollingworth and the Speyer School staff favored homogeneous grouping, the whole notion of a group's homogeneity contradicts the progressive educator's assertion that the group comprises unique individuals, each with his or her own needs and endowments. The definition of homogeneity becomes increasingly out of focus when any group's diversity becomes clear. (With this thought in mind, Bank Street faculty member Leah Levinger, in her child development class, asks students to consider an imaginary classroom of homogeneously grouped gifted students who include Norbert Wiener, W. A. Mozart, and Virginia Woolf.) In addition, homogeneous grouping of gifted and slower learners spotlighted the differences between people, in direct opposition to the stated goals of Speyer School progressive educators, who aimed to forge bonds of commonality. In effect it seems, they instituted an educational design that might easily increase rather than minimize tensions within a society, where differences and inequalities often lead to friction and strife. In her attempts to refute the widely held nineteenth-century belief of hereditary determinism, Hollingworth was inconsistent. On the one hand, her recruitment policies reflected ethnic, racial, and gender diversity. Yet, by relying on testing and tracking, she did not escape the distinctions she hoped to overcome. Her sympathy failed to overcome her expectations that the slow learners were destined for a life of menial labor.

Scientific Basis of Education

The practice and consequences of the use of tests present a challenge to present-day progressive educators. They rightfully claim that the I.Q., standardized aptitude, and competency tests have been widely misinterpreted as culturally biased and producing data that, when overinterpreted, can have enormous consequences.

Without question, progressive educators recognize the need to develop more accurate methods of assessment. There is, however, some debate over the degree to which educators should acknowledge and influence test performance, particularly in determining future educational opportunities of their students. As one educator describes it, a teacher who completely disregards the teaching of skills needed to score well on standardized tests does her students a disservice, given that poor test scores channel students into less challenging classes and less competitive colleges (Delpit, 1992).

Contrary to current retrospective views of progressive education, its early proponents believed in the value of I.Q. tests and other forms of scientific measurements (Cremin, 1964). At the Speyer School, intelligence tests were used to track students—the manifestation of Hollingworth's belief in a strong correlation between high test scores and life achievement. Candidates for the Speyer School who scored 130 on a series of aptitude and I.Q. tests were considered eligible for the gifted program; those who scored between 75 and 90 fell into the "dull/normal" range and were possible candidates for the slow learners program. Speyer School staff also conducted parent interviews and teacher recommendations to determine the suitability of prospective students. In this way, Hollingworth recruited 225 pupils, ages 6.6 to 12.10 including 50 gifted students (growing to 90 over the five-year period of the school's existence) and 175 slow-learning children (Board of Education, 1941).

In the most positive sense, Speyer School planners used tests and measurements to address the needs of individual students and to adopt an appropriate teaching approach. On the one hand, as progressive educators, while they believed in the equality of all people, they acknowledged the superiority of some children over others by separating high and low test scorers. Despite the limits of testing, Hollingworth and her

Teachers College colleague, Arthur Gates, argued that testing was an excellent method of determining intelligence and potential. They went so far as to claim, along with other progressives such as E. L. Thorndike, who supported the "scientific approach" to evaluation of a person's potential, that intelligence testing was key to preparing children for productive membership in a democracy where people were given equal opportunity and intelligence ruled (Antler, 1987, p. 208; Cremin, Shannon, & Townsend, 1954, pp. 43-45; Spring, 1986, pp. 178-180, 240). In addition, they believed that high test scores correlated with the realization of a child's brilliant future, in contrast to current belief that intelligence testing cannot predict life achievement (Tolan, 1990).

Design and Curriculum

For progressive educators, the issues of curriculum design and implementation raise questions concerning what children learn, how they learn, and the importance of recognizing and building upon the experiences children bring with them. Unlike traditional approaches that concentrate on specific subjects and discrete bits of information within a specific period, usually 40-45 minutes per subject, progressive approaches usually incorporate a core curriculum spanning several subjects and using larger blocks of time. In experimental curricula, children's diverse experiences and knowledge are given validity, and a wide variety of resources and activities are used.

Yet, in progressive curricula design and implementation, there are ambiguities and tensions. There is no agreement as to the "appropriate" subject matter children should learn or, when integrating curricula, which subject should take precedence. Moreover, progressives disagree as to what *child-centered* or *child-generated curricula* means (Irwin, 1991). While children's experiences are clearly important, it is unclear which experiences are educative and their particular role in the curriculum. In addition, for progressives, process is thought to be critical. Delpit (1992), however, for example, questions the devaluation of skills, particularly for minority children.

Inconsistencies inherent in progressive educational practice at the Speyer School surfaced in the design and implementation of curriculum for both types of learners, rapid and slow. While academic requirements as specified by the board of education dictated some of the curriculum content for both groups, other curricula were targeted specifically for the separate groups. Curriculum for the gifted combined a carefully planned incorporation of enrichment and acceleration. Mornings were devoted to the learning of academic subjects, which students were taught in half the time usually allotted in a regular public school setting. In the afternoons, they generally planned and engaged in projects or worked on specific curriculum units. As part of a unit on aviation, for example, the students planned a trip to the airport and were given a tour, which included a lecture and demonstration on how planes worked. They saw a film on Admiral Byrd's flight over Antarctica and took out books on aviation at the local library (Speyer School *Curriculum Bulletin* 1).

Curriculum decisions for the gifted program grew out of Hollingworth's personal vision. Influenced by the strand of progressive ideology that encouraged Americans to help better society through active, thinking participation within a democracy (Cremin, 1964), Hollingworth anticipated that these gifted children would one day assume leadership positions, and she and her staff created curricula that she believed would help them take on that responsibility. Hollingworth believed, for example, that learning a foreign language gave breadth to a child's experience, and she required that the gifted students learn French. In addition, French was a college requirement and she assumed that these children would go on to college (Hollingworth, 1938).

Another subject that Hollingworth felt was important for gifted children was history, believing as she did that a study of history required a developed imagination. She believed that gifted students possessed the formal operational skills necessary for an understanding of the past. In addition, she thought a solid historical knowledge base would help these future leaders to analyze more fully contemporary society. One particular design, "The Evolution of Common Things," attempted to span the history of civilized man and included such units as the Evolution of Art, Literature and Music, the History of Aviation, the Story of Clothing, the History of Communication, the Development of Health and Sanitation Measures, the Story of Shelter, the Evolution of Toys and Games, and the Evolution of Transportation.

In contrast, the curriculum for the slow learners was designed around practicability, current experience, and activity. Reading was not the conventional method of learning. Because they were considered far more concrete than the gifted, "incapable of imagination," according to W. B. Featherstone (1937), the slow-learner program's director, these students were not introduced to historical inquiry or to the study of foreign language. Instead, their social studies centered on a study of public utilities, banks, and the post office, institutions that the staff and administration felt directly affected their lives. The use of problem solving was employed throughout the curriculum; the use of drill, however, varied from classroom to classroom, depending upon individual teaching styles. For slow learners, the class trip formed the meat of their curriculum; the classroom supplemented these experiences through heavy use of visual materials, discussions, and other language arts activities. A unit on public utilities and banks included a class trip to a neighborhood factory and bank, a number of guest speakers, and much classroom discussion about how increased prices, unemployment, and other aspects of U.S. life, caught in the grips of a national depression, altered the child's everyday experience (Featherstone, 1939).

Underlying curriculum decisions for both groups was a clear recognition of the need to develop strong interpersonal relationships and cultivate a spirit of classroom cooperation. To help overcome feelings of alienation and poor self-esteem, which afflicted slow and rapid learner alike, teachers encouraged children to talk about their own personal experiences. Within the context of a curriculum unit, for example, students were given ample opportunity to talk about how their families coped with difficulties such as housing and money (Hollingworth, 1938).

Another way the Speyer School incorporated the affective side of the child in its curriculum plan centered on the way Hollingworth structured classroom activities. Not only did she encourage children to establish themselves as part of the group in preparation for their participation in a democratic society, but she also believed group interaction promoted character development. She organized several group projects, created the Games Club, which mixed both gifted and slow learners, and wholly supported other combining of groups through student government, assemblies, sports teams, and mutual playground use.

Despite attempts to establish cohesive curriculum, ambiguities of progressivism emerged and were expressed in the dichotomy of the school's expectations. Gifted students experienced roles as leaders and followers in group work. Slow learners experienced the heterogeneity of society (in microcosm) in extracurricular activities, but their function as leaders was not discussed. Hollingworth believed the mixed group experience helped the gifted learn tolerance. One might ask: For whom? Although she would assert that it was tolerance for each other, attitudes of superiority based on I.Q. led to assumptions about the slow learner's abilities and came into direct conflict with the progressive belief that each child should be viewed as an individual. For the gifted, Hollingworth instituted debate as part of the curriculum because she believed it would teach, together with language, logic, and critical thinking skills, ways to argue constructively. For the slow learners, whom she and others believed incapable of critical thinking skills, debate was not taught (Hollingworth, 1938).

Despite the fundamental differences in approach and expectation toward the two groups, Speyer School educators were able to incorporate certain aspects of progressive educational theory. Using Dewey's theories of an experientially based, child-centered approach to education, for example, staff and administration designed integrated curriculum for both types of learners. In both cases, they involved the child in the planning and organizing of curriculum, experiences that, they believed, empowered children, giving them a greater sense of self-determination and responsibility. The first curriculum implemented in the slow learners' program, for example, "We Visit the Orient," resulted from the fact that the school contained several Chinese students, one of whom in a younger grade became the focus of the group's interest (Featherstone, 1938).

In almost every situation, Speyer School staff encouraged students to express their individual interests. Even room decoration became a vehicle for a student's creative self-expression. Each classroom had movable furniture, courtesy of Teachers College, so that the room design accommodated individual needs and abilities and so that curriculum could be more easily integrated. As one teacher described it,

> The school no longer presents a new situation to the children. They are a part of that situation—the very substance of it. The use of movable furniture, the privileges of moving about the classroom freely, . . . of planning with teachers what work they will do, are now familiar matters. . . . Our experiment begins and ends with our children. (Board of Education, 1941)

School and Community

Progressive educators realize that there exists a relationship between the school, the family, and the community and student achievement and success. In creating a climate conducive to learning, they agree about the importance of including students, parents, and the community in the educational process. Schools that treat students, parents, and community as important develop attitudes that enhance student achievement. By seeing schools as extensions of the families, progressive schools reinforce the continuity between home and school. When actively involving itself in the affairs of the community, schools can help forge bonds between families and between students and teachers (Henderson, 1988).

The Speyer School promoted a deep connection between staff and students by allowing one teacher to remain with his or her class throughout the five years of the school's existence. For the most part, children remained the full five years. In some instances, however, older children graduated after four years: the average age for gifted students upon graduation was 13 years, for slow learners, 14 to 16 years of age. In a few cases, students left for other reasons including transfers to parochial school, family relocation, or poor adjustment to the school (Board of Education, 1941).

By giving the relationship between teacher and child time to develop, the Speyer School accomplished another important part of its overall plan as well as testing an underlying tenet of progressive education. Again influenced by Dewey and other progressive educators, Speyer School staff believed that, for both rapid and slow learners, teachers needed to work with the whole child. As part of their efforts to design curriculum around the affective needs of a child, Hollingworth and Gates stressed the importance of approaching students first on a human level—with kindness, acceptance, and respect. Treating children in a humane way, teaching them to treat one another with humanity, had direct, palpable benefits. Visitors to the school noted little tension, particularly among children in the slow learners' program, a striking improvement over the stressful atmosphere in similar regular public school classes (Gates & Bond, 1936).

Both the Speyer School and the Board of Education were acutely aware of the negative social ramifications of allowing the needs of these children to remain unaddressed. An unresponsive school environment often resulted in truancy, which frequently led to juvenile delinquency and criminal behavior (Campbell, 1934-1935; Hollingworth, 1936). Therefore a warm, caring school environment and developmentally appropriate curricula were needed to turn these alienated children into eager learners and involved members of a group. The planning board limited class size to 25 pupils, a sizable decrease from regular school classes, which often contained 40 or more children. Transforming students from potentially disruptive members of society into contributing productive citizens within a democracy tied in with the school's purpose of promoting social change and social stability (Featherstone, 1939; Hollingworth, 1936).

The Speyer School also considered as one of its primary goals the developing of a close, working relationship between itself and the community, another example of the school's progressive ties. The planning board viewed education as socially interactive and the school as an agent for social change. It felt a moral obligation to improve the quality of society through the education of children who, it believed, would assume the role of members and, in some cases, leaders of that society in the future. Speyer School staff saw parent involvement as critical to achieving success and therefore instituted as one key aim the development of the relationship between parent and school. To this end, teachers served as social workers, making home visits and helping families obtain aid from social agencies (Board of Education, 1941).

Allowing the curriculum to grow from student interest also necessitated the school's involvement in the child's life outside the school, integrating the role of the school more fully within society. In realizing one aspect of the multicultural component of the curriculum, for example, the school reached out into the community and included parents as part of the unit. These parents were invited to speak before student groups, sharing their childhood experiences of growing up in other cultures. Students were also encouraged to bring examples of objects representative of their ethnic backgrounds. One curriculum schema culminated in an exhibition of these objects, which included a Hebrew prayer book, a Chinese scroll, a pair of Dutch shoes, and lace from Czechoslovakia (Board of Education, 1941).

Professional Development

Rather than being used as agents for the implementation of standardized, predesigned curriculum, teachers need to become creative, vital participants within a school structure. "What has been lost [today] is the focus of teachers as thinking, feeling human beings who are choice-makers and the instrument of their own practice," asserts Ayers (1991). For progressive educators, professional involvement suggests the creation of schools in which teachers are involved in the decision-making process, have a sense of ownership, develop their own curriculum, and select as well as create their own material. Administrators of such schools motivate teachers and support each teaching situation as unique with individualized curriculum.

Hollingworth and other Speyer School planners made a commitment to teacher training. To accomplish this, the Speyer School used Columbia Teachers College as a resource. The college waived its fees and extended invitations to special lectures and seminars. Speyer School teachers were given "professional days" as well during which they visited other progressive schools to observe different methods and approaches. The fruits of such exposure were shared at staff meetings.

In addition, teachers were encouraged to experiment and be creative. They initiated "activity programs" within the context of comprehensive curriculum units. The teaching of reading, writing, and mathematics skills were integrated whenever possible into these units. Because Speyer School teachers often lacked the appropriate materials needed for this "unconventional" approach, they were given the freedom to create their own. To help the teachers accomplish this, the school turned to the Works Projects Administration (WPA) for help. The WPA Remedial Reading workers assisted Speyer School teachers to prepare their reading material, later published by the Board of Education, along with entirely teacher-created curriculum units (Speyer School *Curriculum Bulletin* 1). The WPA was instrumental in other ways as well, specifically, for example, in providing funds to augment teacher salaries (Tyack, Lowe, & Hansot, 1984).

Finally, from its inception, administrators and teachers alike contributed to supervision and policymaking decisions. The school aimed to create an atmosphere in which all staff members felt comfortable voicing opinions and concerns and were completely clear about the school's philosophical goals, which they helped define. The Speyer School also tried to provide support for staff members as they tested new methods of handling difficult educational problems. Examples of topics discussed at staff meetings included the instructional effectiveness of traditional public schools as well as an analysis of truancy patterns. The cooperative spirit further promoted the belief that the human relationship among coworkers, among students as well as between teachers and students, formed a fundamental component of the learning process (Board of Education, 1941).

Outcomes

As an experiment, the Speyer School was a limited success. On the most fundamental level, evaluations, final reports, and student-parent feedback attest to the fact that the Speyer School experience provided vast improvement in a number of areas. A decrease in truancy rates and an increase in reading scores, specifically among slower learners, exemplify two important goals in the school's curriculum, which it undeniably met. This group also scored higher than their public school counterparts on a general information test, which included questions about locations in New York City and other practical matters. Because the test was devised by the school staff, its measure of student achievement was selective. Math scores, however, showed no difference compared with those of similar traditional public school classes. Students in both programs exhibited a far greater enthusiasm and interest in school and learning, noted in the attendance records of children, who were able to remain with one teacher for an extended time period. The longer the time period, it was observed, the greater the improvement (Board of Education, 1941).

The students themselves also related their positive feelings toward school in interviews conducted by Speyer School staff and board of education evaluators. An interesting point on this score is that only gifted students participated in follow-up interviews. There was general agreement among the gifted that school was "a fun and happy place," in which they were able to move among peers. The students refer to their discontent before attending the Speyer School, about how it presented learning as discovery and a vehicle for self-expression. As one student indicated, "Nobody tried to regiment me and I was never any good at being regimented." They talked about how the school nurtured a strong social conscience and a love of art and music. They also appreciated the multicultural diversity of the student population (White, 1990).

Follow-up reports also tracked the gifted to their high school choices, another criteria used for measure of success. Most students attended the High School of Music and Art; however, there were Speyer School graduates at Bronx High School of Science, Stuyvesant High School, and other competitive public schools throughout New York City as well as such private schools as the Dalton School. Equally important to Speyer School evaluators as a measure of a student's academic achievement was his or her emotional adjustment. Reports indicated that in this area, as well, students adjusted well, even though many were younger than traditional high school age (Board of Education, 1941).

Final evaluations also included the opinions of parents. As many of the children came from working-class homes, there was an initial apprehension from parents over the methods of progressive education that the school employed. Characteristically, working-class parents have expressed ambivalence toward progressive education, mistrusting the relative freedom and nontraditional approaches it espouses (Apple, 1982). In the case of the Speyer School, however, most parents reported, through questionnaires that teachers from the school devised, that the experience had made a marked positive difference in the lives of their children (Board of Education, 1941).

Outside evaluators from the Board of Education also made note that the teachers themselves benefited from the progressive environment the school promoted. Not only were Speyer School teachers more well rounded than those generally found in traditional public schools, but they showed themselves to be "better learners," able to assimilate and incorporate a wide variety of curriculum material to meet the needs of their students (Board of Education, 1941).

When envisioning the Speyer School as a model for system-wide reform, public school educators experienced a number of difficulties. They believed that the implementation of a child-centered curriculum tailored to the unique needs and capabilities of individual students, teachers, and community would require too massive and rapid a reorganization of the existing system to be considered on a broad scale. They believed chaos would result were traditionally trained administrators and teachers required to reorient their whole approach to teaching. Not only would expanded responsibilities such as developing new curriculum materials or, when applicable, functioning as a liaison between city agency, student, family, and community prove overwhelming to the traditional public school teacher, but they also would necessitate a redefinition of a teacher's role, a school's role, and finally the role of education in society. Whereas progressive educators saw their role, in its simplest terms, as one of agent for social change, the Board of Education viewed the whole notion of change with great caution. The Board's purpose was to promote continuity, and any type of change should occur slowly after careful and deliberate consideration. In this way, Speyer School proposals clashed with the underlying philosophical and structural tenets upheld by the Board of Education. Other difficulties concerned ordering supplies—the immediate unavailability of the visual materials, special supplies, and manipulatives required for a dynamic integrated curriculum. These obstacles supported the Board's fundamental belief that this type of structure could succeed most effectively only within a small school setting (Board of Education, 1941). Even today, ways to effect widespread change within the bureaucracy of the New York City public school system remain an issue.[1]

Summary

Despite the tensions evident in both the Speyer School design and progressive education, the above examination reaffirms my belief that it is vital to continue creating and implementing alternative ways to reach our children through education. Rather than providing simple answers, an analysis of the Speyer School raises a series of considerations for the progressive educator: In many ways, these points focus our attention on the need to find answers to the long-standing questions that progressive educators continue to address, questions surrounding the key issues of cultural pluralism, student grouping, and evaluation of ability, to cite a few examples.

In addition to eliciting questions, the school confirms the effectiveness of certain progressive tenets. For example, it points out the value of parent-community involvement in providing a warm, nurturing environment for disaffected children. It also illustrates the benefit of an affectively based, child-centered curriculum in allowing these children to actively engage in learning. Finally, it gives testimony to the importance of supporting teachers and encouraging their involvement in the design and implementation of a school.

It is clear that the current public school system has many faults and that instituting change is an ambitious, multifaceted endeavor. Rather than give in to the excuse that progressive education techniques are only for the privileged and too problematic to impose, educators need to learn from past efforts in alternative public education such as the Speyer School.

Note

1. In her book *The Troubled Crusade* (1983), educational historian Diane Ravitch describes the general trend in education from World War II to the current time as discontinuous, citing the progressive education movement as the disrupting factor. Other historians, such as David Tyack, view these trends as continuous, claiming that twentieth-century education remains fundamentally traditional. Alternatives such as progressive education have never really changed the thrust of public education.

References

Antler, J. (1987). *Lucy Sprague Mitchell: The making of a modern woman.* New York: Yale University Press.

Apple, M. (Ed.). (1982). *Cultural and economic reproduction in education* (pp. 32-78). London: Routledge & Kegan Paul.

Ayers, W. (1991). Grounded insight. In K. Jervis & C. Montag (Eds.), *Progressive education for the 1990s: Transforming practice* (pp. 125-132). New York: Teachers College Press.

Banks, J. A. (1983, April). Multiethnic education and the quest for equality. *Phi Delta Kappan*, pp. 582-585.

Board of Education of the City of New York. (1941). *Final report of the Speyer School, 1935-1940*. New York: Author.

Campbell, H. G. (1934-1935). *All the children: The thirty-seventh annual report of the superintendent of schools*. New York: Board of Education.

Cremin, L. (1964). *The transformation of the school: Progressivism in American education, 1876-1957*. New York: Vintage.

Cremin, L., Shannon, D., & Townsend, M. (1954). *A history of Teachers College: Columbia University*. New York: Columbia University Press.

Delpit, L. (1992, March/April). Teachers, culture and power: An interview with African-American educator Lisa Delpit. *Rethinking Schools*, pp. 14-16.

Featherstone, W. B. (1937, February). The Speyer School for "slow-reading" children. *Teachers College Record, 38*, 365-380.

Featherstone, W. B. (1938). An "experience-curriculum" for slow learners at public school 500 (Speyer School). *Teachers College Record, 39*(4), 287-295.

Featherstone, W. B. (1939, March). Social education of the non-academic. *Social Education*, pp. 163-168.

Gates, A. I., & Bond, G. L. (1936). Some outcomes of instruction in the Speyer experimental school (P.S. 500). *Teachers College Record, 38*(3), 206-217.

Henderson, A. (1988, October). Parents are a school's best friends. *Phi Delta Kappan*, pp. 148-153.

Hollingworth, L. S. (1936, November). The founding of the Speyer School. *Teachers College Record, 38*(2), 19-128.

Hollingworth, L. S. (1938). An enrichment curriculum for rapid learners at public school 500 (Speyer School). *Teachers College Record, 39*(4), 296-306.

Irwin, K. (1991). The eight year study. In K. Jervis & C. Montag (Eds.), *Progressive education for the 1990s: Transforming practice*. New York: Teachers College Press.

Kerr, B. (1990, March). Leta Hollingworth's legacy to counseling and guidance. *The Roeper Review, 12*(3), 178-181.

Montralto, N. V. (1981). Multicultural education in the New York City public schools, 1919-1941. In D. Ravitch & R. Goodenow (Eds.), *Educating an urban people: The New York City experience* (pp. 67-83). New York: Teachers College Press.

Ravitch, D. (1983). *The troubled crusade: American education 1945-1980*. New York: Basic Books.

Silverman, L. K. (1990). The social and emotional education of the gifted: The discoveries of Leta Hollingworth. *The Roeper Review, 12*(3), 171-177.

Speyer School. (1937). *Curriculum Bulletin, 1*. Board of Education.

Spring, J. (1986). *The American school 1642-1985*. New York: Longman.

Tolan, S. (1990). From production to nurturing: Hollingworth and parental perspectives today. *The Roeper Review, 12*(3), 203-207.

Tyack, D., Lowe, R., & Hansot, E. (1984). *Public schools in hard times: The Great Depression and recent years*. Cambridge, MA: Harvard University Press.

White, W. L. (1990, March). Interviews with child I, child J, and child L. *The Roeper Review, 12*(3), 222-227.

Lewis, once a student and still a faculty member at Bank Street, was part of the exciting revolution in children's literature. She sets the stage for Marcus's description, in this excerpt from his biography, of Margaret Wise Brown and her early experience in writing for children. Stimulated by Lucy Sprague Mitchell, Brown's introduction to the "here and how" approach to writing for children she experienced at Bank Street as a student and, later, as a member of the writing group, was the springboard for her many wonderful books. Marcus identifies Brown's learning to rely on children's expressions and ways of making their world as well as her own ability to combine fantasy and reality in picture books for the very young.

10. The Here and Now Comes of Age: Margaret Wise Brown, Lucy Sprague Mitchell, and the Early Days of Writing for Children at Bank Street[1]

LEONARD S. MARCUS

Prologue

"The picture book," Margaret Wise Brown once said, "should have the power to jog the child with the unexpected and

AUTHOR'S NOTE: From *Margaret Wise Brown: Awakened by the Moon*, by Leonard S. Marcus, copyright © 1992 by Leonard S. Marcus. Reprinted by permission of Beacon Press, Boston.

comfort him with the familiar." Did she learn this at Bank Street, where she came in 1935 as a complete novice, to study with the innovative educator, Lucy Sprague Mitchell? Certainly the story of Margaret Wise Brown, poet among picture book authors, is inextricably interwoven with the story of early Bank Street, that radical new school where teachers were trained without courses in pedagogy and young children were given stories created right out of the stuff of their familiar worlds. Trucks and tugboats were the characters, not giants and princes.

Bank Street College in the early 1930s was part of the progressive movement strongly influenced by John Dewey. But Lucy Sprague Mitchell, who had studied with Dewey, was adding her own ideas, particularly in the realm of literature for children. In her Writer's Laboratory, established in 1937, she and a group of young Bank Street writers—Margaret Wise Brown included—were plunging into the midst of a controversy. Respected librarians at that time were staunchly promoting classic fairy-tale literature, even for preschool children. And here came Lucy Sprague Mitchell and her talented staff urging writers to listen to children, watch them, study the development of their interests, and give them stories about the world they knew.

Margaret Wise Brown's particular talent for listening to children and catching their own words placed her at the very center of this movement. And of course she was not only a listener, she was a creator with an astonishing talent to jog, delight, and comfort small children with the stories she seemed to create effortlessly. Was it the hundred stories she had written by the time of her early death that played a large part in turning the tide—convincing the librarians that "here and now" products could have great charm? Certainly today it is taken for granted that young children want, need, and love literature from the here and now world—if it is truly literature, full of surprises, suspense, and words that delight. Actually, though Margaret Wise Brown was indeed a "here and now" writer, she added her own touches of fantasy, perhaps pulling the here and now movement along to a richer and fuller conception of the meaning of "here and now" in the young child's world.

The excerpts that follow, from Leonard Marcus's fully detailed and sensitive biography of Margaret Wise Brown, center on her beginning days as a writer learning from and working with Lucy Sprague Mitchell. They tell the story of two influential women, both of them laying tracks to be followed far into the century. "Brownie," as she was always called at Bank Street, went on to make her own life in her decidedly individual style. (See the biography for this fascinating account.) But her stories for children, all along the way, retained the poetic, childlike touch that was her signature from the start.

Claudia Lewis

Three years out of college, in the fall of 1935, Margaret Wise Brown enrolled in the teacher training program of New York's progressive Bureau of Educational Experiments (popularly known as Bank Street). There, under the inspired tutelage of Lucy Sprague Mitchell, she immersed herself in childhood development studies, learned to focus her own wild, poetic instincts for language, and, by a "happy accident" (Brown, 1951, p. 81), as she later said, found her vocation as a writer for young children.

Margaret's Bank Street mentor was an iconoclast who during the 1920s had proposed a bold new "here and now" literature for the very young, an approach based on her empirical studies of preschoolers. Nursery-aged children, Mitchell believed, preferred rhythmic, gamelike stories about the everyday world of clocks and socks and modern cities—not (as the children's library establishment had long assumed) romantic, once-upon-a-time fantasies. Mitchell's ideas gave Margaret a sturdy foundation upon which to grow and, before long, to depart from creatively. By the start of 1938, she had become a published author who was much in demand, and with Mitchell's blessing she had been chosen editor of an experimental new juveniles publishing house in the "here and now" mold, William R. Scott, Inc. Lucy Mitchell had been the "here and now" literature's inventor, instigator, and guiding spirit. As author and editor, Margaret Wise Brown was to become its chief impresario.

Within a few short years of the bureau's founding in 1916, Mitchell had begun channeling a good portion of her prodigious energy into an intensive study of childhood language development and its relationship to other aspects of the child's emerging self. Her investigations in this field were of pathfinding importance. Among the more striking insights to emerge early on was the observation that "communication is not the earliest impulse that leads to the use of language"—a discovery that ran directly counter to the most basic assumptions of traditional pedagogy, with its emphasis on vocabulary building and mastery of the mechanics of grammar, syntax, and spelling. "Children," she was convinced, "begin to play with sounds long before words have any meaning to them" (Mitchell, 1953, pp. 119-120). Their first semantically meaningful utterances, Mitchell believed, continued to reflect their total immersion in the "here and now" world of the sensory realm. A 4-year-old did not speak (or think) of "climbing a hill"—remote adult conceptualization—but of going up "the place where the legs ache" (Mitchell, 1953, p. 279), as one child had put the matter to her in conversation. For Mitchell, the lesson to be drawn from the evidence was that young children made such highly vivid direct observations as a matter of course, provided only that they were encouraged to express themselves freely.

Mitchell soon felt confident enough in her findings to take a second ambitious step as a researcher and reformer: the creation of a prototype book for an entirely new kind of literature for young children, a developmentally sound "here and now" literature based on her own research.

Mitchell's introduction to the *Here and Now Story Book*, which Dutton published in 1921, combined a vigorous summary of its author's theories with practical advice addressed to the teachers and parents who would be reading the book to their children. As she well realized, the *Here and Now Story Book* was certain to be regarded as a strange and controversial work, challenging as it did conventional assumptions about the form and content of stories and poems appropriate for small children. For one thing, she had made extensive use of children's own invented phrases and sound-alike words—"toot, toot" and the like—less with a view to creating memorable literary works than to providing stories that children would recognize as their own. Mitchell's formal emphasis on rhythmic repetition was another attempt to take a direct lead from children's own speech patterns.

More striking, however, than these features of the stories (traditional folk tales and rhymes also employed repeating devices and contained some play words) was the emphatically modern urban setting of the *Here and Now Story Book*'s pieces. Much of the children's literature of the period remained rooted in nineteenth-century Romanticism, with its idealized imagery of the happy child at home in harmonious natural surroundings. In stark contrast, Mitchell's stories about skyscrapers and airplanes, tugboats and trolleys, acknowledged the demographic and social reality that in 1921 the majority of American children lived in cities.

Lucy Mitchell's imaginative writing could be witty but was more often overwrought and a bit dull. She made no exaggerated claims for herself in the literary sphere. Her primary objective was to provide other, more gifted writers with a model on which to base fresh experiments in the virtually neglected field of literature for the nursery ages.

The Cooperative School for Student Teachers, the Bank Street program that Margaret Wise Brown entered in the fall of 1935, had not been envisioned in the bureau's original plans. Its establishment in 1930 marked an important shift in emphasis away from quantitative studies of child development; the new focus was on preparing the next generation of teachers for work in child-centered experimental schools. Significantly, courses in pedagogy were excluded from the curriculum. When student teachers were not engaged in actual on-the-job training, they came to the bureau's new headquarters at 69 Bank Street for classes intended not so much to teach them how to teach as to help them become more experientially grounded, self-aware human beings.

Mitchell and her colleagues felt that traditional schooling, with its emphasis on rote learning, had a deadening effect that rendered most adults ill equipped to respond with sensitivity to children's own needs. If, as William James (1958) had said, young children were little empiricists whose "native interests" lay "altogether in the sphere of sensation," student teachers would have to undergo a wholesale reeducation of the senses, a kind of second childhood, before they would be ready to do their jobs well. For, as James had also said, "The child will always attend more to what a teacher does than to what the teacher says" (p. 73).

To heighten their sensory awareness, trainees were given classes in painting, dance, pantomime, music—all activities also offered to Bank Street's nursery school youngsters. Mitchell's abiding faith in learning from firsthand experience had inspired her to attempt her *Here and Now Story Book.* Pursuing the logic of the experiment a step further, she resolved that each of the trainees in the Cooperative School should try her hand at writing as well. The students' efforts might not be very accomplished, but the primary goal was simply to make them more aware of the range of children's experience as listeners and readers.

Mitchell taught the children's literature workshop herself, and it was as a member of that class, in the fall of 1935, that Margaret first considered the possibility of becoming a children's author. Mitchell's immense learning, her fiercely independent and playful manner, and her selfless dedication to her work all seem to have impressed Margaret from the start. The questions she posed about childhood development in the literary sphere, as in others, stirred Margaret's curiosity deeply. And Margaret was grateful for her new mentor's eagerness to encourage her in her determination to find some place for herself in the literary world.

The first piece Margaret produced in Mitchell's class was, she said afterward, a "silly story" that "tried too hard to sound like a children's story." It had been "all decked out like a Christmas tree with echoes of all the fairy stories I had ever read" (Brown, 1951, p. 79). Nevertheless, Mitchell soon spotted something special in "Brownie" (as Margaret was known to her Bank

Street colleagues): "crazy, penetrating, blind instincts and feeling for language" (personal communication, May 27, 1941), as she later told the critic Louise Seaman Bechtel.

Margaret's arrival at Bank Street could hardly have been better timed. By temperament and training, Lucy Mitchell was a teacher supremely suited to guiding Margaret toward a vocation worthy of her extraordinary talents. In turn, Margaret's rapid emergence as a promising writer for the very young presented the Bank Street founder with an opportunity to advance her own life work a step further. Mitchell realized that "Brownie" and a handful of others then at the school represented the potential core of a whole new generation of "here and now" authors. Early in 1936, she proposed that a sequel to the landmark *Here and Now Story Book* be written as a collaborative effort in which Margaret and some of her fellow students might all participate.

Always a steady seller, the original *Here and Now Story Book* was in its eighteenth printing in 1936. It is not surprising that the publisher, E. P. Dutton, was quite receptive to Lucy Mitchell's new idea. In typical fashion, Mitchell threw herself completely into all phases of the project, with Margaret as her assistant. "I am in the process of looking over recent publications for children" (personal communication, June 3, 1936), Mitchell wrote Dutton's president John Macrae, who was editing the anthology personally. She was determined to hold the retail price of the book to two dollars (about average for the time) to make it widely affordable and was studying similar books to determine how much color art might be feasible at the price.

Taken together, Mitchell's introductions to each age-graded section of the new volume constituted a book in themselves, a substantial monograph composed of subtly observed, year-by-year developmental profiles of children from 2 to 6. Describing a typical 2-year-old, Mitchell (Mitchell et al., 1937) wrote:

> Mollie . . . has got her legs, though she often loses them. For she still has a baby's legs—short and weak. . . . She has not far to fall, and her frequent sudden sitting-downs seem to amuse

rather than to discourage her. . . . "Da, Mollie, da," she says solemnly each time. To whom? To herself, of course. For at two Mollie's conversation is not cramped by lack of an audience. It burbles on, accompanying almost every activity. To practice new words? To reinforce the emotional quality of the activity? Who but two-year-olds know? And they never tell us! . . . Sometimes Mollie's remarks are repeated over and over until they trail off into a rhythmic chant. . . . Mollie is changing. . . . But while she is two, the stories that Mollie seems to enjoy (presumably because she understands them) are about Mollie and Mollie's emotional waverings between dependence and independence, her adventure with her own bed, her own dinner, her own blocks, her own places to sit, her own kitty. . . . She enjoys very brief stories about her intimately personal world. (pp. 1-9)

The import of these observations was not lost on the future author of *Goodnight Moon*, but little by Margaret and her fellow contributors to the anthology proved memorable. There were, to be sure, occasional flashes of wit and signs of promise—Margaret's "Fifteen Bathtubs," for example (a story about a young contrarian who for all the numerous tubs in his parent's house managed never to get washed); Edith Thacher's "The Elephant's Delicate Taste," a droll satirical piece in the *Just So* vein; and Lucy Mitchell's own buoyantly titled "How Jimmy Jim Jam Got His Name."

In a prefatory note to *Another Here and Now Story Book* (1937), Mitchell addressed critics of the earlier volume who had "felt that [her] philosophy might be jeopardizing something precious to children—the sheer beauty of classical literature." After restating unequivocally that children under the age of 7 were not yet ready to appreciate classical mythology and folklore, she wrote:

If the stories in this book are less lovely than Cinderella or Little Red Riding Hood or Pandora's Box, it is because we lack the requisite artistry, not because we do not value loveliness. The great writer for the young children of the "here and now" period is still to come. (pp. xxiii-xxiv)

By almost any standard, *Another Here and Now Story Book*, which Dutton published in the spring of 1937, was a striking success. Sales of the book were excellent, with a third printing required within a month of its publication in March, and reviews were generally favorable. *The New York Times* in its thoughtful and balanced appraisal found the book better than the earlier collection, which the reviewer noted had pioneered a significant new kind of literature for young children:

> Sixteen years ago, . . . [Mitchell's] idea was so new as to be startling, even a little shocking, but with the passage of time this type of story has come to be better understood. What the story of everyday things does for the little child is recognized; also the fact that its advocates are not bent on driving out the tale of imagination and fancy. (Eaton, 1937, p. 10)

The progressive education movement itself seemed a good deal less startling to large segments of the American public than it had just 15 or 20 years earlier. In the early 1920s, when Mitchell's first *Story Book* was published, there were perhaps two dozen nursery schools in the United States; by 1936, such schools numbered well into the hundreds. A *Time* magazine cover story would soon declare that progressive education had entered the American mainstream.

A striking indication of this shift in attitudes was to be found in the *Horn Book* magazine's May/June 1937 number. The journal's editor, Bertha E. Mahony, hailed the new Bank Street book with respectful appreciation and a changed mind. Recalling that when Mitchell's first story collection appeared she had been among the doubters, Mahony (1937) explained, "We feared that, if the boundaries in the content of stories for little children were fixed too tightly to familiar and *seen* things, the element of wonder would be lost" (p. 166).

The *Horn Book*'s May/June issue also included a poem by Lucy Mitchell and a profile of her coauthored by Margaret and a fellow *Story Book* contributor, Mary Phelps (Phelps & Brown, 1937). Seizing the moment, they proclaimed that

> when Mrs. Mitchell began to publish, in 1921, there appeared a new kind of author for children. Combining a scientist's command of modern child study with the insight of an unusually gifted teacher, she knew children well enough to understand what is their reality, what their confusion, at different levels of growth. Believing the art experience in all its beauty and delight is their proper heritage, she realized that it can be given them in full measure only by writers in whom the creative genius unites with real understanding of how children grow. (p. 159)

It had largely been a matter of chance that enough more or less talented writers were available to Mitchell in the spring of 1936 to produce *Another Here and Now Story Book*. The following year, she moved to replace chance with something like scientific predictability. Mitchell conceived of creating an elite group within the school whose primary objective would be to develop their craft as writers. Margaret and her colleagues became charter members of the Bank Street Writers Laboratory. The group met for the first time in October 1937.

In principle, the Bank Street community had always aspired to ethnic and racial diversity. But, in practice, as most of the school's active recruitment of teacher trainees was done at Radcliffe and the other Seven Sisters colleges, nearly all of the 20 to 30 annual entrants to the program were white, middle-class women.

Mitchell saw the Writers Laboratory as an opportunity to take a concrete step toward rectifying this imbalance. Early in the summer of 1937, she established a special scholarship to support a young black writer interested in joining the new workshop. In her usual practical-minded, well-intentioned, and proprietary way, she dispatched Margaret as an envoy to Harlem to recruit a suitable candidate.

Margaret headed uptown to West 136th Street, to the Countee Cullen Branch of the New York Public Library, where she found the children's librarian, Augusta Baker, waiting for her. Baker, who was well known to the city's children as a storyteller, escorted Margaret past the ranges of shelves answering her many questions.

On the whole, Baker explained, Harlem children read what other city youngsters read: *Peter Rabbit, Peter Pan, The Wind in the Willows*, Andrew Lang's Rainbow fairy tale collections—the "classics," most of them imported from England. There were pitifully few books that reflected black children's own experiences and cultural heritage. Only a handful of black writers attempted such books. James Weldon Johnson, the patriarch of the Harlem literary renaissance, was not among them, although he took a keen personal interest in the young people of the Harlem community, and Johnson's bravura creation poem, "God's Trombones," was read by older children who came to the library.

The classic work of African American folklore, the *Brer Rabbit* stories, sat unread on the shelves. The children, Baker reported, found it hard to make out the dialect of the centuries-old tales, which had been written down and published during the 1880s by a white southern journalist, Joel Chandler Harris. In most important respects, Harris had been faithful to the traditional black storytellers' narrative art and to the Gulla dialect. But there had also been patently racist blackface *Brer Rabbit* parodies, like *Uncle Pappy Sings*, a copy of which Baker showed Margaret. The children that the librarian read to did enjoy the stirring poetry of Paul Laurence Dunbar, even though Dunbar himself sometimes resorted to dialect and did not write specifically with children in mind. A few African adventure stories were also available. Baker expressed her delight in Lucy Mitchell's eagerness to encourage the writing of books about black children's own lives. The librarian, whose husband was a local WPA administrator, promised to pass the word about the Writers Laboratory scholarship.

Baker's comments on the *Brer Rabbit* tales were of particular interest to Margaret, who was just then working on her own edition of the stories—attempting a simplification of the dialect that she hoped would make the tales more accessible while still retaining the flavor and energy of the originals. Baker invited her to return to Harlem to test her manuscript, Bank Street style, at the library's story hour.

This Margaret did from time to time over the summer of 1937, which she spent partly in New York and partly on a rented potato farm, Ploughed Fields, at the far end of Long Island. Struggling with the knotty problem that Augusta Baker had alluded to, Margaret wondered how much of the dialect as set down by Harris to leave intact. She wavered on this point, fearful of draining the tales of their character.

Margaret's versions of the stories gradually emerged. In "The Wonderful Tar-Baby Story," the best known of all *Brer Rabbit* tales, Harris's (1880/1924) line "Brer Rabbit come prancin' 'long twel he spy de Tar-Baby" (pp. 7-8) became "Brer Rabbit he came prancing along until he spied the Tar-Baby" (Brown, 1941, p. 7). Harris's (1880/1924) "Youer stuck up, dat's w'at you is . . . " (p. 9) became "You're stuck up, dat's what you is . . . and I'm gwineter cure you" (Brown, 1941, p. 7).

In addition to modifications of the dialect, Margaret made another, more significant change, eliminating the narrative frame that Harris had devised to render the tales more palatable to his overwhelmingly white audience. Harris had interposed a 7-year-old "little white boy" who was heard to converse with the old slave storyteller in the passages introducing each tale. One by one, Remus told his beguiling tales for the boy's amusement. By discarding Harris's device and presenting the stories on their own, Margaret brought them a full step closer to their authentic origins in the culture of African Americans and their African ancestors. She proudly told Augusta Baker when the manuscript began to assume its final form, "Now we are taking them [the stories] out of slavery" (A. Baker Alexander, personal communication, January 31, 1985).

Starting in October 1937, the dozen or so women of the Bank Street Writers Laboratory met on Wednesdays throughout the school year for late afternoon sessions that generally stretched on into the evening. In a top floor room with a battered green plush sofa as its centerpiece, Lucy Mitchell, a stack of papers in hand, took her place each week in the sofa's shapeless depths as the others gathered round. Mitchell rarely seemed in a hurry on these occasions, and for everyone in the group the meetings were eagerly anticipated events.

A heady, informal workshop atmosphere prevailed, with less rivalry among the participants than one might have expected from ambitious young writers routinely putting their work on the line for their fellows' scrutiny. Mitchell's fair-mindedness and contagious enthusiasm did much to set the cooperative tone. Sherry, tea, and pastries also helped. When Margaret acquired a Kerry Blue terrier, she began bringing the dog to meetings. Curling up at her feet, Smoke often dozed through the literary discussions, but, if a manuscript being read aloud happened to bore Margaret, a little kick to the dog's ribs produced a mournful howl that spoke volumes for them both and gave the group as a whole a few tension-shattering moments of laughter.

Because the members all had regular contact with young children, there were always fresh nuggets of language data to report: "I come from Alabama," a 3-year-old had warbled into one researcher's ear, "with a Band-aid on my knee" (Bank Street, n.d.). "The Emotional Effect of Stories on Children" and other prearranged discussion topics also provided a focus for a portion of some meetings.

Distinguished guests periodically sat in—Pearl Buck, psychologist Alice Keliher, Max Lerner, poet and folklorist Sterling Brown, and many others. They commented on the members' work and spoke about their own contributions to the fields of literature, child development study, intelligence testing, and current affairs. Such encounters were considered an integral part of the "here and now" writer's education. Talks by Margaret's Harper editor, Louise Raymond, and by respected illustrators like Kurt Wiese kept the group grounded in the practical realities of writing for publication. The main business of each meeting, however, was the critiquing of work. The effectiveness of a particular image, the appropriateness of this or that word, and similar matters of craft were ardently debated as the group explored the central issue of how purely literary considerations and those brought to light by developmental research might be reconciled in the new kind of children's literature.

The writings of Gertrude Stein, Virginia Woolf, and other modernists excited them greatly and were understood to have a particular relevance to writing for young children. The modernist aesthetic of re-creating in art the immediacy of sensory impressions seemed to coincide with young children's natural reliance on their senses as the primary means of both experiencing and expressing themselves about the world.

Lucy Mitchell generally listened more than she spoke and resisted the temptation to take charge, except to propose occasional group assignments of one kind or another, her "five-finger exercises." She once asked everyone to rewrite a finished story for an age group other than the one for which it had been originally intended. Such experiments forced Margaret and the others to test their most basic assumptions. It was Mitchell's gift as a teacher to make doing so seem like a form of play.

Among the parents of the toddlers enrolled at Bank Street in the fall of 1937 was William R. Scott, an engaging man in his late 20s with a serious interest in books. An English major at Yale, Scott was a skilled letterpress printer and book designer. He had a great reserve of family money at his disposal and was eager to become a publisher. But a publisher of what? Scott had brought out a miscellany of limited edition art books and poetry broadsides, and he had discussed possible future directions with his wife, Ethel, and his brother-in-law, John McCullough, but without coming to any decisions. Then he met Lucy Mitchell.

Mitchell and Jessie Stanton, who directed the Bank Street nursery school, told Scott that in juvenile publishing a chance lay open to him to make a significant contribution to the book world, the education field, and society as a whole. They urged him to become the first publisher to devote his list to experimentally tested, "here and now"-style children's books.

The two women argued that the growing public interest in progressive education and the emergence throughout the United States of nursery schools for children as young as 18 months of age meant that a sizable market existed for the type of book they had in mind. Scott might therefore expect to earn a reasonable return for his efforts. He would not have far to go for publishable material. The Writers Laboratory produced a steady stream of manuscripts, some of them quite fine. Any manuscript that the firm was considering might first be tried out on Bank Street's nursery school children or on the older children at the affiliated City & Country School and Little Red School House. A firm that specialized in child-tested books was bound to arouse the book-buying public's curiosity and establish its name rapidly.

Overwhelmed by Mitchell and Stanton's enthusiasm and sense of mission and by the simple logic of their idea, Scott agreed to the plan. With all the daring and determination of a young Crusoe (a Crusoe who happily had the freedom to choose the ground on which to prove his resourcefulness), Scott set up shop, partly in the projection closet made available to him at 69 Bank Street, partly in the dining room of his Greenwich Village town house, and partly at his farm in North Bennington, Vermont, where the barn became the company's warehouse and summer quarters.

Mitchell could not, she told Scott, serve as the fledgling firm's editor. She was pleased, however, to recommend a suitable substitute. Margaret was offered the job and accepted it gladly and was soon energetically applying herself to the search for new authors and illustrators.

Then and afterward, Margaret "collected" illustrators, as Bill Scott (personal communication, September 10, 1981) recalled. While visiting a friend in Connecticut, for example, she became curious about the artist who had painted a series of whimsical bathhouse murals—semiabstractions featuring grinning sharks, an outsize octopus, and other "Perils of the Sea." The murals, she was told, were the work of a young artist recently returned from Paris named Clement Hurd. Margaret asked to meet him.

The painter in question proved to be a tall, lanky man with a boyish, shy, patrician manner and dry, off-tempo sense of humor. He earned his living, he explained, by making decorative hooked rugs and executing other such commissions for society clients. He considered painting and scenic design his serious work. Hurd had never thought about illustrating a children's book but was willing to give it a try.

Early in 1938, Margaret presented him with a simply structured text composed of big/little comparisons ("Once upon a time/there was a great bumble bug/and a tiny little bumble bug/And there was a great big butterfly/and a little tiny butterfly"; Brown, 1938). This manuscript, which she had written to order for Hurd, became their first collaboration, *Bumble Bugs and Elephants.*

The artist soon learned that illustrating a picture book, at least a picture book for Scott, involved more than producing a sequence of suitable paintings. The art, like the text, had to be tested on groups of actual children. Accustomed to submitting his work to the scrutiny of art directors, private clients, and his Paris teacher Fernand Léger, Hurd was understandably ill at ease when he arrived for his appointment at the Bank Street nursery school and was accosted by a swarm of clamoring critics who barely reached his knees.

The classroom teacher instructed the visitor to arrange his paintings on the floor and step back while the children examined them. The waiting period that followed was unnerving. When the children finally dispersed with what seemed like a killing indifference to the work laid before them, Hurd's heart sank. The teacher's cheerful verdict soon revived him.

"Congratulations!" she said. "You held their attention for five minutes! I timed them with my watch" (C. Hurd, personal communication, July 13, 1982). Hurd modestly accepted the accolade, collected his pictures and his hat, and strode out the door.

Hurd's illustrations for *Bumble Bugs and Elephants* were a splendid piece of work. The paintings were images of a fundamentally benign world, a sort of "here and now" peaceable kingdom with a sense of fun. Thereafter, Margaret turned primarily to him to illustrate those manuscripts of hers—including, eventually, *Goodnight Moon*—which investigated the child's elemental feelings of attachment to home.

When Margaret Wise Brown died in 1952 at the age of 42 of a blood clot following a routine operation, she had been publishing her work steadily for 15 years. Though her formal association with Bank Street had come to an end by the early 1940s, she continued throughout her brief, protean career to value, and make good use of, her journeyman training in Lucy Mitchell's Writers Laboratory. In books like *Red Light Green Light* (1944), *Five Little Firemen* (Brown & Hurd, 1948), *The Important Book* (1949), and many others, Margaret spun inventive, fresh variations on the central Bank Street theme of "here and now" realism. In her most expansive and compelling variation on that theme, *Goodnight Moon* (1947), she suggested that from the young child's point of view the "here and now" might even encompass its apparent opposite—the sheer fantasy of say bears in chairs and a cow jumping over the moon. Margaret's major contribution to the "here and now" idea was her recognition that dreams and fantasies could be just as real to children as were their material surroundings.

Margaret, who had come to Bank Street in 1935 with no clear idea about her future, had gone on to become a mentor to numerous writers and illustrators, including Alvin Tresselt, Esphyr Slobodkina, Charles Shaw, Clement Hurd, and Ellen

Tarry, all of whose careers she helped along in the critical early stages. Harper and Brothers' great juveniles editor Ursula Nordstrom likewise credited Margaret with having taught her all that she knew about picture books.

Lucy Mitchell was equally aware that her former student had much to teach others. In March 1951, the two women met for a nostalgic reunion in New York. Mitchell had lost her beloved husband, Robin, little more than two years earlier and was starting to feel her age. Writing afterward to thank "Brownie" for the visit, she told her: "Your things . . . have a magic power that words *can* have but so seldom do. I sometimes wonder— now that my chance has passed—whether I could have made words magical if my civic conscience had been less domineering?" (personal communication, March 29, 1951).

Margaret (1951) for her part would observe that same year in the *Book of Knowledge 1951 Annual:* "We speak naturally, but spend all our lives trying to write naturally" (p. 77). Forty years after her untimely death, more than one in three of her more than one hundred books remain in print—the living legacy of much tenderness and insight and good-hearted mischief and of the sheer gallantry with which she and Lucy Sprague Mitchell and their colleagues and collaborators set out to make the picture book new.

Note

1. I wish to thank Dr. Andrew C. Mitchell for permission to quote from his mother Lucy Sprague Mitchell's unpublished papers. LSM's letter to Margaret Wise Brown, dated March 29, 1951, is also used by permission of the Memorial and Library Association of Westerly, Rhode Island. LSM's letter to John Macrae, dated June 3, 1936, is found in the E. P. Dutton Records, George Arents Research Library for Special Collections at Syracuse University, Syracuse, New York, and is used by permission. LSM's letter to Louise Seaman Bechtel, dated May 27,

1941, and the Bank Street observer notes titled "Words and Meanings," are a part of the Lucy Sprague Mitchell Papers, Rare Book and Manuscript Library, Columbia University, New York, New York, and are used by permission; the latter is also used by permission of the Bank Street College of Education, New York, New York.

References

Bank Street. (n.d.). [Words and meanings: Unpublished raw data]. New York.

Brown, M. W. (1938). *Bumble bugs and elephants: A big and little book* (C. Hurd, Illustrator). New York: W. R. Scott.

Brown, M. W. (1941). The wonderful tar-baby story. In *Brer Rabbit* (A. B. Frost, Illustrator). New York: Harper & Brothers.

Brown, M. W. [Pseudonym, Golden MacDonald]. (1944). *Red light green light* (L. Weisgard, Illustrator). New York: Doubleday, Doran.

Brown, M. W. (1947). *Goodnight moon* (C. Hurd, Illustrator). New York: Harper.

Brown, M. W. (1949). *The important book* (L. Weisgard, Illustrator). New York: Harper.

Brown, M. W. (1951). Creative writing for very young children. In E. V. McLoughlin (Ed.), *The book of knowledge 1951 annual* (pp. 77-81). New York: Grolier Society.

Brown, M. W. (1952). Stories to be sung and songs to be told. In E. V. McLoughlin (Ed.), *The book of knowledge 1952 annual* (pp. 166-170). New York: Grolier Society.

Brown, M. W., & Hurd, E. T. (1948). *Five little firemen* (T. Gergely, Illustrator). New York: Simon & Schuster.

Eaton, A. T. (1937, May 2). [Review of *Another here and now story book*]. *New York Times Book Review*, p. 10.

Harris, J. C. (1924). The wonderful tar-baby story. In *Uncle Remus: His songs and his sayings* (A. B. Frost, Illustrator; pp. 7-11). New York: D. Appleton. (Original work published 1880)

James, W. (1958). *Talks to teachers*. New York: Norton.

Mahony, B. E. (1937, May/June). [Review of *Another here and now story book*]. *Horn Book*, p. 166.

Mitchell, L. S. (1921). *Here and now story book*. New York: E. P. Dutton.

Mitchell, L. S. (1953). *Two lives: The story of Wesley Clair Mitchell and myself*. New York: Simon & Schuster.

Mitchell, L. S., et al. (1937). *Another here and now story book*. New York: E. P. Dutton.

Phelps, M., & Brown, M. W. (1937, May/June). Lucy Sprague Mitchell. *Horn Book*, p. 159.

Sherman's chapter presents, at once, a historical study and ideological critique of vocational choice during the early part of this century. She identifies the social construction of vocational choice as very much a part of what was then the prevailing progressive sensibilities, assumptions, and agenda. Vocational choice, Sherman demonstrates, existed at the intersection of the burgeoning needs of a growing industrialized economy requiring efficient workers and a preoccupation with ensuring social harmony. Vocational choice, translated in schools into early tracking, masked the influence of class and gender on the options presented to students. This is a story of how our society organized itself to prepare individuals differentially while maintaining the illusion of equal and free choice. Traces of this approach to school guidance in today's school are noted.

11. What Do You Want to Be When You Grow Up? The Ideology of Vocational Choice

PATRICIA ROGAN SHERMAN

Many of the modern social professions were formed or radically restructured during the Progressive Era (1890-1920). This is true for education in general and the associated profession of

AUTHOR'S NOTE: I wish to thank Berenice Fisher, Mary Sue Richardson, Daniel Walkowitz, Gerald Markowitz, Dennis Sherman, and the Business and Professional Women's Foundation for their support in completing this research.

vocational guidance in particular. The foundations of these professions, and particularly their ideological underpinnings, are, however, not always well understood.

This remains important, for, almost a full century later, the educational and counseling professions continue to be tied to the same ideological roots formed in interaction with the economic, social, and political forces of the Progressive Era. Moreover, while the lines to the Progressive Era may lead us to think of these professions in their early stages as *progressive* in today's sense of the word, in fact, they were not. There was often a split between theory and practice or, at least, between rhetoric and effect. While many progressive educators argued at length for equal opportunity and the importance of individual intellectual and moral development, in the long run, these goals of education were secondary to the reality of preparing youth to take their place in "the various occupational, political, familial, and other adult roles required by an expanding economy and stable polity" (Bowles & Gintis, 1976, p. 21). This should not be surprising given the power of industrial capitalism at the turn of the century and the corresponding ability of corporate industrialists to form a social vision and influence social thinking to support their economic needs (Weinstein, 1968). In spite of the extensive concern for equality and personal development on the part of progressive educators, professions were often formed and developed in accord with principles that would have the effect of limiting opportunities and access to the occupational structure for the working classes, immigrant groups, people of color, and women.

The notion of "vocational choice" was at the core of the vocational guidance movement and was also of crucial importance to ideas for educational reform during the Progressive Era. To understand what is meant by *vocational choice*, it might be helpful to examine a question often asked of children.

"What do you want to be when you grow up?" Adults seem to delight in the innocent responses of children. For girls born into families with little education and lifelong economic struggle, the more accurate question is never asked: "Given that you are a girl born into a life of poverty, what are you most likely to become when you enter the work force?" The first question propagates the belief that we are all free to choose an occupation—that vocational choice is based on free will. It reinforces democratic ideals—that individuals have equal access to all vocations and that any limitations are due to individual differences and deficits. The second wording of the question introduces the variables of gender and class as inhibitors of free will. The question could be rephrased to include race or ethnicity.

The first question's assumption of free will also underlies the construct of vocational choice in more current counseling psychology or vocational guidance journals (Ginzberg, Ginsburg, Axelrad, & Herma, 1951; Holland, 1959, 1973; Roe, 1957). This concept of choice has been central to the theories of vocational counselors and many educators for decades (Gottfredson, 1981; Lazerson, 1991). Yet, there is something alarmingly real about the rephrasing of the question implying that issues of free will in occupational selection can be strongly influenced by issues of gender, race, ethnicity, and class.

To understand the ways these rather contradictory perspectives of occupational choice or selection can both appear to have merit, we need to examine the origins of the idea of occupational choice. This idea emerged within a sociohistorical context. The field of vocational guidance and the notion of vocational choice evolved in interaction with multiple forces during the Progressive Era.

Education and the Progressive Era

The Progressive Era was a time of tremendous social, economic, and political upheaval associated with the explosive growth of industrial capitalism during the last half of the nineteenth century. From the 1890s through World War I, "the country faced a fateful choice between order and chaos" (Williams, 1966, p. 3). The forces of industrialism were affecting all phases of everyday life (Hays, 1957). Violent labor strikes and occasional riots became a part of life in urban areas (Hays, 1957; Williams,

1966). Immigration expanded and reached unprecedented numbers from 1900 to 1915, in large part because of the response to the need for more industrial workers. Newly arrived immigrants were willing to work, but to varying degrees they experienced conflicts between the skills, values, and life-styles of their previous lives and their new milieu that led to serious transition problems in the new industrial cities. More established citizens were fearful that social conditions could lead to economic collapse and social revolution as problems with recessions, poverty, crime, slums, and violent strikes assaulted their sensibilities. Although many of these same middle-class citizens wished to improve conditions for the poor, they also sought to protect their own hard-won status and even carve out new roles for themselves in the turn-of-the-century industrial order. Many opposed unrestricted immigration (Mann, 1974). In New England, racial, ethnic, and religious prejudice was extensive in urban areas and many progressive leaders were not free from such prejudice (May, 1959).

Some citizens emerged as spokespeople advocating reform. Many corporate leaders feared economic chaos and worked to replace laissez-faire economic policies with government regulation that would support their interests (Weinstein, 1968). Powerful and middle-level business interests joined with reformers and labor leaders to ensure a social, economic, and political climate that would sustain and nourish corporate interests and improve social conditions (Weinstein, 1968). Many in the middle class formed and joined professions believing that this would facilitate enlightened reform and give them a voice in the new industrial order (Bledstein, 1976).

One of the issues of importance to both businessmen and reformers was the issue of schooling. Businessmen, responding to the increasingly hierarchical subdivision of jobs in business and industrial operations, argued that changes in education and training were needed to ensure internationally competitive workers for the industrial economy (Fish, 1907; Gilbert, 1977). Labor leaders called for equitable access to occupations as it was feared that the children of skilled and unskilled workers would become members of a permanent working class (American Federation of Labor, 1912/1974; Kessler-Harris, 1982; Massachusetts Commission, 1906). Reformers were interested in education as a way to ameliorate the social ills they saw in urban centers (Mann, 1974). The result was a new connection between the public schools and the industrial economy's need for workers to fill jobs.

To understand that connection more fully, we need to look at some of the dramatic changes in methods of production that were implemented by industrialists in the last half of the nineteenth century. During that period, industrial competition led to the "scientific management techniques" of Frederick Winslow Taylor (Braverman, 1974), an efficiency expert hired by industrialists seeking a competitive edge in both national and international markets. Taylor's techniques dramatically organized the production process and therefore the occupational structure along increasingly hierarchical lines. Jobs were divided into two correspondingly distinct groups: managers and manual workers. Scientific management techniques also stressed the importance of dividing labor within these two basic groups into more and more specialized and hierarchical tasks, referred to as "rationalizing labor." The goal was industrial efficiency and the key was to find the right laborer for each particular task and train him or her accordingly (Taylor, 1911).

Industrial manufacturers and businessmen needed a broad base of workers with the "right industrial values" and skills (Alexander, 1909). They needed workers who would accept different levels of employment—employment that varied dramatically in terms of monetary and social rewards. They also wanted workers who would remain with one job instead of changing jobs frequently (Munsterberg, 1910; Woolman, 1909). A way to train workers for the new industrial order was needed and a way to sort workers into occupations that were appropriate for them was essential. Public schooling and vocational counseling became closely tied to the industrial occupational structure during this time.

Education and Training

These changes in methods of production led to the need to train workers prior to work and separate from production sites (Donnelly, 1907; Fish, 1907). The issue of private versus public education of workers was strongly debated (Fisher, 1967). Although some industrial values had been taught in the last decade of the nineteenth century in the public schools, specific industrial work skills had not been a part of the public curriculum.

By the turn of the century, the National Association of Manufacturers (NAM), an organization of medium-sized businessmen, founded in 1885, became interested in setting up private trade schools as models for how workers should be trained (Lazerson & Grubb, 1974). They took up the issue of technical industrial education in 1904, in part as a reaction against militant trade unions (Parry, 1903). NAM members argued for a general elementary education that would include prevocational and manual training (Fisher, 1967; NAM, 1912). Once youths reached the age of 14, however, they would need more intensive skill-related industrial training if they were planning to enter industry. NAM members discussed questions about who should financially support industrial education. Some wanted direct control over training, while others argued that the financial responsibilities for industrial training should be absorbed by the larger community (Fisher, 1967; NAM, 1905).

Meanwhile, a coalition group had been organized to promote the cause of public industrial education. The National Society for the Promotion of Industrial Education (NSPIE) was organized in 1906 to bring to public attention the importance of industrial education and to promote the establishment of institutions for industrial training. The group was conceived of by industrial educators and included important people in labor and business in its membership (Lazerson & Grubb, 1974; Wright, 1909). The NAM joined the efforts of this group and played a strong role in setting its policies (Parry, 1903). The NSPIE argued for public acceptance and financial support of industrial education.

The industrial education movement, then, was directly related to the need to train workers with "appropriate" industrial skills and values for an increasingly subdivided occupational structure, at public expense. Many civic reformers and educators supported the move as a way to keep adolescents off the streets and channel immigrant working-class youths into productive labor. They favored public support of industrial education as a way to ease the urban ills of poverty, crime, and delinquency (Cremin, 1961).

With the introduction of industrial education into public schools, two distinct school curricula would be offered. These curricula reflected the basic divisions in scientific management; Taylor's managers would be trained in liberal arts programs while manual workers would study industrial subjects. This thrust the school into the role of primary selecting agent for the hierarchical occupational structure and led to questions about the democratic nature of assigning children to the different programs of study (Lazerson & Grubb, 1974).

Political Ideas and Educational Reform

Although industrialists, manufacturers, and many educators involved in manual training advocated public support for industrial education, the idea of public training for industry met with opposition from some people in the labor movement and the general population (Gilbert, 1977; Winship, 1910). This happened, in part, because established notions about the meaning of democracy and equality conflicted with some of the needs of the industrialists. It is important to understand the ways democratic ideals and industrial needs finally merged in the area of industrial training, given that the ideology of vocational choice emerged from that interaction.

Throughout most of the nineteenth century, school curriculum had been uniform (Cremin, 1961) as all students studied the same traditional classical subjects. Equality in public education meant that each student received equal treatment, though social groups did not have equal educational opportunity. As the public school population became more heterogeneous with the influx of immigrant children, and industry was increasingly rationalized, ideas about the innate differences of adults and children emerged first from psychologists and then from educators. Educational reformers began to focus on individual differences and argued that even in the same family no two individuals had the same abilities and interests (Munsterberg, 1910). At the same time, many educators and social reformers recognized that the children of workers and immigrants dropped out of school long before the completion of high school (Cubberly, 1909). Critics, especially those favoring public support of industrial education, argued that the schools were undemocratic because they failed to offer curricula that would meet the needs of individual students (Cubberly, 1909).

The solution was unique. The very definition of democratic education would focus on each individual receiving a formal education adapted to his or her needs and abilities (Lazerson & Grubb, 1974). This fit well with the thinking in psychology about individual differences. Hugo Munsterberg overtly argued that psychology could be "placed at the service of commerce and industry" (Munsterberg, 1913, p. 3); most other psychologists inadvertently supported industrial needs by arguing that people differed in terms of ability as well as personality (Borow, 1964). Rather than workers being divided into the hierarchical occupational structure by class, race, ethnicity, or gender, the solution was that students would be divided based on "innate" individual differences. Ironically, democracy in education now meant two different systems of education, one for manual workers and one for managers (Lazerson & Grubb, 1974). The basic division in curriculum reflected the basic structure of occupations associated with scientific methods of production and the rationalization of labor. Ideas about democracy in education and individual differences had been modified by psychologists, educators, and social reformers as they sought to fit educational ideas with industrial needs.

With this new division in the public school curriculum, concern about developing a permanent working class emerged anew among critics and reformers. Labor union officials, in particular, argued that industrial education would be used to flood the labor market—devaluing labor and limiting the occupational mobility of the children of workers (American Federation of Labor, 1912/1974; Kessler-Harris, 1982; Massachusetts Commission, 1906). With industrial education, these concerns became focused on the schools and reflected a recognition that the school was becoming the training and selecting agent for the occupational structure. Questions about selection—on what basis should people be chosen for specific occupations—needed to be resolved (Lazerson & Grubb, 1974).

Frank Parsons and the Ideology of Vocational Choice

In 1908, Frank Parsons, a lawyer, professor, independent economist, and freelance intellectual reformer, founded the Vocation Bureau in Boston and outlined his vocational work in progressive journals and a book (Parsons, 1908a, 1908b, 1908c, 1909/1967). At that time, the field of vocational guidance and the ideology of vocational choice became firmly established (Brewer, 1942).

As an avid reader, prolific writer, and energetic reformer, Parsons was well aware of the issues of his day. He understood much of the impact of industrialism on his world (Flower, 1901). He accepted some of the basic tenets of the economic system while believing that steady but gradual reform could improve the many urban social problems spawned by that same economic system (Flower, 1908). He was a man immersed in his social environment—a man of the times influenced by many of the conflicting values and ideas of his day.

In his publications, Parsons clearly described his ideas and methods of working with clients around the choice of a vocation (Parsons, 1908a, 1908b, 1908c, 1909/1967). Most of Parsons's clients were young immigrant workers attending an evening school that taught civic values and industrial skills. The school was connected with a settlement house in Boston's poverty-stricken

North End. In Parsons's work with immigrant youths, there was a fundamental contradiction between his ideas and his methods. Parsons's ideas stressed the rights of the individual in making a vocational choice, while his methods demonstrated that occupational selection would be made largely on the basis of assessing ability and character. The ideology of vocational choice implied that the individual client would be making a free choice, while, in reality, experts would be used to aid clients in making a connection between their abilities and the needs of the labor market.

Parsons used the words "choosing a vocation" in the title of his book, and choice was emphasized in his ideas. He argued that "no step in life, unless it may be the choice of a husband or wife, is more important that the choice of a vocation" (Parsons, 1909/1967, p. 3). He underscored the individual's right in making a free choice when he argued that vocational choice was so important that "no person may decide for another what occupation he should choose" (Parsons, 1909/1967, p. 4). The emphasis on rights and choices, and the idea that only the individual client can make a vocational choice, fit with strong democratic traditions, ideas supporting individual rights, and older religious ideals connected with vocations being determined by a calling from God (Gilbert, 1977). The idea of free will, implied in Parsons's ideology of vocational choice, seemed to address concerns about restricted access to higher-level occupations voiced by labor union leaders and many reformers.

While stressing the right of the individual to make a vocational choice, Parsons argued, however, that making a wise vocational choice meant "choosing" an occupation in which one was likely to succeed. The "fundamental question" was "the question of adaptation—the question of uniting so far as may be possible, the best abilities and enthusiasms of the developed man with the daily work he has to do" (Parsons, 1908a, p. 12). Vocational choices were to be based on clients discovering their niche in the labor market. The right to make a personal vocational choice came down to the right to ascertain where one's personal attributes, such as ability and character, fit in the hierarchical occupational structure.

Parsons's methods were designed to fulfill this function. He wrote:

> In the wise choice of a vocation there are three broad factors: 1) a clear understanding of yourself, your aptitudes, abilities, interests, ambitions, resources, limitations, and their causes; 2) a knowledge of the requirements and conditions of success, advantages and disadvantages, compensation, opportunities and prospects in different lines of work; and 3) true reasoning on the relations of these two groups of facts. (Parsons, 1909/1967, p. 5)

In step one, by having "a clear understanding of yourself," Parsons meant understanding one's "aptitudes," "abilities," and "character" (Parsons, 1908a, p. 4). Aptitudes and abilities included "verbal memory, visual memory, facility with language, delicacy of touch and coordination of hand and eye" (Parsons, 1908a, p. 5). *Character* was a general term for the personal attributes most valued by the middle class (Horlick, 1975). For Parsons, character included attributes such as being "careful, thorough, prompt, reliable, persistent, good-natured, and sympathetic" (Parsons, 1909/1967, p. 6). Many of these character traits would be considered the "right industrial values" by industrialists. By "resources and limitations," Parsons was referring mainly to financial resources and the time and money to study. Understanding oneself also meant comparing oneself with others. As Parsons encouraged his clients—"look yourself in the eye. Compare yourself with others" (Parsons, 1908a, p. 4). "A clear understanding of yourself" then involved knowing where you stood in a hierarchy of abilities and character traits that were important in the work world.

To accomplish step two, knowledge of the occupational structure and "different lines of work," extensive information would be needed regarding occupational opportunities. Parsons proposed that analyses be made of the varied industrial occupations and training opportunities in the Boston area (Parsons, 1908c). The vocational counselor would need to have occupational descriptions that included conditions of success, worker qualifications, opportunities, and demand for workers (Parsons, 1908c). Although not explored here, it should be mentioned that, following Parsons's lead, vocation bureaus across the country seriously and extensively surveyed industry regarding qualifications for specific occupations over the next decades.

Step three involved putting together information about one's personal attributes with knowledge about qualities needed to be successful in different occupations. The underlying assumption for the entire vocational process in general and step three in particular was that workers' skills could be and needed to be matched with particular occupational qualifications.

> For example, an artist needs, among other things, good visual memory and delicacy of touch; a dentist should have keen sight, delicate touch, correlation of hand and eye, and plenty of nerve; and if the verbal memory is defective or the auditory reactions are slow, it would probably be difficult to become a stenographer. (Parsons, 1908a, p. 5)

So, when Parsons spoke of the vocational counselor's role in helping the client toward "true reasoning on the relations" between step one and step two, he was speaking mainly about particular skills and attributes of character being matched with particular occupations.

Parsons was aware that industrialists needed a stable and efficient work force and he argued that careful vocational work would provide more stable and efficient workers. He wrote that

> boys generally drift into some line of work by chance, proximity, or uninformed selection; and the high percentage of inefficiency and change in the working force experienced by many employers in many lines of industry, and the resulting cost in employment expense, waste of training and low-grade service, are largely due to the haphazard way by which young men and women drift into this or that employment with little or no regard to adaptability. (Parsons, 1909/1967, p. 4)

Taylor's scientific management led to the specialization and subdivision of jobs, a hierarchically divided labor force, and the "scientific selection of the workman." Parsons would use "scientific" techniques with young people to help them understand their abilities and interests so that they themselves would "choose" an occupation at which they could succeed. Workers who believed that their own personal "efficiency and success" in the labor market depended on their "choosing a vocation" for which they were suited would make happier and more stable workers.

Parsons proposed that this work could only be done with the help of a vocational counselor employing scientific methods (Parsons, n.d., chap. 12). Parsons's scientific methods were rather simple and straightforward by present-day standards. The vocational counselor would administer paper and pencil inventories, test memory, physiological reactions, and general intelligence, and further would "read between the lines" as they evaluated the "special characteristics of the young man's character and ability" (Parsons, 1909/1967, p. 6). The vocational counselor would be there to help the client accept his limitations and make the objective evaluation of himself. Parsons believed that the counselor needed to be quite candid and tough with clients—pointing out their personal limitations "with a helpful attitude" (Parsons, 1908b, p. 26). To do this, Parsons often described ways the clients could improve themselves. For example, if Parsons noted a harsh voice, an expressionless face, or a listless clammy handshake, he would discuss the value of well-modulated tones in conversation, the economic value of a smile, or the importance of a firm dry hand (Parsons, 1909/1967). In fact, this was often a way of pointing out client limitations and deficiencies related to class and ethnic background.

Parsons overtly ignored any discussion of class and ethnic background in his publications, choosing to focus on individual differences and limitations instead. For example, he asked immigrant young people to respond to questions about texts read in English, and, when they came up lacking, they were given books to improve their memory (Parsons, 1908b). The client was left with the impression that his individual memory was faulty rather than the realization that reading in English was problematic due to his early ethnic affiliation. Although his assessment measures were simple, Parsons managed to use his tests effectively to convince clients that their limitations were the result of individual rather than group differences.

What about Parsons's methods relating to helping individuals understand their enthusiasms, interests, and ambitions? It is clear in looking at Parsons's case studies that interests should be subordinate to abilities. For example, a young immigrant boy of 19 said he wanted to be a doctor but lacked what Parsons believed to be the appropriate abilities as well as physical and character attributes. Parsons compared his health, manners, and expression with those of other doctors and then told him that "any man who lives a useful life, does his work well, takes care of his family, is a good citizen, . . . will be respected and loved whether he is a farmer, carpenter, lawyer, doctor, . . . or factory worker" (Parsons, 1909/1967, p. 116). Parsons suggested that the young man "visit stock and dairy farms, carpenter shops, shoe factories, wholesale stores, etc." (Parsons, 1909/1967, p. 118).

Gender and Vocational Choice

While Parsons often seemed to center on abilities as being more important than interests, with female clients it was the focus on interests and values in vocational guidance that seemed to narrow options. To understand the ways in which this focus on interests and values narrowed women's vocational options, we need to look briefly at the ways industrialism affected women's lives.

Women's "duties" in reproduction and production had changed dramatically in the nineteenth century in response to industrial organization. Although women and children had been the original industrial workers, as men were still needed in agriculture, by the 1830s, middle-class women were being told that their place was in the home (Kessler-Harris, 1982). Increasingly, production was taking place outside the boundaries of the family. There was a growing split between the home and the work world. The home, a site of more traditional communal and religious values, stood in contrast to the secular world, where individual rights, competitiveness, and ambition were rapidly becoming accepted values (Lasch, 1977; Zaretsky, 1973). A consensus grew on the part of doctors, ministers, and miscellaneous authors that women should protect the essential values and that women's duty was to remain at home taking care of their husbands and children (Cott, 1977; Lasch, 1977; Lerner, 1969/1980; Welter, 1980). Women were told that they were naturally noncompetitive, selfless, caring, and nurturing. This set of ideas about women, which has been labeled the "cult of domesticity," was pervasive and has been well documented by twentieth-century historians (Cott, 1977; Epstein, 1981; Lerner, 1969/1980; Welter, 1980).

By the time Parsons worked with female clients in 1908, women's interests, values, and skills were defined in terms of their domestic duties and their interest in people, interpersonal relations, caring for others, teaching others, and imparting religious values. Their values were communal. Women were thought to require education to raise children with the right interests, values, and skills in the new industrial order. As a result, there was much discussion about appropriate high school classes for women (Massachusetts Commission, 1906), classes that should not lead women away from their essential domestic responsibilities (Bonney, 1901; Dean, 1910). Vocational classes for women centered on domestic training (Marshall, 1909).

So, when Frank Parsons and his trained counselors helped elicit interests, values, and skills from individual female clients, what emerged was a list of female attributes that fit with the ideas expounded in the ideals of domesticity. The focus on the individual client brought forth gender-constructed ideals, not individual differences.

Parsons counseled female clients at the Women's Educational and Industrial Union (WEIU) in 1909 (Brewer, 1942). The WEIU was founded in 1877 to investigate occupational opportunities and locate jobs for poor young girls (Kessler-Harris, 1982). In 1910, the WEIU established an Appointment Bureau (Donham, 1955), which used Parsons's ideas and methods in their initial on-site work with women (Brewer, 1942). From 1922 to 1924, the

Appointment Bureau sent female clients to the Psychological Laboratory at Harvard University for testing and vocational counseling. The laboratory at Harvard followed Parsons's methods and summarized the results of more than 100 vocational-guidance evaluations (Appointment Bureau, 1922-1924; Donham, 1955).

Parsons, himself, documented only one case of his work with women, in contrast to the numerous documented cases of his work with male clients. In this case, Parsons described the woman as young, "beautiful," "charming," "cultured," "careful," "cooperative," and "perseverant" (Parsons, 1909/1967, p. 145). Parsons had organized a list of more than 200 occupations open to women in the Boston area (Parsons, 1909/1967). Upon reading the list to his client, she "chose" journalism, social work, or secretarial work, all considered appropriate for women. The client specifically stated that she was not interested in housework. Parsons suggested that, because she was so young, she might change her mind in five years time and find herself "as interested in homekeeping as you are now in writing and social work" (Parsons, 1909/1967, p. 147). By presenting the young woman with a list of "women's occupations," Parsons began with occupations tied to women's domestic role. He then assumed that her interests would "mature" and she would become more interested in domestic issues. He clearly was influenced by the ideology of domesticity in his work and assumed that female clients would have interests in line with their domestic orientation.

The new focus on occupations being selected according to gendered interests, values, and abilities constricted women's options. Furthermore, this focus disguised the fact that women were being channeled into certain occupations by concentrating on individual women's personal attributes rather than society's role in defining women in certain ways.

Another important aspect of a counselor's job was character assessment. Character assessment for men and women during the Progressive Era, however, involved the evaluation of different attributes. For men, Parsons refers to honesty, ambition, confidence, and industriousness (Parsons, 1909/1967). For women, turn-of-the-century descriptions of character usually referred to "gentility" or maintaining a certain virtue to remain eligible for marriage and raising children (Marshall, 1909; Woolman, 1909). Women's occupations were organized around "notions of propriety and role," and "successful job experiences for women were defined in terms of values appropriate to future home life such as gentility, neatness, morality, and cleanliness" (Kessler-Harris, 1982, p. 128). Occupations for women were hierarchically subdivided into levels based on their ability to protect women's virtue. Certain occupations were described as having "a coarsening influence" because women were forced into "intimate association with a few men" (Kessler-Harris, 1982, p. 136). Much of the focus on industrial training for immigrant girls was a "means for developing a girl's character" (Marshall, 1909).

Parsons Vocation Bureau, in association with the Girls Trade Education Association of Boston, published a series of pamphlets titled "Vocations for Boston Girls" (Girls Trade Education League, 1911). The Appointment Bureau in conjunction with the research department at WEIU, following Parsons's lead, produced a pamphlet titled "Vocations Open to Women" (Donham, 1955). Occupations open to women fit with ideals of domesticity in some way.

Some WEIU female clients interested in career exploration were sent to Harvard University's Psychological Laboratory for testing and vocational counseling in 1922-1924. The work there was quite similar to Parsons's original counseling methods. The majority of these women were high school graduates with some additional training (usually business school work), and a large number had graduated from good women's colleges, some with master's degrees. Most of the clients chose occupations appropriate to their gender such as secretarial jobs, clerical/office work, business occupations (usually higher-level secretarial work), social work, teaching, selling, and writing (Appointment Bureau, 1922-1924). Most of the time, vocational counselors directed women toward traditionally female occupations.

Women were led to believe that they had made personal vocational choices, not choices limited by their gender.

In short, the crucial elements of the ideology of vocational choice meshed with the ideology of domesticity to distort the meaning of "choice," "interests," "values," and even "character" for women. Indeed, the meshing of these two ideologies helps explain the popularity of Parsons's ideas.

Parsons's Appeal and Influence

Parsons's ideas caught on immediately. In response to some newspaper articles, he received hundreds of letters from school personnel all across the country asking for information about vocational counseling and his Vocation Bureau (Brewer, 1942). Within a very short time, vocational counselors were using his ideas and techniques in public schools (Brewer, 1942; Davis, 1969). Parsons's ideas were timely. The schools were rapidly adapting industrial education programs and school personnel needed a "democratic" method of selection for the various training programs they offered.

Parsons's ideas were accepted because they fit the needs of industry, but also because they responded to different strands of current social and political thinking as well as the concerns of the middle class. Public industrial education and vocational guidance promised to keep youths in school, off the streets, and out of the labor market for a period of time. It was hoped that more schooling for the unprecedented numbers of immigrants who arrived between 1900 and 1915 would ameliorate the social problems of the urban centers. Parsons's ideas about free will and choice fit middle-class concerns about equality and social mobility, thereby easing fears about social unrest in the cities.

Parsons's focus on individual differences fit with current thinking in psychology and education. This concentration on immutable individual differences suited the scientific management needs of industrialists. The focus helped Parsons ignore issues of power. He did not acknowledge the hierarchy of the occupational structure in his writings, and his focus on individual differences masked the ways social class, race, ethnic background, and gender influenced personal development. This fit the sensibilities of established citizens and many progressive reformers in 1908.

Parsons believed that each individual had a unique place to fill in the occupational structure. If that place could be found, the individual would find happiness, fulfillment, and success. Parsons argued that this would lead to social harmony and efficiency. In other words, Parsons believed that the needs of industrialists for a stable and efficient work force were not at odds with the needs of workers. Many in the middle class, longing for social harmony, accepted this reasoning.

Conclusion

During the first two decades of the twentieth century, the vocational guidance movement was born. Although sometimes quite removed from the practice of vocational counseling, the ideology of vocational choice emerged and was developed within this movement, offering a democratic rationale for the selection of workers into a hierarchically organized labor force.

The democratic ideals in the ideology of vocational choice stressed the right of the individual to make a choice. In practice, however, experts were used in the vocational selection process to "help" individuals select occupations that corresponded to their individual "abilities" and "character traits." For those whose abilities and characteristics matched the more prestigious and economically rewarding occupations, choice was meaningful because a range of vocations were open to them. For clients whose abilities and character traits narrowed their occupational possibilities, however, the idea of individual free choice masked the ways that their gender, class, race, and ethnic background interacted with abilities and character traits to limit their occupational options. The democratic ideology of vocational choice fit mainly the reality of white, male, middle-class vocational clients, while offering a systematically distorted picture and rationale for others being selected for lower level occupations.

In the past 70 years, the field of vocational guidance has grown and changed, often with the help of the federal government. Many people in the field have introduced more sophisticated scientific assessment measures, refined theories of occupational choice, and expanded comprehensive classification systems of occupations. Researchers have applied scientific methods in the social sciences to accomplish much of the above. The basic work in vocational guidance continues, however, to strongly resemble Parsons's early work. Individual assessments of ability, interests, and values are matched with the requirements of different occupational roles in industry. In short, we are not encouraged to think of the ways our class, race, ethnic background, or gender affect our options. Rather, we are supposed to believe that we, as free and equal individuals, choose our occupations, careers, or educations.

Thus the ideology of vocational choice remains part of mainstream thinking, much as "choice" itself remains an ideological fixture in professions such as education. Today, many of us believe that we chose our occupations, careers, or educations— we don't think of the ways our options may have been limited based on our class, race, ethnic background, or gender. In the field of vocational guidance and counseling, Parsons's ideas have been so well accepted that some readers may have had difficulty seeing "choosing a vocation" as separate from understanding personal skills and matching them with the requirements of different occupations.

References

Alexander, M. W. (1909). The apprenticeship system of the General Electric Company at West Lynn, Massachusetts. *The Annals of the American Academy of Political and Social Science, 33,* 141-150.

American Federation of Labor. (1912). Reports of the Committee on Industrial Education and Commission of Industrial Relations. (Reprinted in M. Lazerson & W. N. Grubb, Eds.,

1974, *American education and vocationalism: A documentary history 1870-1970*, pp. 101-114, Washington, DC: Author)

Appointment Bureau. (1922-1924). [Vocational guidance evaluations] (Women's Educational and Industrial Union Collection, Schlesinger Manuscripts). Boston: Radcliffe College.

Bledstein, B. J. (1976). *The culture of professionalism: The development of higher education in America.* New York: Norton.

Bonney, W. L. (1901). Women and the wage system. *The Arena, 26,* 172-177.

Borow, H. (1964). *Man in a world of work.* Boston: Houghton Mifflin.

Bowles, S., & Gintis, H. (1976). *Schooling in capitalist America: Educational reform and the contradictions of economic life.* New York: Basic Books.

Braverman, H. (1974). *Labor and monopoly capital: The degradation of work in the twentieth century.* New York: Monthly Review Press.

Brewer, J. (1942). *History of vocational guidance: Origins and early development.* New York: Harper.

Cott, N. (1977). *The bonds of womanhood: "Woman's sphere" in New England, 1780-1835.* New Haven, CT: Yale University Press.

Cremin, L. A. (1961). *The transformation of the school: Progressivism in American education 1876-1957.* New York: Random House.

Cubberly, E. P. (1909). *Changing conceptions of education.* Boston: Houghton Mifflin.

Davis, H. V. (1969). *Frank Parsons: Prophet, innovator, counselor.* Carbondale: Southern Illinois University Press.

Dean, A. D. (1910). *Vocational education.* Albany: New York State Education Department, Division of Trade Schools.

Donham, A. G. (1955). *History of the Women's Educational and Industrial Union.* Unpublished manuscript, Women's Educational and Industrial Union Collection, Schlesinger Manuscripts, Radcliffe College, Boston.

Donnelly, S. B. (1907). Address. *National Society for the Promotion of Industrial Education Bulletin, 1,* 33-36.

Epstein, B. L. (1981). *The politics of domesticity: Women, evangelism, and temperance in nineteenth-century America.* Middletown, CT: Wesleyan University Press.

Fish, F. (1907). Address. *National Society for the Promotion of Industrial Education Bulletin, 1,* 24-30.

Fisher, B. M. (1967). *Industrial education: American ideals and institutions.* Madison: University of Wisconsin Press.

Flower, B. O. (1901). An economist with twentieth century ideals: Frank Parsons, C.E., Ph.D., educator, author and economist. *The Arena, 26,* 157-171.

Flower, B. O. (1908). Professor Frank Parsons, Ph.D.: An appreciation. *The Arena, 40,* 171-183.

Gilbert, J. B. (1977). *Work without salvation: America's intellectuals and industrial alienation, 1880-1910.* Baltimore, MD: Johns Hopkins University Press.

Ginzberg, E., Ginsburg, S. W., Axelrad, S., & Herma, J. L. (1951). *Occupational choice: An approach to a general theory.* New York: Columbia University Press.

Girls Trade Education League. (1911). *Vocations for Boston girls.* Boston: Author.

Gottfredson, L. S. (1981). Circumscription and compromise: A developmental theory of occupational aspirations [Monograph]. *Journal of Counseling Psychology, 28*(6), 545-579.

Hays, S. P. (1957). *The response to industrialism, 1885-1914.* Chicago: University of Chicago Press.

Holland, J. L. (1959). A theory of vocational choice. *Journal of Counseling Psychology, 6*(1), 35-45.

Holland, J. L. (1973). *Making vocational choices: A theory of careers.* Englewood Cliffs, NJ: Prentice-Hall.

Horlick, A. S. (1975). *Country boys and merchant princes: The social control of young men in New York.* Lewisburg, PA: Bucknell University Press.

Kessler-Harris, A. (1982). *Out to work: A history of wage-earning women in the United States.* New York: Oxford University Press.

Lasch, C. (1977). *Haven in a heartless world: The family besieged.* New York: Basic Books.

Lazerson, M. (1991). Democracy, progressivism, and the comprehensive high school. In K. Jervis & C. Montag (Eds.), *Progressive education for the 1990s: Transforming practice* (pp. 41-50). New York: Teachers College Press.

Lazerson, M., & Grubb, W. N. (Eds.). (1974). *American education and vocationalism: A documentary history, 1870-1970*. New York: Teachers College Press.

Lerner, G. (1980). The lady and the mill girl: Changes in the status of women in the age of Jackson. In E. Katz & A. Rapone (Eds.), *Women's experience in America: An historical anthology*. New Brunswick, NJ: Transaction. (Work originally published in *Midcontinent American Studies Journal, 10*, 5-15, 1969)

Mann, A. (1974). *Yankee reformers in the urban age: Social reform in Boston, 1880-1900*. Chicago: University of Chicago Press.

Marshall, F. M. (1909). The industrial training of women. *The Annals of the American Academy of Political and Social Science, 33*, 144.

Massachusetts Commission on Industrial Education and Technical Education. (1906). *Report of the Massachusetts Commission on Industrial Education and Technical Education*. Boston: Author.

May, H. F. (1959). *The end of American innocence: The first years of our own time, 1912-1917*. Oxford: Oxford University Press.

Munsterberg, H. (1910). *American problems from the point of view of a psychologist*. New York: Moffat, Yard.

Munsterberg, H. (1913). *Psychology and industrial efficiency*. Boston: Houghton Mifflin.

National Association of Manufacturers (NAM). (1905). Report on industrial education. In *Proceedings NAM* (Vol. 10). Washington, DC: Author.

National Association of Manufacturers (NAM). (1912). Report on industrial education. In *Proceedings NAM* (Vol. 17). Washington, DC: Author.

Parry, D. M. (1903). Annual report of the president. In *Proceedings of the Eighth Annual Convention of the NAM* (pp. 13-15, 80-81). Washington, DC: NAM.

Parsons, F. (1908a). The Vocation Bureau, part I. *The Arena, 40*, 3-16.

Parsons, F. (1908b). The Vocation Bureau, part II. *The Arena, 40*, 171-183.

Parsons, F. (1908c). First report to the executive committee and trustees. In *Vocation Bureau papers*. Boston: Harvard University Archives.

Parsons, F. (1909/1967). *Choosing a vocation.* Boston: Houghton Mifflin. (Reprint of original work, New York: Agathon, 1909)

Parsons, F. (n.d.). *Youth and the world.* Unpublished manuscript, Yale University Archives, New Haven, CT.

Roe, A. (1957). Early determinants of vocational choice. *Journal of Counseling Psychology, 4,* 212-217.

Taylor, F. W. (1911). *The principles of scientific management.* New York: Harper.

Weinstein, J. B. (1968). *The corporate ideal in the liberal state: 1900-1918.* Boston: Beacon.

Welter, B. (1980). The cult of true womanhood. In E. Katz & A. Rapone (Eds.), *Women's experience in America: An historical anthology* (pp. 193-218). New Brunswick, NJ: Transaction.

Williams, W. A. (1966). *The contours of American history.* Chicago: Quadrangle.

Winship, A. E. (1910). Vocational training in the public schools. *The New England Journal of Education, 71,* 58-65.

Woolman, M. S. (1909). The relative value and cost of various trades in a girl's trading school. *The Annals of the American Academy of Political and Social Science, 33,* 127-140.

Wright, C. D. (1909). The work of the National Society for the Promotion of Industrial Education. *The Annals of the American Academy of Political and Social Science, 33,* 13-22.

Zaretsky, E. (1973). *Capitalism, the family, and personal life.* New York: Harper & Row.

In this final chapter, Silin explores the role psychology has played, with its developmental focus, in the formation of a progressive pedagogy. Drawing upon both postmodern social theory and a strand of progressive education that stressed social transformation, Silin is particularly concerned about the pedagogical consequences that result from a limited formation of the self. Specifically, Silin argues that an overly psychologized reading of childhood, in effect, marginalizes the social construction of identity and casts a progressive pedagogy in an unwarranted, unrealistic light. We ought, he argues, to recognize the regulatory functions that result from scientific techniques and that find their way into ordinary classroom practices, practices as apparently benign as observation. By so doing, it may be possible to construct a more subtle educational discourse that theorizes about the self from a multiplicity of perspectives and social contexts.

12. New Subjects, Familiar Roles: Progressive Legacies in the Postmodern World

JONATHAN G. SILIN

True reflection presents me to myself not as idle and inaccessible subjectivity. But as identical with my presence in the world and to others, as I am now realizing it: I am all that I see, I am an intersubjective field, not despite my body and historical situation, but, on the contrary, by being this body and this situation, and through them, all the rest.

Maurice Merleau-Ponty
(*Phenomenology of Perception*)

This is an essay about the self, about the changing notions of self that inform postmodern thought and their implications for education. It is an essay that seeks to honor the progressive tradition out of which it is written at the same time as it raises questions about the particular progressive legacy dominating early childhood practices today. Specifically, I want to explore how our highly psychologized understanding of childhood fosters a belief in individuals as autonomous, self-determining agents, separate and distinct from the social world they inhabit. I will argue that adopting a more complex, multivocal concept of subjectivity, one that posits the individual and the social not as binary oppositions but as parts of a single regime of truth, would encourage us to rethink our ideas about age-appropriate curriculum. How might our programs change if the self were seen as constituted in and through the social rather than in opposition to it? This is not to attempt an exhaustive catalogue of recent developments in psychology but more simply to signal a new directionality in theorizing subjectivity. My immediate purpose is to frame our resistance to talking about pressing social issues with young children as a function of the reliance on traditional child development research for the knowledge base of the field (Silin, 1988). My larger goal is to remind us that the progressive movement was not only about individual growth and social efficiency but also about the power residing within the group and possibilities of societal transformation, messages as vital today as they were a century ago.

The Standard of Practice: Development as the Aim of Education

I came of age as an educator within a liberal, progressive context, at a time when Piaget was just beginning his ascension into the pedagogical sphere and the most popular article summarizing contrasting approaches to early education was titled "Development as the Aim of Education" (Kohlberg & Mayer, 1972). My professional training was dominated by a broad array of psychologists who were used to interpret children's behavior and to make decisions about curriculum. With a singular emphasis on individual development, there was little space for consideration of the political and ethical ramifications of our work. Those, like myself, who looked for a thread of social analysis within these discussions of developmental ages and stages were drawn to educational philosophers like Counts (1932) and Dewey (1916), early childhood specialists like Caroline Pratt (1971) and Lucy Sprague Mitchell (1934). Grounded in an appreciation of rapid economic changes, they viewed social transformation rather than instructional efficiency to be at the center of our educational interests. It is the tension between the dominant focus on developmentally appropriate practice and the minor but persistent chord of social advocacy to which this chapter is addressed.

For evidence of the ongoing nature of this tension, one need only turn to a most recent exchange of ideas in the *Early Childhood Research Quarterly*. Here Kessler (1991) has initiated an unusually acrimonious dialogue by suggesting that developmentally appropriate practices should no longer be the end point of our work but must be subsumed under a broader set of social goals. She proposes that our ultimate educational purposes have to do with preparing active citizens for a democratic society, reflecting the more social reconstructionist aspect of the progressive tradition. The majority position is articulated by Bredekamp (1991), of the National Association of the Education of Young Children. Bredekamp argues that we must continue a singular focus on the developmental rationale as an effective strategy to gain legitimation as professionals with recognized standards of practice that can resist the imposition of inappropriate academic programming from those who do not understand or value young children. Yet, never in this debate is it suggested that we examine the nature of developmental claims themselves, only that we place them in a context that gives them social purpose. Our gaze need not leave the individual children who through our guidance can become autonomous participants in political life. But what if this individual, whose growth we so carefully monitor and autonomy we promote, is no more a permanent fixture of the social landscape than the U.S. Constitution is universal to the political world? What if our belief in a rational subject only functions as a mechanism to control our behavior, as a most subtle means to govern the soul?

An important caveat is necessary before pursuing this question further. What we call the progressive movement was a complex, pluralistic, and contradictory set of ideas and practices (Cremin, 1964). My particular concerns are not with the more technocratic aspects of this legacy that have left educators the tasks of measuring, classifying, and sorting children to promote a more productive America. A well-articulated critique of this tradition has been with us since the 1960s (Katz, 1971; Tyack, 1974). Rather, I choose to focus on an aspect of the progressive movement in which I and readers of this book may be more directly implicated, the belief in psychological knowledge as the basis of educational decision making. For here the interdiscursive relationship between child development research and humanistic movements for individual liberation too often mask the regulative function of our work. Here we assure ourselves that we act in the best interests of the children, freeing their potential by promoting autonomy and self-actualization. Always striving to respond to individual differences, comfortable in our assessments of what is needed, we tend not to ask about how these judgments may confound the biological and the social, the pregiven and the constructed.

The Language of Individual Needs

Or are we so comfortable? As a new teacher, I remember only too well my most frequent response when confronted by the oppositional behavior of one of my young students. The words ring in my ears even today: "You *need* to sit down now." "You *need* to be alone for a while." My demands for compliance were always couched in terms of what children needed to do. In retrospect, I think this was an attempt to mask what in fact was the coercive imposition of my will by drawing attention to the child's lack of restraint or internal control. This might also be read as a substitution of power for authority.

Woodhead (1990) has recently suggested that the language of needs veils our uncertainty about what is right for children. We manage to cloak decisions based on personal values and specific cultural locations in a vocabulary that appears factual, universal, and timeless. To speak of the other's need is to speak of an objective description that is driven by an emotional imperative. For the child is understood as unable to recognize that which makes such evident common sense to the adult. The empirical and evaluative are combined so as to assure us that the needs are intrinsic to the child rather than socially constructed in our daily interactions and encoded in the pedagogical canon. The teacher's claim to truth lies not in the ambiguously negotiated realm of intersubjectivity but in the objectivity of the scientific gaze that obliterates both the observer and the observed.

At our weekly staff meetings and at endless parent workshops, we would talk about what children needed, here cast as a matter of curriculum. The need for play, social interaction, or learning by doing were uppermost on the agenda for children of sophisticated, middle-class urban families. Seldom did we stop to wonder if these needs attributed to the children themselves might more accurately be found in ourselves, the culture of the school, or its community. Such considerations would suggest the more fragile, situated nature of the discourse in which we engaged and the power arrangements on which it was built. The discourse, which at that time had not been fully infused with the vocabulary of multiculturalism, only reinforced a polarity between the interests of the individual and the interests of the group. Steeped in a plethora of psychological theories explaining children's development and studies documenting their growth, we reproduced what seemed to be an inevitable conflict between the personal and the social, the private and public worlds of childhood.

Limitations of the
Developmentalist Perspective

To be honest, it was not until I left the classroom that I became uneasy about the extent to which early education had been colonized by developmentalists and the limits of the language they imposed. As a doctoral student, I explored two critical streams of thought. The first, going back to the 1920s, has always raised questions about psychological studies that decontextualize learning, miscalculating children's capabilities because they ask them to perform in situations that are abstracted from the multidimensional realities of everyday experience (Isaacs, 1966). The second and more recent tradition calls attention to the ways that psychological theories exist within the framework of the positivist sciences (Egan, 1983; Spodek, 1970). It is this critique that seeks to reintroduce a concern for the ethical foundations of our educational commitments and to shift attention toward questions of purposes as well as of technique, to the why as well as the how and when (Cuffaro, 1984).

I argued that, as a professional knowledge base, the exclusive use of psychological theories devalues alternative ways of knowing children—aesthetic, symbolic, imaginative (Silin, 1987). It seemed to me that, no matter what the domain of childhood life on which scientists focused, they all shared a common belief in the developmental metaphor itself. This is very much a metaphor of the Enlightenment, borrowed from the biological sciences and superimposed on discussions of human change. Its use implies not only a continuity of physical and psychological growth but also an adult-centered perspective in relation to children. Research making this assumption most often begins with a set of adult characteristics, defined by male, middle-class, Western standards of maturity, and examines growth as progress toward their achievement (Speier, 1976). The imposition of these standards is rationalized through the understanding that, because developmental processes are biologically based, as exemplified in Piaget's assimilation/accommodation model of adaptation, they are also universal. Although environment or experience may affect the speed of development, the attainment of higher levels of thought, or even the way that specific tasks are accomplished, the sequence of stages, the laws of development, are construed as cross-culturally valid.

The most incisive analysis of the way that the developmental metaphor functions to ensure the absolute distinction between adult and child is offered by Merleau-Ponty (1964) in his critique of Piaget. To Merleau-Ponty, the Piagetian focus on rational, cognitive structures sacrifices the immediate, visceral knowledge of self and others that we possess before being overwhelmed by language and rules of perception. Rejecting any hierarchy of stages that posits an artificial separation of the child and adult, Merleau-Ponty prefers to look for the continuities, the child as neither absolute other nor as exactly the same as ourselves. Such continuity can only come from assuming the centrality of preconceptual knowledge, knowledge that is neither objective nor subjective but that emerges through direct participation in the world. This is a knowledge that would allow us to know both the child in the classroom and the child within ourselves. It is a knowledge that would allow us access to the questions that really matter. Paley (1991) places this search for the right questions and the challenges it entails at the heart of the pedagogical project.

> In the matter of the self we are not connected to one another by accumulations of skills and facts, but, rather, by inner fears and fantasies, impulsive urges and pleasures. That which every child feels we all feel; that which every child fears we all fear. The challenge is to uncover what we seek and fear and fantasize and desire, so we may proceed toward the understanding of another person. And if that person happens to be a child in our classroom, we will need some strict rules to go by, for the roles we play in a classroom are too unequal. It is hard enough to find common cause in the faculty room, but in the classroom we automatically become judge and jury and there is seldom a witness for the defense. (p. 155)

Only at the Request
of the Children

What are the "common causes" of the contemporary world? What kinds of questions are on the minds of children and teachers? In the past several years, my interest in AIDS and drug education has brought me back into the classroom, if not quite into the faculty room. When called to assist schools with the process of formulating AIDS curriculum, it was natural for me to begin by asking what children were saying about the subject. The responses of teachers clearly indicated that AIDS had entered their classrooms through the voices of their students regardless of formal instruction. Many of these opportunities occurred in classrooms with young children, classrooms in which the prospect of talking about AIDS seemed most daunting. Sometimes these voices had been heard at the most unexpected moments, sometimes on more predictable occasions. Almost always, teachers had felt unprepared to take advantage of the moment to begin a dialogue that could have led to more structured learning. The children's concerns were met by a lethal silence (Silin, in press).

This is not to blame teachers, for they are part of a larger culture of denial. Although New York has mandated K-12 AIDS education since 1987, its *AIDS Instructional Guide* refers to the disease only twice in the K-3 section. The lessons actually deal with general health concepts, not very realistic preparation for living in a city where it is estimated that more than 70,000 children will lose one or both parents to HIV in the next few years and where some classrooms already contain several children who have seen family members and friends die of AIDS. While it may be naive to expect an official government document to reflect a progressive position, might we not expect more from a book titled *Engaging Children's Minds: The Project Approach* (Katz, 1989)? Perusing this work, I was drawn to the discussion of teacher planning. An example of a curriculum based on the hospital is illustrated with a wonderful diagram including spokes and topic headings like "people," "materials," "operations," and so on. I notice, feeling hopeful, that AIDS is listed under "illnesses" and then, upon closer inspection, see an asterisk leading me to the bottom of the page where, if the book were in color, I would have seen a little red flag instead of the words: "only if raised by the children." Apparently we are allowed to initiate discussion about transplants, diabetes, jaundice, even having a baby, but not AIDS. It seems to me that this project web teaches the teacher that among other things there are acceptable and unacceptable or less acceptable reasons for going to the hospital. Of what are the authors afraid? Are teachers only left to soothe the anxious child as suggested in the only *Young Children* (Skeen & Hudson, 1987) article to appear on this subject during the 1980s?

In my work with teachers, I hear the reluctance to initiate subjects such as AIDS, substance abuse, and homelessness couched in the language of the developmentally appropriate curriculum. Echoing my own teaching vocabulary, they tell me that their children have more pressing needs—the need to play and to make sense of their immediate family lives. They imply that these needs are somehow separate from rather than enmeshed in the social world. I am repeatedly told that it is the children who aren't ready for these difficult topics. What can they understand of such complex and disturbing phenomena? I am always left to reflect on whose readiness is really in question. For, in the end, we are probably most disturbed by the questions for which there are no answers and the ethical dilemmas raised by a society that is all to ready to desert those who are ill, poor, or otherwise deemed marginal. I am also left to wonder how progressive educators of an earlier era might have interpreted this resistance to raising critical social issues with children, to keeping the daily realities of our lives outside of the classroom.

In a paper addressing the restructuring of social studies for the middle years, Minuchin (1990) highlights two obstacles to creating more relevant curriculum. The first is the traditional program with its sequence of topics based on child development principles designed to reflect changes in cognitive capacity, meaningful content, and thinking styles. This familiar sequence begins with family, moves outward to neighborhood and community, and eventually leads to cultures of other times and places. The second impediment is our desire to present a manageable world to children when we as adults feel increasingly powerless and ineffective to influence the direction of modern life. While Minuchin makes an important contribution to demystifying what appear to be radical shifts in the family and offers concrete suggestions for new curriculum, I think her most incisive comments have to do with differences in adult and child perceptions about social change.

> "Social change" is an interesting concept, implying that we all approach "then" and "now" with the same framework. But, of course, our perceptions vary, and the differences are particularly important in the teaching-learning enterprise. What represents "change" for teachers, who are adults, is simply "now" for children. That's how it is; this is the world. One implication of this difference in perspective is that we may be more impressed or disturbed by changing elements of social reality than the children are. They may be readier than we think to make their reality a subject of study. (p. 4)

That is how it is; this is the world. But early childhood educators have always been selective in their re-presentation of the world. The desire to sanitize the curriculum is an enduring theme in our work. For example, in 1980 I tried to understand why the field appeared to be largely immune to the diverse, often politically inspired critiques of the school that had emerged in the prior decades (Silin, 1988). In large part, I interpreted this resistance as an unwillingness of many to go outside of the developmental sciences to ground their pedagogy, a gendered refusal to acknowledge the political nature of schooling. Interviewing teachers, I found that they defined their roles in terms of protective control whether they favored behaviorist, cognitive structuralist, or psychoanalytic frameworks. They all saw young children as open to the world, curious, and eager to learn yet vulnerable to the threats posed by either internal emotional turmoil or external sources of influence. Their response was to offer protection to their charges by controlling the educational environment. They viewed themselves as unbiased, objective practitioners who only acted in the best interests of the child.

While teachers today have a heightened sense of the external dangers, I believe that they are motivated by a similar desire to cordon off a safe space in which children can grow at their own pace. Bettye Caldwell, a leader in the field during the 1960s and 1970s, summarized this perspective when referring to early childhood education as the "applied side of the basic science of child development" (1984, p. 53). Yet some psychologists express concern about the continued development of "a nursery ideology of extra-ordinary dogmatism" that even resists advances in developmental theory (Bruner, 1980, p. 203). Bruner's words do not lead me away from my original interest in the apolitical nature of teacher thinking, but they do suggest a growing space between changes in developmental knowledge and daily practice. Recent developments in theorizing subjectivity, for example, might recast our understanding of the individual-social dichotomy and the language of needs in which it is expressed. This is not to say that I agree with the message implicit in Caldwell's earlier statement that knowledge flows only from theoretician to practitioner as if each worked in separate discursive fields. Rather, I want to place the question of child-adult relations in the context of the distances we have created between the individual and the social, the mind and the body. How is it that we fail to hear and/or respond to children's questions? Why do we act sometimes as if we live in such a different world than our students?

Governing the Soul

With psychometrics, psychology had begun to establish its claim as the appropriate authority to adjudicate upon the lives of individuals, to administer them in such a way that would maximize their social utility and minimize the social danger their difference might represent. In the conception and technology of intelligence, for perhaps the first time, a science of the soul was combined with a strategy for the government of the individual (Rose, 1990, p. 140).

In the last decade, a group of European scholars has begun to make problematic the coherent, unitary subject that has been the object of our most intensive educational efforts (Henriquez, Hollway, Urwin, Venn, & Walkerdine, 1984; Rose, 1990). Locating the origins of this subject in the Cartesian cogito of seventeenth-century humanism and tracing its development into the multiplication of nineteenth-century scientific discourses, these critics force us to set aside any belief in a fixed, pregiven subject. It is the "tutelary complex," as Danzelot (1977/1979) refers to the interlocking governmental technologies produced in these discourses, that inscribes the citizen as an individual with rights as well as with responsibilities. Through the new legal, medical, and pedagogical practices, the individual comes to recognize the needs, desires, and wishes consistent with governmental control. Social regulation is less about overt coercion or limitation than about the production of emotions and attitudes that will enable us to claim our rights and adhere to our responsibilities as members of the body politic. Our sense of self, the multiple identities to which we respond, is constructed in and through the social institutions—courts, school, hospital, and clinic—that define the nature of the individual.

The conditions that gave rise to a nursery school practice focusing on the developing child are historically specific, part of the larger process through which the idea of mental health has achieved its hegemony. Foucault (1980) has laid the groundwork for understanding the way that scientific discourses produce subjectivity, extending our recognition of power beyond the boundaries in which we usually see it exploited or trapped. It is not that he spoke of early education. Despite the omnipresence of a pedagogical vocabulary in Foucault's work (for who but Foucault has brought to our attention the multiple meanings of the examination, discipline, and power/knowledge?), there is little direct attention given to the institution of schooling. He does, however, attend to the nineteenth-century penchant for quantitative measurement of human characteristics. This mania for measurement was most often used to establish distributive statistical norms within specific populations (Gould, 1981). It was this drive to normalize human growth and behavior that allowed specialists to pass judgment on the normal as well as the abnormal, to create exemplary case studies, and to define the subject as the object of developmental surveillance.

Only recently has there been a spate of attempts to deconstruct the ever popular developmental paradigms from this Foucauldian perspective. Polakow's (1989) work exemplifies this search to understand how those who want only to nurture the young may unwittingly be implicated in a regulative project. She is insistent in her claim:

> To talk of child development is also to talk of motherhood and domestic ideology, of family and patriarchy, of power and control. In the case of childhood, it is also to link power and the site of control—the body—to a social history of surveillance, classification, and regulation: in short, to the "bio-power" (Foucault, 1984) that we, as child developers, increasingly employ in our discursive practices as we chart taxonomies of thinking skills, scale norms of psychosocial and cognitive development, and assess the staged progression of performance outcomes. (p. 75)

Foucault and Polakow teach us that control is not always about limits and boundaries. Rather, it functions through the proliferation of knowledges that allow us to "know" the individual with ever greater certainty. Through the observation and classification of psychological characteristics, we not only record the socialization of those in our charge; we also describe the very domains in which to seek expressions of individual differences. In this sense, we participate in the production of subjectivity, that which is considered essential to the self.

The nursery school has not only become an essential site for the identification of developmental differences. It is also a site that reinforces the expert/practitioner dichotomy by instructing parents on the appropriate methods of home care that will ensure the leveling of the expert-identified differences. In the twentieth century, even normal development is problematic, a mine field of potential hazards posed by uneducated parents and societal ills. It can be navigated, however, with professional assistance. The more there is to be known about the child, the more knowers there must be. The process of measuring and assessing is as much about the lives of children as it is about ensuring the growth of a professional hierarchy.

The laying down of this developmental mine field was begun in the nineteenth century with the new mental measurement technologies and child study movements and it escalated in the early twentieth century with the popularity of behaviorist, Freudian, and normative research studies such as those Gesell conducted at Yale. It is a mine field continually being planted with new points of danger such as the importance of a single, maternal caregiver in the 1950s, the role of early intellectual stimulation in the 1960s and 1970s, or the significance of mutually regulated communication patterns in the 1980s. Although we have learned to chart the path of individual growth with greater specificity, we have also increased the distance that must be traveled. With the accumulation of empirical and theoretical knowledge, the accomplishment of adulthood appears to be ever more complex and far from the haunts of early childhood. It requires the help of more experts, longer periods of institutional life, and stronger family support.

The Developing Child

Ironically, as science tells us how different we are than children, the immediate social world seems to be providing us with quite another message. The problems we once thought hidden from view are now too readily part of children's experience, the life of the body more directly threatened, and the press of economic events experienced by all regardless of age. Yet in our classrooms we continue to collude in a silence that would suggest otherwise. Perhaps it is this very silence that designates the distance between the developing child and the social world of which he or she is a part. The children we have inscribed in our pedagogy are a priori individuals with capacities that mature over and against the world into which they are born. That is, when early childhood educators define their work as the application of the science of child development, they commit themselves to the idea of the developing child. This is an idea premised on the location of certain capacities within the individual—and therefore within the domain of psychological knowing—and others that are not. Factors external to children may shape development and ultimately influence their educability but remain outside of the teacher's control. What the teacher can do is monitor the child's natural development. We can look for indicators of the understandings and concepts that underlie the acquisition of knowledge. Contemporary progressive pedagogy is based on a structuralist epistemology that leaves the educator an observer of the child's growth through largely predetermined stages. The goal is not the transfer of information to groups of children or the promotion of social transformation but the fostering of individual change. Knowledge has become development, development the aim of education.

This emphasis on the teacher's role in observing and recording information about the developing child has its most trenchant roots in the experimental progressive schools of the early twentieth century. Designed as laboratories for the scientific study of children's growth, with particular emphasis on the social and emotional aspects of development, their goal was to foster a curriculum based on the objective data gathered by teachers. This method is described in detail by Antler (1982) and is best summarized in the 1919 report from the Bureau of Educational Experiments:

> We are working on a curriculum, checking it by our growth records; and working on how to record growth, evaluating our records by the children's reactions to our planned environment. . . . We were perforce recording growth of parts of children; but we were living with whole children as that each

half of our thinking constantly served as a check for the other half. (Antler, 1982, p. 571)

A number of the experimental schools had a stronger commitment to social change and placed less emphasis on the study of individual children (Cremin, 1964). In the case of the bureau, later known as Bank Street College of Education, the more tenuous aspects of its social philosophy may have suffered an ironic death knell with the monies brought into the field by the 1960s War on Poverty. This was a moment that called for formalization, rationalization, and simplification of an otherwise flexible, sophisticated, and complex perspective to ensure institutional participation in an increasingly competitive educational arena.

Indeed, the War on Poverty and the many early intervention programs that it engendered turned public attention toward an appreciation of the cognitive abilities of young children. A minority of progressive educators tried to maintain a balanced perspective on the role of cognitive growth (Biber, 1977). But the dominant child-centered pedagogy that emerged in the 1970s found its theoretical underpinnings in Piaget's genetic epistemology (Walkerdine, 1984). This was a pedagogy that gave precedence to the individual over the group, the cognitive over the socioemotional, the concept over the content.

His [Piaget's] personal role in the movement towards naturalization of mathematical and scientific knowledges as individual capacities, developing in a quasi-spontaneous fashion given the correct environment, was a central part of that movement which permitted the curriculum to be understood as spontaneous and permitted the teaching of facts to disappear in favor of the monitoring of the learning of concepts. Recognizing such a movement is absolutely crucial to understanding how the present pedagogic common-sense "facts" themselves have become concepts, structures—stripped of their content and located in individuals. (Walkerdine, 1984, p. 178)

As Walkerdine points out, the English were particularly susceptible to the Piagetian influence. Practicing their own form of intellectual amnesia, they disregarded the critical analysis of Piaget's work done by educators in the 1920s such as Isaacs (1966). In the United States, there has also been an alternative, if weaker, tradition to offset the focus on the individual inherent in Piaget's work. Both Mead and Vygotsky, the former from a social interactionist and the latter from a Marxist perspective, attempted to more fully account for the functioning of the social within the individual.[1] And Dewey is seldom appreciated for the subtlety and complexity with which he approached philosophical inquiry and the special contribution that he makes toward understanding the realities of early childhood teaching (Cuffaro, 1982). He most frequently adapted a dialectical methodology to resolve the many apparent contradictions in our educational thinking. Thus in discussing the movement between the child and the group, the individual and the social, heredity and environment, he initially used the term *interaction*. Later, to emphasize the transformational relations of these elements rather than their fixity or discreteness, he began to substitute the concept of *transaction*. It is the social individual that emerges from Dewey's work. Cuffaro makes this clear.

> In Dewey's actuality, social and individual are not an issue of static rest or even a question of balance. It is a spatio-temporal affair of a whole which has "phases and emphases marking its activity." As Dewey presents the evolving person, the social and the individual may be said to be "two names for the same reality." It is not either the social or the individual but the social individual, each element functioning within the whole, named as separate elements for the purpose of analysis but in actuality transactionally related. Such a view ensures continuity and connections. It attends to process. (p. 95)

New Subjects, Familiar Roles

Researchers have expressed increasing interest in the history of this alternative tradition that moves beyond individualism and rationalism to the embodied nature of self (Hermans, Kempen, & van Loon, 1992). Its earliest forerunner, the seventeenth-century historian Giambattista Vico, rejected the ahistorical conception of the human mind embedded in Descartes's famous dictum, "I think therefore I am" in favor of a view of mind and body as inseparable—"because I consist of body and mind, therefore I think." This understanding of self as moving through space and time and able to imaginatively occupy a number of positions that permit dialogical relations is one that has found new support within the postmodern world. Hermans et al. (1992) comment on its many subtle variations.

The dialogical self can be seen as a multiplicity of *I* positions or as possible selves (see Markus & Nurius, 1986). The difference, however, is that possible selves (e.g., what one would like to be or may be afraid of becoming) are assumed to constitute part of a multifaceted self-concept with one centralized I position, whereas the dialogical self has the character of a decentralized, polyphonic narrative with a multiplicity of *I* positions. This scene of dialogical relations, moreover, is intended to oppose the sharp self-nonself boundaries drawn by Western rationalistic thinking about the self (Holdstock, 1990; Hsu, 1985).

Postmodern psychologists locate a theoretical basis for their work in discourse theory. Discourse might best be defined as "sets of concepts and the language through which they are thought as inseparable from and fused with social practices and institutions. Ideas, concepts, knowledge, modes of speaking, etc. codify social practices and in turn constitute them" (James & Prout, 1990, p. 25). Urwin (1984) theorizes that subjectivity is produced as we assume different positions in a variety of discursive practices. In contradistinction to traditional psychologists, she does not presume a universal set of developmental processes or a "real" child that might be revealed by peeling back the layers of social meanings attached to childhood. We are no more nor less than the accumulated subject positions we learn to occupy as participants in various discourses.

The goal of the postmodernists is to abolish the individual/social dualism inherent in formulations that pose a pregiven subject, one that is discrete, coherent, and existing prior to social experience. In its place, they seek to define a more complex, decentered, at times contradictory, subject embedded in the social world. The challenge is to maintain the tension between individual agency and the limits imposed by material constraints. It is a perspective that becomes most problematic when the child is read only as a social text, the biological body reduced to an effect of socially constructed interpretations. Urwin (1984) tries to avoid this pitfall by drawing both on Lacan's semiotically driven description of development and on Foucault's analysis of power/knowledge. From the former, she understands that coming into subjectivity is disjunctive and discontinuous, the struggle for continuity and identity ongoing rather than a completed accomplishment of adulthood. With the assistance of the latter, she is able to conceptualize a historically situated subject and to account for the possibility of social change lacking in purely linguistic explanations. Focusing on the behavioral regularities that precede language, but that are part of larger discursive practices through which we learn to occupy subject positions, Urwin is able to link the psychic and the cultural, power and desire, continuity and change.

The Child-in-the-World

It has not been my purpose to unpack all of the meanings the new theories of subjectivity might bring to the work of early childhood education. I am only too aware of the gap between expert knowledge and pedagogical acts as they occur in specific, concrete situations. But I have wanted to outline the limitations of the developmentalist perspective that dominates the field today. Specifically, I have been concerned by the way that the concept of developmentally appropriate curriculum is being used to rationalize the avoidance of discussing pressing social issues with young children. When the individual and the social are seen as discrete domains, we construct two significant, often unbridgeable distances. The first is the distance between adults and children created by stage theories of development that has been criticized by social phenomenologists. The second is the space between children and the disquieting material realities in which they live that is the subject of this chapter. To decrease these distances, I have suggested we substitute a notion of subjectivity as constituted in the domain of the social for the accepted individual/social dualism. This would also be to recognize the role of our own discursive practices in producing the subjectivity that heretofore appeared to prefigure our educational interventions.

In short, I contend that we undermine our best intentions when we consider the child and the world as separate entities. The subject of our pedagogical attentions might better be construed as the child-in-the-world. And this is where we turn from progressivism understood to be the effective realization of individual human potential to progressivism as social reconstruction. Rather than fearing the loss of professional objectivity by grounding our work in an articulated social philosophy, we might choose to understand this as the route to fulfilling our educational responsibilities. In 1932, Counts articulated just such a position. He reasoned that education is of necessity about imposition and all our methodological concerns—and here I include considerations of developmental appropriateness—useless unless employed to achieve larger social purposes. We cannot live with response-ability in the current time or understand the past without projecting a future toward which to strive. In a society that undervalues and marginalizes children, to promote a more equitable distribution of material wealth and the social transformation that this would require is simply to understand our role as advocates for the young and a more just vision of the future.

Note

1. Postmodern theorists (Henriquez et al., 1984) have criticized Mead and Vygotsky for relying on a concept of the subject as autonomous and rational, prefiguring the social rather than emerging through it. This critique hinges on the claim that they both, albeit in different ways, fail to adequately account for how the outside gets inside the individual. According to Henriquez,

it is the mechanisms of internalization that appear most awkward and problematic in their work.

References

Antler, J. (1982). Progressive education and the scientific study of the child. *Teachers College Record, 83*(4), 559-593.

Biber, B. (1977). Cognition in early childhood: A historical perspective. In B. Spodek & H. Walberg (Eds.), *Early childhood education: Issues and insights.* Berkeley, CA: McCutchan.

Bredekamp, S. (1991). Redeveloping early childhood education: A response to Keller. *Early Childhood Research Quarterly, 6,* 199-209.

Bruner, J. (1980). *Under five in Britain.* London: Grant McIntyre.

Caldwell, B. (1984). Growth and development. *Young Children, 39*(6), 53-56.

Counts, G. (1932). *Dare the school build a new social order?* Carbondale: Southern Illinois University Press.

Cremin, L. (1964). *The transformation of the school.* New York: Vintage.

Cuffaro, H. (1982). *Unfolding and connecting Dewey's thought from a teacher's perspective.* Unpublished doctoral dissertation, Teachers College, New York.

Cuffaro, H. (1984). Microcomputers in education: Why is earlier better? *Teachers College Record, 85*(4), 559-568.

Danzelot, J. (1979). *The policing of families* (R. Hurley, Trans.). New York: Pantheon. (Original work published 1977)

Dewey, J. (1916). *Democracy and education.* New York: Macmillan.

Egan, K. (1983). *Education and psychology.* New York: Teachers College Press.

Foucault, M. (1980). *Power/knowledge: Selected interviews and other writings 1972-1977* (C. Gordon, Ed.; C. Gordon, L. Marshall, J. Mepham, and K. Soper, Trans.). New York: Pantheon.

Foucault, M. (1984). *The Foucault reader* (P. Rabinow, Ed.). New York: Pantheon.

Gould, S. (1981). *The mismeasure of man.* New York: Norton.

Henriquez, J., Hollway, W., Urwin, C., Venn, C., & Walkerdine, V. (1984). *Changing the subject: Psychology, social regulation and subjectivity.* New York: Methuen.

Hermans, H., Kempen, H., & van Loon, R. (1992). The dialogical self: Beyond individualism and rationalism. *American Psychologist, 47*(1), 23-33.

Holdstock, T. (1990, August). *The African self: An holistic cosmology.* Paper presented at the William James Principles Congress, Amsterdam, the Netherlands.

Hsu, F. (1985). The self in cross cultural perspective. In A. Marsella, G. de Vos, & F. Hsu (Eds.), *Culture and self: Asian and Western perspectives* (pp. 24-55). New York: Tavistock.

Isaacs, S. (1966). *Intellectual growth in young children.* New York: Schocken.

James, A., & Prout, A. (1990). A new paradigm for the sociology of childhood? Provenance, promise and problems. In A. James & A. Prout (Eds.), *Constructing and reconstructing childhood.* New York: Falmer.

Katz, L. (1989). *Engaging children's minds: The project approach.* Norwood, NJ: Ablex.

Katz, M. (1971). *Class, bureaucracy and the schools.* New York: Praeger.

Kessler, S. (1991). Alternative perspectives on early childhood education. *Early Childhood Research Quarterly, 6,* 183-197.

Kohlberg, L., & Mayer, R. (1972). Development as the aim of education. *Harvard Educational Review, 42*(4), 449-496.

Markus, H., & Nurius, P. (1986). Possible selves. *American Psychologist, 41,* 954-969.

Merleau-Ponty, M. (1962). *Phenomenology of perception* (C. Smith, Trans.). New York: Humanities Press.

Merleau-Ponty, M. (1964). *The primacy of perception.* Evanston, IL: Northwestern University Press.

Minuchin, P. (1990). Social change and social reality: Some implications for social studies. *Thought and Practice, 2*(2), 3-16.

Mitchell, L. (1934). *Young geographers.* New York: John Day.

Paley, G. (1991). The heart and soul of the matter: Teaching as a moral act. *The Educational Forum, 55*(2), 155-166.

Polakow, V. (1989). Deconstructing development. *Journal of Education, 171*(2), 75-87.

Pratt, C. (1971). *I learn from children.* New York: Cornerstone Library.

Rose, N. (1990). *Governing the soul: The shaping of the private self.* New York: Routledge.

Silin, J. (1987). The early childhood educator's knowledge base: A reconsideration. In L. Katz (Ed.), *Current topics in early childhood education* (Vol. 7). Norwood, NJ: Ablex.

Silin, J. (1988). Becoming knowledgeable professionals. In B. Spodek, O. Saracho, & D. Peters (Eds.), *Professionalism and the early childhood practitioner.* New York: Teachers College Press.

Silin, J. (in press). Children, teachers and the human immunodeficiency virus: Authorizing AIDS education in the curriculum. *Journal of Education.*

Skeen, P., & Hudson, D. (1987). What we should and should not tell our children about AIDS. *Young Children, 42*(4), 65-71.

Speier, M. (1976). The adult ideological viewpoint in studies of childhood. In A. Skolnick (Ed.), *Rethinking childhood.* Boston: Little, Brown.

Spodek, B. (1970). What are the sources of early childhood curriculum? *Young Children, 26*(1), 48-58.

Tyack, D. (1974). *The one best system.* Cambridge, MA: Harvard University Press.

Urwin, C. (1984). Power relations and the emergence of language. In J. Henriquez et al., *Changing the subject.* New York: Methuen.

Walkerdine, V. (1984). Developmental psychology and the child-centered pedagogy: The insertion of Piaget into early education. In J. Henriquez et al., *Changing the subject.* New York: Methuen.

Woodhead, M. (1990). Psychology and the cultural construction of children's needs. In A. James & A. Prout (Eds.), *Constructing and reconstructing childhood.* New York: Falmer.

Index